Temptations
OF THE **WEST**

How to be Modern in India,
Pakistan and Beyond

Also by Pankaj Mishra

Butter Chicken in Ludhiana:
Travels in Small Town India

The Romantics:
A novel

An End to Suffering:
The Buddha in the World

Temptations
OF THE WEST

How to be Modern in India, Pakistan and Beyond

PANKAJ MISHRA

PICADOR

For Barbara Epstein

First published 2006 by Picador
an imprint of Pan Macmillan Ltd
Pan Macmillan, 20 New Wharf Road, London N1 9RR
Basingstoke and Oxford
Associated companies throughout the world
www.panmacmillan.com

ISBN-13: 978-0330-43467-6
ISBN-10: 0-330-43467-5

1 3 5 7 9 8 6 4 2

A CIP catalogue record for this book is available from
the British Library.

Typeset by IntypeLibra, London
Printed and bound in Great Britain by
Mackays of Chatham, Chatham, Kent

Foreword

Over the last five years I have travelled to places as far apart as Buddhist Tibet, Bollywood and Taliban-ruled Afghanistan. *Temptations of the West* describes these journeys in South and Central Asia, through countries that differ radically from each other in many ways but that seem to experience the same dilemma: how do people with traditions extending back several millennia modernize themselves?

Recent events have ensured that this is no longer an academic question. Western ideologies, whether of colonialism, or of communism and globalization, have confronted the countries I visited – India, Pakistan, Afghanistan, Nepal and Tibet – with the same challenge: modernize or perish. But the wrenching process of remaking life and society in all their aspects (social, economic, existential) frequently collapses in violence, affecting not just South Asia, but also, as the horrific events of 9/11 showed, even the apparently remote and self-contained worlds of the West.

Needless to say, the societies I travelled through are too internally diverse to be summed up by broad generalizations of the kind preferred by policymakers and op-ed columnists. These interconnected narratives do not presume to offer solutions to their great problems, or dwell abstractly on democracy, religion, and terrorism. Rather, they seek to make the reader enter actual experiences: of individuals – Hindus, Muslims, Buddhists trying to find a way in the modern world – and of the traveller, as, confronted with a bewildering complexity, he moves from ignorance and prejudice to a measure of self-awareness and knowledge.

Contents

Prologue

Benares:
Learning to Read

I SPENT FOUR MONTHS in Benares in the winter of
1988. I was twenty years old, with no clear idea of my
future, or indeed much of anything else. After three idle,
bookish years at a provincial university in a decaying old
provincial town, I had developed an aversion to the world
of careers and jobs which, having no money, I was destined
to join. In Benares, the holiest city of the Hindus, where
people come either ritually to dissolve their accumulated
'sins' in the Ganges, or simply to die and achieve liberation
from the cycle of rebirths – in Benares, with a tiny allow-
ance, I sought nothing more than a continuation of the life
I had led as an undergraduate.

I lived in the old quarter, in a half-derelict house owned
by a Brahmin musician: a tiny, frail, courteous old man.
Panditji had long ago cut himself off from the larger world,
and lay sunk all day long in an opium-induced daze, from
which he roused himself punctually at six in the evening to
give sitar lessons to German and American students. It was
how he maintained his expensive habit, and also staved off
penury. His estranged, asthmatic wife lived on the floor
above his – she claimed to have not gone downstairs for

fifteen years – and spent most of her time in a window-less kitchen full of smoke from the dung-paved hearth, conversing in a low voice with her faithful family retainer of over fifty years. The retainer, a small reticent man in pleated khaki shorts, hinted, in that gloomy setting, at better days in the past; even a kind of feudal grandeur.

The house where I lived and the melancholy presence of Panditji and his wife were part of the world of old Benares that was still intact in the late 1980s, and of which the chess games in the alleys, the all-night concerts in temples, the dancing girls at elaborately formal weddings, the gently decadent pleasures of betel leaves and opium, formed an essential component. In less than two years, most of this solid-seeming world was to vanish into thin air. The old city was to be scarred by a rash of fast-food outlets, video-game parlours, and boutiques, the most garish symbols of the entrepreneurial energies unleashed by the liberalization of the Indian economy, which would transform Benares in the way they had already transformed other sleepy small towns across India.

But I didn't know this then, and I did not listen too closely when Panditji's wife reminisced about the Benares she had known as a young woman; when she told me about the time her husband came to her family home as a starving student; or when she described the honours bestowed on her father by the Maharajah of Benares. I was even less attentive when she complained about her son and his wife; more particularly the latter, who, though Brahmin, had in her opinion the greedy, grasping ways of the merchant castes.

I didn't pay much attention to the lives around me. I was especially indifferent to the wide-eyed Europeans drifting about on the old ghats, each attached to an ash-smeared Guru. I was deep in my own world, and, though I squirmed at the word and the kind of abject dependence it suggested, I had found my own Guru, long dead but to me more real than anyone I actually knew during that winter I spent slowly making my way through his books.

On an earlier visit to the library at Benares Hindu University, idly browsing through the stacks, I had noticed a book called *The American Earthquake*. I read a few pages at random, standing in a dark corridor between overloaded, dusty shelves. It seemed interesting; I made a mental note to look it up on my next trip to the library. Months passed. By then I had moved to Benares, and one day while looking for something else in the same section of the stacks, I came across the book again. This time I took it to the reading room. An hour into it, I began to look at the long list under the heading, 'Other books by Edmund Wilson'. Later that afternoon, I went back to the shelves, where they all were; dust-laden, termite-infested, but beautifully, miraculously, present: *The Shores of Light, Classics and Commercials, The Bit Between My Teeth, The Wound and the Bow, Europe Without Baedeker, A Window on Russia, A Piece of My Mind* . . .

It was miraculous because this was no ordinary library. Wilson's books weren't easily accessible. I had always lived in small towns where libraries and bookshops were few and far between, and did not stock anything except a few standard texts of English literature: Austen, Dickens, Kipling, Thackeray. My semicolonial education had made me spend much of my time on minor Victorian and Edwardian writers. Some diversity was provided by writers in Hindi and the Russians, which you could buy cheaply at communist bookstores. As for the rest, I read randomly, whatever I could find, and with the furious intensity of a small-town boy to whom books are the sole means of communicating with, and understanding, the larger world.

I had realized early on that being passionate about literature wasn't enough. You had to be resourceful; you had to be perpetually on the hunt for books. And so I was: at libraries and bookshops, at other people's houses, in letters to relatives in the West, and, most fruitfully, at the local paper recycler. There I once bought a tattered old paperback of Heinrich Mann's *Man of Straw*, which – such were the gaps in my knowledge – I dutifully read and made notes about, without knowing anything about his more famous and distinguished brother. Among this disconnected reading I had certain preferences, a few strong likes and dislikes, but they did not add up to coherent standards of judgement. I knew little of the social and historical underpinnings to the books I read; I had only a fleeting sense of the artistry and skill to which certain novels owed their greatness.

I had problems, too, with those books of Edmund Wilson I had found at the library, some of which I read in part that winter, others from cover to cover. Many of them were collections of reviews of books I could not possibly read at the time, or else they referred to other books I hadn't heard of. Proust, Joyce, Hemingway, Waugh, yes; Malraux and Silone, probably; but where in India could one find John Dos Passos? Wilson's books also assumed a basic knowledge of politics and history I did not have. They were a struggle for me, and the ignorance I felt before them was a secret source of shame, but it was also a better stimulus to the effort his books demanded than mere intellectual curiosity.

I was never to cease feeling this ignorance, but I also had a sense as I groped my way through Wilson's work that my awareness of all these unread books and unknown writers was being filtered through an extraordinarily cohesive sensibility. Over the next few months, it became clear to me that his powers of summary and explication were often worth more attention than the books and writers that were his subject. There was also a certain image that his lucid prose and confident judgements suggested, and that I at once found very attractive: that of a man wholly devoted to reading and thinking and writing. I thought of him at work in his various residences – Provincetown, Talcottville, Cambridge, Wellfleet – and in my imagination these resonant names became attached to a promise of wisdom and serenity.

The library where I found Wilson's books had, along with the university, come out of an old, and now vanished, impulse: the desire among Hindu reformists in the freedom movement to create indigenous centres of education and culture. The fundamental idea was to train young Hindu men for the modern world; and, like many other idealisms of the freedom movement, it hadn't survived long in the chaos of independent India, where even the right to education came to be fiercely fought over under the banner of specific castes, religions, regions, and communities.

Sectarian tensions were particularly intense in North India, especially in Uttar Pradesh, the province with the greatest population and second highest poverty rate in the country, where caste and political rivalries spread to the local universities. The main political parties, eager to enlist the large student vote in their favour, had begun to put money into student union elections. Politically ambitious students would organize themselves by caste – the Brahmin, the Thakur (the so-called warrior caste), the Backward, and the Scheduled (the government's euphemism for former untouchables). The tensions were so great that academic sessions were frequently interrupted by student strikes; arson, kidnapping, and murder among students became common features of campus life.

Miraculously, the library at Benares had remained well stocked. Subscriptions to foreign magazines had been renewed on time: you could find complete volumes of the *TLS*, *Partisan Review*, and the *New York Review of Books* from the 1960s in the stacks. Catalogues of university presses had been dutifully scrutinized by the library staff; the books, as though through some secluded channel untouched by the surrounding disorder, had kept flowing in.

The library was housed in an impressively large building in the style known as Hindu–Saracenic, whose attractive pastiche of Indian and Victorian Gothic architecture had been prompted by the same Indian modernist aspirations that had created the university. But by the late 1980s chaos reigned in almost every department: few books were to be found in their right places; the card catalogue was in complete disarray. In the reading room, students of a distinctly criminal appearance smoked foul-smelling cigarettes and noisily played cards. Some of them chose to take their siestas on long desks; bored young women spent hours scratching their initials into table tops.

It was hardly a congenial place for long hours of reading, but since I wasn't enrolled as a student at the university, I could not take books out of the library. I was, however, allowed to sit in the reading room, and I was there almost every day from the time it opened in the morning. Since I had little money, I walked the four miles to the library from my house. For lunch I had an omelette at a fly-infested stall outside the library, and then a glass of sticky-sweet tea which effectively killed all hunger for the next few hours. In the evening, I would walk home along the river and sit until after dark on the ghats, among a mixed company of touts and drug-pushers; washermen gathering clothes that had rested on the stone steps all afternoon, white and sparkling in the sun; groups of children playing hopscotch on the chalk-marked stone floor; a few late bathers, dressing and undressing under tattered beach umbrellas; and groups of old men, silently gazing at the darkening river.

Many of my days in Benares were spent in this way, and when I think of them they seem serenely uneventful. But what I remember best now are not so much the clear blue skies and magically still afternoons, glimpsed from my window-side perch at the library, as the factors that constantly threatened to undo that serenity. For a radically different world existed barely a few hundred metres from where I sat, reading about Santayana.

The university in those days was the scene of intense battles between students and the police. Anything could provoke them: a student who was not readmitted after being expelled, an exam that a professor refused to postpone. A peculiar frenzy periodically overtook the two sides, whereupon the students would rampage through the campus, smashing furniture and any windowpanes left unbroken from their last eruption of rage. Challenged by the police, they would retreat to the sanctuary of their hostels and fire pistols at the baton-charging constables. In retaliation, the policemen would often invade the hostels, break into locked rooms, drag out their pleading, wailing occupants, and proceed to beat them.

I once saw one of their victims, minutes after the police had left, coughing blood and broken teeth, his clothes torn, the baton marks on his exposed arms rapidly turning blue. Another time I saw a policeman with half of the flesh on his back gouged out by a locally made hand grenade. Anxious colleagues watched helplessly from behind their wire mesh shields as he tottered and collapsed on the ground. Terrified bystanders like myself threw themselves to the ground in a defensive reflex we'd seen in action movies. The grenade thrower – a scrawny boy in a big-collared shirt and tight polyester trousers who, I learned later, had targeted the policeman after being tortured by him in custody – stood watching on the cobblestone road, fascinated by his handiwork.

Such violence, extreme though it seemed, wasn't new to the university, which had long been witness to bloodier battles between the student wings of communist and Hindu nationalist organizations. These two groups tended to be allied with different ends of the caste system: the lower castes tended to be communist; the upper castes tended to be Hindu nationalist. But frequently now, the violence came for no ideological reason, with no connections to a cause or movement. It erupted spontaneously, fuelled only by the sense of despair and hopelessness that permanently hung over North Indian universities in the 1980s. This was itself part of a larger crisis caused by the collapse of many Indian institutions, the increasingly close alliance between crime and politics, and the growth of state-organized corruption – processes that had accelerated during Mrs Gandhi's 'Emergency' in the mid-seventies.

For students poised to enter this world, the choices were harsh – and it didn't matter what caste you belonged to; poverty was evenly distributed across this region. Most of the people I knew were deeply cynical in their attitude toward their future. You could work towards becoming a member of either the state or national legislature and siphon off government funds earmarked for literacy and population-control projects; if nothing worked out, you could aspire, at the other end of the scale, to be a lowly telephone mechanic and make money by selling illegal telephone connections.

Most of the students in this traditionally backward area of India came from feudal or semi-rural families, and aspired to join the civil service, a colonial invention that even in independent India continued to offer the easiest and quickest route to political power and affluence. But there were fewer and fewer recruitments made to the civil service from North India, where the decline in standards, as well as the cheap availability of higher education, had made it possible for millions to acquire university degrees while they had less and less prospect of employment. Bribery and nepotism had played a major part in the disbursement of jobs in the minor government services. Students from the lately impoverished upper castes suffered most in this respect: if poverty wasn't enough, they were further disadvantaged by the large quotas for lower-caste candidates in government jobs.

The quotas, first created by Nehru's government in the early 1950s and meant as a temporary measure, were expanded and used by successive governments as an electoral ploy to attract lower-caste votes. The upper-caste students found themselves making the difficult adjustments to urban life only to confront the prospect of being sent back to the oblivion they had emerged from; and their sense of blocked futures, which they acquired early in their time at the university, was to reach a tragic culmination in 1990 in the spate of self-immolations following the central government's decision to provide even larger quotas in federal jobs for applicants from lower castes.

My own situation was little different from that of the people around me. I had recently spent three years at the nearby provincial university at Allahabad, where I was in even closer, more unsettling, proximity to the desperation I saw in Benares. I was upper caste myself, without family wealth, and in roughly the same position as my father had been in freshly independent India when the land reform act of 1951 reduced his once well-to-do Brahmin family to penury. (The act was another of Nehru's attempts at social equality; it was meant to turn exploited tenants into landholders.) My mother's family had suffered a similar setback. Like many others in my family who laboriously worked their way into the middle classes, I had to make my own way in the world. Looking back, I can see my compulsive pursuit of books, the calm and order it suggested contrasting so jarringly with the rage and desperation around me, as my way of putting off a grimly foreclosed future.

So, during my months in Benares, I was able to live at a slight tangent to the chaos of the university. And I was able to do this, I now see, partly because of Rajesh.

*

I got to know Rajesh early in my stay at Benares. A tall, wiry, good-looking man in his mid twenties, he had continued to live in Benares after finishing his studies at the university. He was eccentric and moody: he would recite Urdu poetry one moment and then denounce its decadence the next, and start to enumerate the virtues of the farming life. 'All these wine drinkers with broken hearts,' he would say. 'You can't compare them to simple peasants who do more for humanity.' He used to claim he would rather be a farmer than join government service and do the bidding of corrupt politicians. On other occasions, he would tell me about the good works that honest civil servants in India could achieve, and how he himself aspired to be one of them. There was also an unexpected mystical side to him. I once saw him standing on the ghats gesturing towards the sandy expanses across the river. 'That,' he was saying to his companion, a slightly terrified young student, 'is *sunyata*, the void. And this' – he pointed at the teeming conglomeration of temples and houses behind us – 'is *maya*, illusion. Do you know what our task is? Our task is to live somewhere in between.'

Rajesh revered Gandhi, and distrusted Nehru, who he said was too 'modern' in his outlook; but then he would change his mind and say that Gandhi wasn't 'tough' enough. All of these opinions he delivered with a faraway look; they formed part of his monologues about the degraded state of contemporary India. 'Where are we going?' he would ask, dramatically throwing up his hands. 'What kind of nation are we becoming?' He loved Faiz, the Pakistani writer whose doom-laden poetry he knew by heart, and he was also fond of Wordsworth, whom he had studied as an undergraduate; he showed me a notebook where he had copied down his favourite poems, 'The Solitary Reaper' among them. But I could never get him to talk about them. He did not listen much; and he did not like anyone interrupting his monologues. It wasn't easy to be with him.

He had been at the university for eight years when I met him, and at first he appeared to be another of the countless students who hung around the campus, mechanically accumulating useless degrees, applying for this or that job. I had come to him with an introduction from a mutual friend at my undergraduate university. This friend believed that 'studious' people like myself needed powerful 'backers' at Benares Hindu University – he used the English words – and that Rajesh was well-placed to protect me from local bullies and criminals. Rajesh himself believed so, and was more than happy to take me under his wing. 'You are here to study,' he told me at our first meeting, 'and that's what you should do. Let me know if anyone bothers you and I'll fix the bastard.'

Part of his concern for me came from an old, and now slightly melodramatic, reverence for 'studious' Brahmins. He was Brahmin himself, but considered himself unequal to what he felt to be the proper dignity of his caste. The feeling was widespread in the region, where the traditional dominance of Brahmins was beginning to collapse in the face of a serious political challenge by assertive lower castes. The decline of Brahmin prestige and authority – intimately linked to their diminishing political importance – was symbolized by a famous family of Benares, which was once very close to the Nehru–Gandhi dynasty, and had been pushed into irrelevance by the new, militant kind of low-caste politician. The members of the family still wore their caste marks on their foreheads; they still observed fasts, regularly bathed in the Ganges, were chief guests at temples on holy days, and would not accept food from low-caste people. But this excessive concern about their public image, and an overdeveloped sense of uncleanliness and contamination, was all that remained of their Brahminness. No crowds of job-seekers and flunkeys gathered at their house any more; the women in the family walked around the bazaars unescorted and unrecognized; visiting journalists went elsewhere for good copy.

Rajesh felt the general change of status differently. He fasted religiously, went to offer flowers at the temple of Hanuman, the monkey god, every Tuesday. His regard for Faiz and love for Urdu poetry spoke of an older Brahminical instinct for learning and the arts. But he also gave the impression that none of the old ways or values mattered any more in a world in which Brahmins were forced to struggle to survive with everyone else. 'Yes, I am a Brahmin, too,' Rajesh would say, and then add, mysteriously, 'but I have done things no Brahmin would have ever done.'

I remember my first visit to his room, which was in one of the derelict-looking hostels with piles of broken furniture scattered on the front quad. The stairs to his room were splattered with blood-red patterns made by students spitting betel juice. In the assorted shabbiness of his room – light from a naked bulb falling weakly on scabby blue walls, unmade bed, discarded slippers, rickety table, cheap denim jeans hanging limply from a solitary nail in the wall, a bamboo bookstand tottering under the weight of old newspapers – I noticed a jute shoulder bag lying open on the ground, bulging with crude pistols. No attempt had been made to conceal the pistols, which seemed to belong as naturally to the room as the green plastic bucket next to them. Their presence made me nervous; so did the hint of instability given by Rajesh's speech and manner, the long monologues, the unconnected references to Wordsworth, to India. I began to wish I saw less of him.

But it was hard to break off contact, even harder to be indifferent to the innocent friendliness he exuded every time I saw him. He often appeared at the library, 'checking up,' he said, on whether I was being my studious self, or whether I was there to 'ogle the girls'. I would try to avoid him by disappearing from the reading room at the time he was likely to show up there, but he would then appear at a later hour. He also took a surprising amount of interest in my reading; surprising, because although he had done an undergraduate course in English, I rarely saw him reading anything more than the Hindi newspapers scattered around the tea-shops on the campus. 'Edmund Wilson! Again! Why,' he would ask with genuine bemusement, 'are you always reading the same man?' He listened patiently while I tried to say a few explanatory words about the particular book or essay he had pointed to. He once caught me reading *To the Finland Station*, and I had to provide a crude summary, in fewer words than used by Wilson, of Trotsky's main ideas. I couldn't, of course, refuse; the thought of Rajesh's instability, the pistols in his room, always forced me to summon up a reasonably friendly response. It could be exhausting being with him at times. Why, I would wonder, did he, who seemed to have read little beyond Faiz and the Romantics, want to know so much about people so distant from us, like Trotsky or Bakunin? (More simply, why couldn't he spend his time with other people in the university?)

Rajesh was well known in student circles. There was a special respect for him among other upper-caste students from nearby villages; lonely and vulnerable in what to them was the larger, intimidating world away from home, they saw Rajesh as a sympathetic fellow provincial and older protector. Rajesh fitted the role rather well: he was physically bigger and stronger than most students on the campus; he had a certain reputation – a lot of people seemed to know about the pistols in his room; and it pleased him to be thought of as a godfather-like figure.

Whenever I went out with him to a tea stall, a small crowd instantly gathered round and eagerly hung on every word he spoke. He often talked about politics, the latest developments in Delhi, the current gossip about the size of a minister's wealth; he would repeat colourful stories about local politicians, the imaginative ways in which they had conned the World Bank or some other development agency, the bridges that were built only on paper, the roads that existed only in files.

Indeed, although he seemed content simply talking about politics, I often wondered if he were not planning to be a politician himself: students with a popular mass base in the university who proved themselves capable of organizing strikes and demonstrations were often hand-picked by local political bosses to contest elections to the local municipal corporation. Rajesh seemed to know people off-campus as well; I once noticed a couple of conspicuously affluent visitors who had driven to see him in a sinister-looking pale-green Ambassador with tinted windows.

But I was preoccupied, particularly with Wilson's writings and their maze of cross-references that sent me scurrying from book to book in an effort to plug at least some of what I felt were egregious gaps in my knowledge. One of the books I came across in this way was Flaubert's *Sentimental Education*, which I had read rather indifferently in a Penguin Classics edition some time back. Wilson's essay on the politics of Flaubert, collected in *The Triple Thinkers*, made me want to reread it. When I did so, I found Flaubert's account of an ambitious provincial's tryst with metropolitan glamour and disillusion full of the kind of subtle satisfactions to which a neurotic adolescent sensibility would be especially susceptible. I identified with Frédéric Moreau, the protagonist, with his large, passionate but imprecise longings; his indecisiveness, his aimlessness, his self-contempt. I cannot ever forget the sick feeling that came over me after I finished the novel late one evening at the library. I was only twenty, and much experience, and many more books, lay ahead of me. But I couldn't fail to recognize the intimations the novel gave me of the many stages of drift and futility I was encountering and was yet to encounter in my own life.

I recommended *Sentimental Education* to Rajesh one evening, and gave him a photocopy of Wilson's essay. I didn't expect him to read all of it; but he had been curious about Wilson, and I thought the essay was a good example of his writing. I didn't hear from him for a few weeks. My life went on as before. I left for the library early in the morning, and came back to a house reverberating with the exuberant jangling of sitars, the doleful twang of sarods, the hollow beat of tablas. I ate every evening with Panditji's wife, sitting cross-legged on the floor in her dark kitchen, awkwardly inhaling thick smoke from the wood fire, over which Shyam dextrously juggled hot chapatis from one calloused palm to another.

Later, back in my room, trying to read in the low-voltage light, I would hear the bells for evening prayers ring out from the adjacent temple. I spoke little to the Americans who, after their lessons with Panditji, came up to the roof to smoke opium. I already knew I could not share my intellectual discoveries with them. They hadn't heard of Edmund Wilson: one of them, a Princeton undergraduate, straining to recognize the name, thought I meant the biologist E.O. Wilson. The cultural figures they spoke about, and appeared to miss in the often oppressive alienness of this most ancient of Indian towns, were then unknown to me; it was to take me a few more years to find out who David Letterman was. But whatever their reasons, the Americans were, like me, refugees from the modern world of work and achievement, explorers of a world that antedated their own, and I was sympathetic to them.

Several weeks after I'd last seen him, Rajesh abruptly reappeared one afternoon at the library. He had been away, he said, on urgent work. Now he was on his way to visit his mother, who lived in a village forty miles west of Benares. Would I accompany him? I thought of making some excuse, but then I realized I needed some diversion and I said yes. Besides, I was curious about Rajesh's background, of which he had told me nothing until then. I could guess that he wasn't well-off, but one could have said the same for most students at the university.

We left one cold foggy morning on the small-gauge, steam-engined train that in those days ran between Benares and Allahabad. A chilly wind, gritty with coal dust, blew in through the iron-barred windows as the train puffed and wheezed through an endless flat plain, with stubbly fields stretching to tree-blurred horizons, and coils of smoke torpid above ragged settlements of mud huts and half-built brick houses. The train was empty, and Rajesh and I stretched out on hard wooden benches, wrapped from head to toe in coarse military blankets, hurriedly sipping the cardamom-scented tea that seemed to turn cold the moment the vendor lifted the kettle off his tiny coal stove.

We got off at a small station populated entirely, it seemed, by mangy dogs. A half-hour tonga ride from there, the horse's hooves clattering loudly against the tarmac road. Mango groves on both sides. Here and there, a few box-shaped houses with large courtyards where men slumbered on string cots; cold-storage warehouses; tiny shuttered shops. At an enclave of mud huts, swarthy blouseless women swept the common yard with brooms made of leafy neem twigs that left the earth raked over with crow's-feet patterns. Finally, at the end of a row of identical roadside buildings, there was Rajesh's own house, brick-walled, one room, poor – but what had I expected?

The door was opened by Rajesh's mother, a tiny shrunken woman in a widow's white sari. She looked frankly puzzled to see me at first, but grew very welcoming when Rajesh introduced me as a friend from the university. After the early morning light, it was dark and damp inside the high-ceilinged room. There was a solitary window, but it was closed. In one corner, partitioned off by a flimsy handloom sari, was the kitchen, where a few brass utensils dully gleamed in the dark, and where Rajesh's mother busied herself with breakfast. In another corner, under a sagging string cot, was a tin trunk, leprous with rust. There were religious calendars in garish colours on the walls: Shiva, Krishna, Hanuman. I recall being unsettled by that bare, lightless room, and its extreme poverty, something not immediately apparent in Rajesh's life in Benares.

During the morning, Rajesh had become silent. Now he left the room while I sat in a straight-backed wicker chair and talked to his mother, both of us forced to speak very loudly to make ourselves heard above the hissing sounds from the kerosene stove. It wasn't easy to express sympathy at that volume; and sympathy was increasingly required of me as she began to tell stories from her past: she had been widowed fifteen years ago when Rajesh was still a child, and soon afterwards her wealthy, feudal in-laws had started to harass her. The house in which she lived with her husband and son was taken away, and they refused to give back what little dowry she had brought with her. Her parents were dead, her brothers too poor to support her. There was only Rajesh, who had worked since he was thirteen, first in the maize fields, and then at a carpet factory in Benares, where he had gone to evening school and done well enough to enter the university. The years had somehow passed.

But now she was worried. Rajesh, she felt, had reached a dead end. There were no more openings for him. All the jobs were going to low-caste people. And not only did Rajesh have the wrong kind of caste, he had no connections anywhere for a government job. She added, with a touch of old Brahmin pride, he had too much self-respect to work for low-caste shopkeepers and businessmen.

How little of Rajesh's past I had known! I knew a bit about those carpet factories; they had been in the papers after some human rights organizations petitioned the courts to prohibit them from using child labourers. There had been pictures of large-eyed, frightened-looking children in dungeon-like rooms, framed against their exquisite handiworks. I was shocked to realize that Rajesh had been one of them. The tormenting private memories of childhood that he carried within himself seemed unimaginable.

On the train back to Benares, Rajesh broke his silence to say that he had read *Sentimental Education*, and that it was a story he knew well. '*Yeh meri duniya ki kahani hai. Main in logo ko janta hoon*,' he said, in Hindi. 'It is the story of my world. I know these people well.' He gave me a hard look. 'Your hero, Edmund Wilson,' he added, in English, 'he also knows them.'

What did Rajesh, a student in a provincial Indian university in the late 1980s, have in common with Frédéric Moreau or any of the doomed members of his generation in this novel of mid-nineteenth-century Paris? As it happened, I didn't ask him to explain. I had already been made to feel awkward by the unexpected disclosures about his past, and the day had been somewhat exhausting. We talked, desultorily, of other things, and parted in Benares.

It was two years later, when I was in Benares again, that I next heard about Rajesh. The man who told me, someone I remembered as one of Rajesh's hangers-on, appeared surprised that I didn't already know that he had been a member of a criminal gang specializing in debt collection on behalf of a group of local moneylenders and businessmen. That explains his mysterious absences from Benares, I thought, as well as the pistols in his room and the sinister-looking Ambassador with tinted windows.

It was, the man said, a good, steady business: once confronted with the possibility of violence, people paid up very quickly, without involving the police. But then Rajesh had graduated to something riskier – and here, although shocked and bewildered by what I had been told, and fully expecting the worst, I could not take it in.

At some stage, the man said, dramatically pausing after every word, Rajesh had turned himself into a contract killer. It was an extremely well-paid profession, and a well-connected one. You worked for small-time contractors who in turn worked for wealthy industrialists and also did favours for local political bosses who did not always rely on their own 'private armies' (the local term for loyal henchmen) for certain jobs. You got to know everyone well after a few years in the business. You worked for all these important people, yet you were ultimately on your own. The chances of survival weren't very high. Sooner or later, the police came to hear of you. Fierce loyalties of caste and clan ensured that every murder would be avenged. It was what would one day happen to Rajesh, his one-time friend predicted. In a typical ambush of the kind often reported in the local papers, he would be on his motorcycle when four men would surround him at a busy intersection in the old city, and shoot him dead. The prurient excitement on the man's face filled me with disgust and anger.

I never did hear what happened to Rajesh. Such stories were in the newspapers every day. But it took me a while to sort out my confused feelings. I kept seeing Rajesh at that busy crossing, trapped in the dense swarm of scooters, cycle rickshaws, bullock carts, cars, buses, trucks, and bicycles, the four men converging upon him, producing crude pistols from their pockets . . .

Rajesh had bewildered me: his self-consciousness about his Brahmin identity, the pistols in his room, his constant talk of the void. I could now see that he had been struggling to make sense of his life, to connect the disparate elements that existed in it; but so, in a different way, was I.

In 1996 I thought of writing something on Edmund Wilson. I had tried before, in 1995, the year of Wilson's centenary, but what I wrote then seemed to me too much like a reprise of what a lot of other people had already said. I realized though that I had been trying to write about him as an American or European writer would have done. What I had in mind was a straightforward exposition of Wilson's key books; it hadn't occurred to me that a separate narrative probably existed in my private discovery of Wilson's writings in a dusty old library in the ancient town of Benares.

Browsing through old papers in preparation for another attempt, I came across a photocopy of his essay on Flaubert's politics. It looked familiar. Idly flipping through the essay, I reached the pages on *Sentimental Education*, where I saw some passages underlined in red. As I'm not in the habit of marking up a printed text, I wondered who had done this. I read the underlined sentences:

> Frédéric is only the more refined as well as the more incompetent side of the middle-class mediocrity of which the dubious promoter represents the more flashy and active aspect. And so in the case of the other characters, the journalists and the artists, the members of the various political factions, the remnants of the old nobility, Frédéric finds the same shoddiness and lack of principle which are gradually revealed in himself . . .

On another page the underlined passage read:

> Flaubert's novel plants deep in our mind an idea which

we never quite get rid of: the suspicion that our middle-class society of manufacturers, businessmen, and bankers, of people who live on or deal in investments, so far from being redeemed by its culture, has ended by cheapening and invalidating all the departments of culture, political, scientific, artistic, and religious, as well as corrupting and weakening the ordinary human relations: love, friendship, and loyalty to cause – till the whole civilization seems to dwindle.

The passage offered a small glimpse of Wilson's way of finding the sources and effects of literature in the overlap between individual states of mind and specific historical realities. But I hadn't noticed this when I discovered the piece. I read it again and thought about the red under-linings. And then, after almost seven years, Rajesh strode back into my consciousness. I remembered the afternoon I had given *Sentimental Education* and Wilson's essay to him; I remembered his words to me on the train, words I dismissed as exaggeration, the determined look on his face as he said, 'It is the story of my world. I know these people well. Your hero, Edmund Wilson, he also knows them.'

What had he meant by that?

The question did not leave me. And there came a time when I began to think I had understood very little, and mis-understood much, during those months in Benares. I recalled the day I went to visit Rajesh's village and I at last saw that there had been a purpose behind Rajesh's invita-tion to his home, his decision to reveal so frankly his life to me. Even the cryptic remarks about *Sentimental Educa-tion* and Wilson on the train: he wanted me to know that not only had he read the novel; he had drawn, with Wilson's help, his own conclusions from it.

In the hard and mean world he had lived in, first as a child labourer and then as hired criminal for politicians and businessmen, Rajesh would have come to know well the grimy underside of middle-class society. What became clearer to me now was how quick he had been to recognize that the society Flaubert and Wilson wrote about wasn't much different from the one he inhabited in Benares: 'It's the story of my world,' he had said. I couldn't see it then but in Benares I had been among people who, like Frédéric Moreau and his friends, had either disowned or, in many cases, moved away from their provincial origins in order to realize their dreams of success in the bourgeois world. Only a handful of them were able to get anywhere near to realizing their dreams while the rest saw their ambitions dwindle away in successive disappointments over the years. The degradation of bribery, sycophancy, and nepotism that people were forced into in their hunt for jobs was undermining in itself: so pervasive was the corruption around them that neither those who succeeded nor those who failed were able to escape its taint.

The small, unnoticed tragedies of thwarted hopes and ideals Flaubert wrote about in *Sentimental Education* were all around us. And this awareness – which was also mine but which I tried to evade through, ironically, the kind of obsessive reading that had led me to the novel in the first place – had been Rajesh's private key to the book. Thus, where I saw only the reflection of a personal neurosis – the character of Frédéric in particular embodying my sense of inadequacy, my harsh self-image – he had discovered a social and psychological environment that was similar to the one he lived in.

That discovery did honour to both Flaubert and Wilson. The world we knew in Benares was many years away from those of the French novelist and the American critic. Yet – and this was a measure of their greatness – they seemed to have had an accurate, if bitter, knowledge of its peculiar human ordeals and futility. It was a knowledge Rajesh himself arrived at by a somewhat different route. 'To fully appreciate the book,' Wilson had written of *Sentimental Education*, 'one must have had time to see something of life.' It sounds like a general sort of adage; but Rajesh exemplified its truth even as he moved into another world, taking what in retrospect look like all the wrong turns. Rajesh had known how to connect whatever little he read to the world around himself, much in the same way Wilson had done in his essay, and in his other writings: a way that revealed a symbiotic relationship between life and literature that I, despite all my reading, was not fully to grasp until long after I had left Benares and thought again of that time of hopeful, confused striving when I first read Edmund Wilson.

Part I

Allahabad:
The Nehrus, the Gandhis
and Democracy

1 The Colonial City and the Countryside

IN SEPTEMBER 2000, INDIA held its third general election in as many years after the coalition government dominated by the Hindu nationalist BJP (Indian People's Party) collapsed in New Delhi. The Hindu nationalists, who had conducted nuclear tests and challenged Pakistan to a final war over Kashmir soon after joining the coalition government in 1998, were expected to strengthen their position and resume their work of turning India into a militant Hindu state. I thought then of returning to Allahabad, the North Indian city where I had lived as an undergraduate student from 1985 to 1988, a time when Hindu nationalism still seemed as marginal in India as it had been for the previous four decades.

Allahabad lies in the heart of the vast North Indian plains, at the confluence of the two sacred rivers of Hinduism, the Ganges and the Yamuna. Flying across the plains on a clear day, you can follow the rivers as they descend from the Himalayas and then meander through great expanses of flat cultivated land, past clusters of ancient cities and towns. Three millennia ago, their waters provided the basis for the civilization of the original Aryan settlers of North India. Each winter, hundreds of thousands of pilgrims still travel to Allahabad from all across India for a religious fair near the confluence, and every twelve years the Kumbh Mela, the largest human gathering in the world, attracts millions of Hindus to the site.

Yet the place isn't easy to get to. Commercial flights have been discontinued; and during the election period, the overnight train from Delhi was overbooked. To get to Allahabad in time for the early campaigning, I had to take the hopping flight from Delhi to Benares, along with a tour group of Italians travelling to see the erotic temple sculpture at Khajuraho, and then drive eighty miles east to Allahabad.

The flight is operated by one of India's private airlines. The breakfast was freshly cooked and warm; the toilets were clean and generously supplied with cologne; and the courtesy and efficiency of the staff were like marvels compared to the resolute badness of the state-owned Indian Airlines. Miles out of Delhi, moving deeper into a part of India still untouched by the entrepreneurial energy and foreign investments of recent years, the flight could seem part of the good things that contact with the global economy had brought to India: higher standards of health and hygiene, a greater alertness to individual needs.

But an older India of caste and poverty is never far away, even on a plane with its western-style amenities, its atmosphere of international ease and luxury. In Khajuraho, after the package tourists had departed, another kind of people came on board: dark-complexioned, barefoot cleaners with little brushes and rags. They filled the cabin with the smell of sweat and chewed tobacco, and as they went scuttling through the narrow aisles on hands and knees – as if their degradation was required by their low caste – the expression on the face of the pretty short-skirted stewardess, who could have been the glamorous poster-girl of a European or American airline, was one of pure distaste.

The long bone-rattling drive afterwards to Allahabad on potholed roads, through calf-deep floods, past the tin-roofed shacks and rain-battered villages of mud and thatch – the cowering huts, so picturesque from the plane, now appearing frail, in danger of collapsing onto the sodden earth from which they had been so arduously raised, the low-caste women paving tiny courtyards with cow-dung, the men spinning rope for the string cots, the sky low and grey over the flat fields and tiny huts and the buffaloes placid in muddy pools – the long drive through a world that belonged to itself as fixedly as it would have done two centuries ago was a reminder of how far even the superficially good things of a globalized economy were from this heavily populated and impoverished part of India.

India, with its severe disparities of income, caste, and religion, is split into so many separate worlds. You can live in one without knowing anything about the others; and no world has an obvious past until you make the effort of dredging it up. I didn't find out until later that the region between Allahabad and Benares, familiar to me from my time as an undergraduate student at Allahabad university, hadn't always been so impoverished. In the early years of the nineteenth century, when the British were still more interested in business than empire, the area had been an important trade centre for North India, and its merchants and moneylenders had been known for their initiative and energy.

But, as always in India, the prosperity so created had been shared out among a very small group of people; it had led to little except the creation of zealously guarded hoards, or, occasionally, an opulent mansion in the midst of a teeming bazaar. When trading routes changed and the region lost its importance, the private fortunes quickly dwindled, the mansions fell into ruin and were taken over by squatters. The region was restored to the wretchedness and cruelties that were probably always there under the gloss of temporary affluence.

Affluence is still a rare achievement; but the gloss has got shinier and deeper. At the time of the elections, my hotel in Allahabad was a new white eight-storeyed building of egregious luxury, built by a local manufacturer of bidis (cheap Indian cigarettes), who had recently begun to dabble in politics. Every effort had been made to make it conform to international specifications. The menu at the coffee-shop offered Mexican and Italian food. A muzak version of 'Sound of Silence' played in the elevators. When the power supply broke down, as it frequently did in the city, a massive basement generator groaned into life. The corridors were thickly carpeted; the double-glazed windows kept out the loud film music from the small slum just outside the hotel, where a rain-fed gutter overflowed onto the tin-roofed shacks and left green stains of slime on the pale earth around them.

The hotel was fated to remain empty, and so it was, most of the time. Its luxury couldn't but seem pointless. It met no local needs; it required no local expertise. In fact, people from as far as South India had to be imported to fill in managerial positions. Its purpose, if you could call it that, seemed to lie in its being an assertion of wealth and power in the midst of general deprivation, quite like the newly built houses with Doric columns and Palladian facades in the area around the hotel.

The solidity of the building, its quiet interiors, the monumental presence of its white facade in the middle of the city – in all its deliberate order and calm, the hotel underlined its separateness from its setting. Its effect was felt most keenly by the menial staff, who travelled each day from their homes in the flood-threatened outskirts of Allahabad, and approached their place of work with something like awe. They looked very ill at ease in their green uniforms, and were obsequiously polite with guests, calling to mind the Indians who had come to serve in the new city of Allahabad built by the British after the rude shock of the Indian mutiny of 1857, the city whose simple colonial geography was plain from my sixth-floor hotel room: the railway tracks partitioning the congested 'black town' with its minarets and temple domes from the tree-lined grid of 'white town', where for a long period no Indians, apart from servants, could appear in native dress.

Allahabad was 'Prayag', a small pilgrim centre, before the British, in the early nineteenth century, began to use it as a military base, guarding the up-country trade on the river Ganges. When, in 1857, Indian soldiers in British-led armies mutinied, the British struggled to retain their power across most of North India, except in Allahabad, where they were not challenged greatly. They quickly put down the few soldiers who did rebel; they razed to the ground those houses in the old quarter that belonged to rich supporters of the insurrectionists. No stories of unspeakable atrocities against British women and children emerged from Allahabad as they did from Kanpur, just 150 miles away to the north on the Ganges.

Nevertheless, the British wished to make a point. The pacifier of Allahabad was a devout Christian colonel called James Neill who believed that 'the word of God gives no authority to the modern tenderness for human life'. Under his direction, some 6,000 Indians were hanged, shot, or tortured to death, in just a few days.

It was in the months following the pacification that eight villages were confiscated, as a senior official stated, from 'dirty Indian niggers' and were turned into the exclusively British enclave of Civil Lines. The great buildings of the city – the Romanesque cathedral, the university tower and dome, the Gothic public library, the baroque High Court – went up in the decades that followed the suppression of the mutiny, a time of serenity for the British in India, when India officially became part of the Empire and the natives remained quiet for the most part.

In Allahabad, the civil and military administration, the hospitals, schools and the High Court produced a small Anglo-Indian society. For these exiled people, the compensations for the city's great heat and isolation were to be had in untroubled leisure, in the clubs, polo grounds and large bungalows with wide verandahs and sprawling lawns where it was common for a family to have fifty to sixty servants. When, in 1887, the young Rudyard Kipling came to work in Allahabad after some exciting years as a journalist in Lahore, he found himself alienated by the 'large, well-appointed club, where Poker had just driven out

Whist and men gambled seriously', stating that it '. . . was full of large-bore officials, and of a respectability all new'.

When you look now at the buildings of the period after 1857, their playfully diverse architectural styles seem to confirm Kipling's vision of a people savouring their privilege. In their rhetorical magnificence – quite like that of my hotel – they stand apart from, and indeed loom over, everything around them; they suggest a people made absolutely secure by wealth and unchallenged power. At the public library – built as a memorial to the official who dispossessed the 'dirty Indian niggers' of Civil Lines – there are relief figures of Indian peasants and potters and silk-weavers on carved capitals. The peasants are wiry, obviously well-fed men with turbans; the physical appearance and settings of the potters and silk-weavers have been similarly improved. They are unsettling, not least because severe British methods of revenue collection had ravaged the countryside, forcing generations of the rural poor into vicious circles of endless debt and bondage to local landlords and moneylenders. It is hard to imagine that the architect was aware of the crude irony of his representations; more likely that he was indulging a fantasy about the Indian countryside, a romantic idea about peasants created at a safe distance from their actual condition.

The romance had gone, but this distance hadn't really diminished with independence; the administrators and the masses still lived in separate worlds. At the commissioner's office, an old sprucely painted bungalow with trimmed hedges in Civil Lines, a middle-aged woman in a torn white sari held a creased piece of paper and pleaded with attendants wearing red-sashed livery. The widow of one of the labourers killed in a mining accident, she had travelled a long way from her village that morning to beg the commissioner to expedite relief money sanctioned more than two years ago by the government. The audience wasn't granted; the woman was told to take her application to a lower official and not bother the commissioner's office with petty requests.

I accompanied the commissioner and the district police chief on their inspection tour of rural police stations two days before the elections in Allahabad. We travelled in two white Ambassadors with blue lights, sirens and official flags on the bonnet. Villagers turned to look at us warily as we raced through a series of traffic jams on narrow country roads. At the first sign of an approaching bottleneck, the driver put on the siren and bodyguards cradling AK-47s, leaned out of the windows, forcing big overweight trucks off the roads and onto muddy ledges where they stood leaning dangerously.

Policemen everywhere stood to attention and saluted the cars as they went past. At official bungalows with little flower beds and manicured lawns, junior officials vied with each other to open the car doors and escort us to dining tables overloaded with warm snacks. More members of the civil service would invariably join us at this point. These were election observers sent to the region from other states, men in their thirties and forties, eager and fluent. A brisk bonhomie would ensue around the dining table as people compared notes on who was posted where and who was about to be promoted. There would be little talk of the election, or the police stations we had visited (some of them in total disarray – small dark rooms full of dusty files and broken furniture, with smells of urine and alcohol emanating from lock-ups – easily imagined as local centres of tyranny, settings for the third-degree torture and custodial deaths and rapes you read about in the papers).

At the beginning of the inspection tour, the police chief, who had the reputation, rare in Allahabad, of not soliciting bribes, looked concerned. His English marked him as a man who had entered the civil service from a modest small-town background; it is difficult to imagine that someone in his position would not have been made aware of what happened in the police stations. Yet, after the first, where he scolded the paunchy official in charge who had been clumsily making up the number of men arrested and guns seized, he hurried through the rest, with a look of distaste on his face. The commissioner looked restless throughout the tour, and found his voice only with the other civil service men. He had earlier spoken to me with feeling about the inconveniences of living in the English town of Hull, where he had been sent by the Indian government to undergo some training. He now spoke mournfully – others around the dining table shaking their head sideways in sympathy – of criminals with hundreds of police cases against them, who had not only entered politics but also become 'honourable ministers' and to whom he was required to show proper deference.

Dignity, and how to hold on to it: that was what preoccupied these men, most of whom the civil service had rescued from a lower-middle-class shabbiness. The dignity whose emblems included the bungalows, the white cars with sirens, the red-sashed attendants and the attentive lower officials; the dignity that came out of asserting one's distance from everything tainted by the ordinary misery and degradation of India: the widow outside the commissioner's office, the criminals working as ministers, the corrupted men in the rural police stations.

In the assertion of that distance lay the self-image of the colonial administrators, and over time this has changed as little as the actual hierarchies and structure of the admin-istration itself. Only the gap between rhetoric and reality – intenser in an India with democratic aspirations – has widened. For people in small towns and villages – the majority of India's population – the sources of power and justice are still somewhere in the larger unknown world, and you can spend all your life waiting for them to work in your favour.

Consider this village thirty miles out of Allahabad: a huddle of huts, unpainted brick houses and narrow mud lanes on a stony slope. My car was the only motorized vehicle on the rutted country road that dusty late after-noon. Its appearance from around an abrupt bend startled the bullock-cart drivers and shepherds, and excited fear among the people at this village, who stood by the side of the road, holding the little green plastic flags of the Samaj-wadi (Socialist) Party, and waited for the local candidate, Mr Reoti Raman Singh, to arrive. They stood stiffly, not daring to come closer, until summoned by the driver, when they moved awkwardly and surrounded the car. Anxious, thin, sun-hardened faces with roughly cut hair, young and old, pressed against the windows; frankly curious eyes quickly took in my camera, diary, pen – glamorous items in this context – and suddenly clouded over with uncer-tainty. When I asked them about the local issues they wished their Member of Parliament to resolve, they shook their heads. One of the best-dressed persons among them, an old man in white kurta and dhoti and thick white moustache, said that there were no problems at all, and resumed his scrutiny of my personal effects. It was only when my exasperated driver – a recent migrant to Allahabad from a nearby village – introduced me as a journalist and urged them to tell me the truth that the old man began to speak.

The others prompted him, in shy whispers at first, and then everyone spoke at once. This village was different from those I had already visited that day only in the quality of its deprivation. It was privileged in having a tube-well for drinking water, but the nearest hospital was nine miles away, and though the government had installed an electric pole, there had never been any 'current'. The biggest problem related to the government's primary school: it had been around for several years, but the teacher only came once a week from Allahabad and even then only for a couple of hours or so. There was no way of predicting when he would come and so the students dressed each morning for school and spent the day waiting for the teacher outside locked doors. That wasn't all: the teacher was accused by the locals of taking all the rice which the government sent for the pupils every year. He had also been accused of carving out personal profits from the building of the new one-room school for girls: the foundation was 9 inches instead of the usual 20 inches, and the building could collapse any moment.

Earlier that day, I had been travelling with Reoti Raman Singh, the candidate for Allahabad's parliamentary constituency from the Samajwadi, or Socialist, Party. Fierce monsoon rains had accompanied us en route from Mr Singh's rambling mansion in the old quarter of Allahabad

to the rural districts. The windshield wipers flailed use-
lessly; the road was reduced to frothy mud. When the rain
stopped, soft parkland rolled out on both sides, the green
of the grass, trees, and bushes brilliantly vivid and separate
in the grey light of the still turbulent sky; water gurgled
through roadside ditches; and for a moment at least it was
possible to take pleasure in the poverty-ravaged landscape,
to see pastoral beauty in the young boys and girls herding
sheep and buffaloes on grassy slopes.

Mr Singh was a tall stooping man; he walked with a
slight limp and gave an impression of some deep debility,
along with a great kindness. He sat impassive in the front
of the jeep, and hardly moved whenever his personal attendant – a thickset man in a safari suit – reached out from
the back seat to adjust the silk scarf around his employer's
neck. The scarf, stiff with starch, was important: Mr Singh
belonged to a old distinguished feudal family of the region,
one that had made its name and wealth in pre-colonial
times, and the external symbols of his prestige had to be
maintained. At a railway level crossing, a blind man in wet
rags came up to the jeep and, hopping a bit on his bare,
calloused feet, sang a devotional song. Mr Singh obliged
with a generous gift of Rs 100, three times the daily wages
of a labourer. There was both approval and envy on the
faces of the small crowd of onlookers as they watched the
rupee note passing from Mr Singh's attendant to the blind
man: Mr Singh, or 'Kunwar Sahib', Prince, as he was
called, had done the thing expected of him.

Early that morning at his house in Allahabad, men from
nearby villages had sat silently in small dark rooms, tense
with the urgency of those matters they waited to lay before
Mr Singh: power and water connections, a clerical job, a

property dispute. Their blank faces cracked and betrayed disappointment when Mr Singh, already running late that morning, was rushed out to the jeep waiting in the front yard. There were many more supplicants at the villages he stopped at – mostly men from the low Nishad, or fisher-men, caste, small-limbed and dark and half-naked, who ran up to the jeep, hands folded, heads bowed. Mr Singh addressed them in the local dialect; his manner was easy yet authoritative. He asked them directly about their prob-lems, and was quick to respond. He promised to fire the policeman who had been extorting money from one vil-lage; he promised to build a culvert linking another two villages across a canal within a month of his election; at villages requiring water, he promised to have tube-wells dug. He reminded them of the electricity and water he had brought to villages in his region. He didn't say that he had done the good work in his official capacity as a member of the state legislature; it was an earlier contract, and not the obligations of elected office, that he was invoking: the con-tract between the upper-caste wealthy feudal lord and his destitute but loyal subjects. The faces in the crowds looked satisfied; they nodded, childlike, as he spoke, and as he pre-pared to leave, people lunged forward and tried to reach through the open window to touch his feet. It was as if after the unmet expectations from the flawed institutions of democratic India, after the many disappointments, an uncared-for people had found some security in the still per-sisting ideals of *noblesse oblige*.

Drinking water, police harassment, electricity, schools and hospitals: these weren't the themes being discussed when I left Delhi, although the media had been as obsessed with the elections as it was with Kashmir, where the Indian army had fought several bloody battles with Pakistan-backed armed intruders over the summer.

The media grew each year, with new newspapers, magazines, and TV channels appearing almost every week. But only a very small part of what it produced could be called journalism. During the battles in Kashmir, it had assumed the role of cheerleader, and worked up a lot of hysteria among the metropolitan middle classes for whom war and jingoism appeared to clarify, if only momentarily, a self-image that had been blurred by eight years of rapid social and economic liberalization. False stories, disseminated by the Indian army about the torture of its soldiers by the Pakistanis, were retold endlessly even after it was revealed that they were false. Correspondents in battle fatigues shouted breathless reports into microphones as shells screamed overhead. Stylish young army officers boasted at length about their plans for the Pakistanis. There was little embarrassment when on national TV one of the officers echoed the Pepsi Cola slogan, *Yeh Dil Maange More* ('This heart wants more'), and was then killed in battle soon afterwards, or when in its haste to convert the skirmishes into a splendid little war for itself the government announced on independence day that its highest military honour was to go posthumously to a soldier who turned out to be alive in a Delhi army hospital.

And then as abruptly as it had started, the war was over, and forgotten. No one seemed to know how much money had been collected for the families of the 266 dead soldiers; many of the countless relief funds and benefit concerts and fashion shows became part of yet another Indian scam. Political pundits and analysts replaced military strategists and experts on television, and seemed to shuttle endlessly between recording studios, chatting about 'swings' and 'anti-incumbency factors' and 'index of opposition unity'. The English-language press was full of opinion polls and analyses; and the suave spokesmen for the two main political parties, the Congress and the Hindu nationalist Bhartiya Janata Party (BJP), exchanged creative insults in daily debates about the foreign origins of Sonia Gandhi, the leader of the Congress, and the alleged failure of the BJP government to act on early intelligence reports about the intruders in Kashmir.

The television experts and newspaper columnists called it an election without issues. But the separation of issues from elections had occurred long before. Elections, held almost yearly, had become a national drama, preceded and followed by even greater dramas of betrayals, defections, buying and selling legislators, no-confidence motions, coalition collapses, new ministries, speculations about who was in and who was out, etc. The drama – created this time by questions like, 'Is Sonia an agent of the Vatican?' and, 'Did our soldiers die in vain in Kashmir?' – helped suppress the real issues, and also brought about a temporary cohesion and passion among a fragmented apathetic population.

Yet, in Allahabad, once known as the most politically minded city in India, the drama was missing. Even as late as the 1980s, politicians and lawyers, dressed in contrasting white and black, gathered at the old coffee house in the heart of the 'white town' every morning and evening to gossip about various political figures, and the size of their wealth. But I found the coffee house empty. Waiters in scruffy white livery and turbans stood around vacantly under fans hung high from cobwebbed wooden beams on the ceiling; and lizards made drowsy by the moist heat clung unmovingly to the faded painting of Gandhi on the walls where the bright-blue paint had peeled off, exposing the solid masonry underneath.

One morning I went to Anand Bhavan, the family mansion of the Nehrus. It is only a five-minute walk from the campus of Allahabad University, where I had lived as an undergraduate; strange to think that I hardly ever went there.

Not that there was much to see. On the morning I went, gaudily dressed peasant women and children sat cross-legged in the long arcades, cautiously running their hands over the cool marble floors. Outside, the posters at pavement stalls were all of fleshy-lipped Indian film heroes. The usual election party banners, the tempos with loudspeakers, and the motorcycle boys with party flags and bandannas, were hardly visible on the streets. I walked through the wide verandahs and balconies and peered into rooms where French meals were once served on Dresden china with Czech glasses, and where, in a more political time, Mahatma Gandhi and Jawaharlal Nehru and other great men of the Congress Party discussed ways of liberating India from colonial rule. In a newer building on the large walled compound, I could see yet more peasant women, also in gaudy nylon saris, shuffling shyly through an ill-lit gallery of photographs from hopeful times: Nehru, the first prime minister of independent India, inaugurating dams and factories – what he called 'the new temples of India'; Nehru with other celebrities of the postcolonial world, Nasser, Sukarno, Nkrumah; and Nehru's daughter, Indira Gandhi, in an elegant silk sari, hugging Fidel Castro at a summit meeting of non-aligned nations.

In Allahabad, a decaying city whose brief moment of glory belonged to the anticolonial struggle, you couldn't but feel distant from these celebrations of postcolonial nationalism and Third World solidarity. It was also hard not to wonder what, if anything, the peasant visitors made of the photographs. Most of them came on day trips from the vast rural region around Allahabad where the young Jawaharlal Nehru had, after his seven years at Harrow and Cambridge, first been exposed to 'the degradation and overwhelming poverty of India'. Their parents and grandparents were probably among the enthusiastic voters who, after independence, repeatedly elected Nehru to the Indian parliament from a rural constituency near Allahabad – though they themselves had remained close to destitution.

Things hadn't changed much even for those with privileged access to the owners of Anand Bhavan. In the late 1970s, Dom Moraes, the Indian writer and poet, met an old couple, Becchu and his wife Sonia, who had worked there for much of the century. Moraes was then researching a semi-authorized biography of Indira Gandhi; the officials in charge of the mansion let him remove the leatherbound books from the shelves and discover Nehru's interest in Balzac, Dickens, Maugham, and Koestler. The same officials, one rainy day at Anand Bhavan, brought Becchu and Sonia to see Moraes, and told him that 'Becchu was beating Sonia too much. Now he is not beating. Since she is becoming blind, he is taking care.'

The two of them sat before Moraes, 'dripping and shivering after coming in from the cold.' The interview wasn't a success. Moraes got only a blurred picture of the 'splendour, hedonism, and ostentation' that had marked life at Anand Bhavan until the early 1920s (when Gandhi, the charismatic new leader of the freedom movement, partly converted the Nehrus to his ascetic and defiantly Indian lifestyle); Becchu, a 'skinny old man', kept shouting at his wife in between fits of crying. His 'convulsive sobs turned into positive roars of sorrow' when Moraes mentioned Indira Gandhi's defeat in the national elections she had held in 1977, two years after imposing a 'state of emergency' on India and suspending civil rights.

Becchu's grief, however, was more personal. During her nine years as prime minister of India, Mrs Gandhi had promised him a pension; it hadn't been paid and after her defeat it now looked very unlikely indeed. An unsettled Moraes tried to console the servant with a big tip. Becchu stretched out a 'wizened hand' for the rupee notes; but his wife, 'blind or not', was quicker. 'She whipped the money away and stuffed it in her blouse', and Becchu started to wail.

2 *The Dynasty*

Nehru was often perceived by foreign visitors as a 'lonely Indian aristocrat . . . presiding over his deficient but devoted peasantry'. But the description 'aristocrat', which Nehru himself encouraged, is too easily achieved in India: you only need to be placed slightly above the general wretchedness.

The Nehrus were Brahmins from Kashmir who in the early eighteenth century became minor courtiers to Mogul emperors in Delhi. After the British destroyed Muslim power in India in the nineteenth century, the Nehrus found roles in the new imperial dispensation. Motilal Nehru, Jawaharlal's father, was trained as a lawyer; and he moved to Allahabad in 1886 to practise in the high court that the British had established. He first lived in Allahabad's old 'native' quarters – a brothel filled with very young Nepalese women now stands on the site of his house. But he outgrew these modest beginnings very quickly: at the same pace, in fact, as Allahabad's importance as an administrative and educational centre. There was much money to be made from representing in court the decadent and exuberantly litigious landed gentry of North India – the upstart men rewarded with grants of land by the British for their loyalty during the mutiny of 1857 – and soon after buying Anand Bhavan, Motilal acquired liveried servants, horses, an English chauffeur for his imported car, and an Irish tutor for his son, and started to order his clothes from Savile Row.

These were also the affectations of the half-literate landlords he represented. In Bengal, where India's first modern culture was almost a century old, these aspirations to respectability would have been met with sarcasm: Rabindranath Tagore and then Nirad Chaudhuri wrote witheringly of the shallow and ostentatious Anglicization of socially ambitious Indians. In feudal North India, which possessed little of the self-confident egalitarian spirit of the Bengal Renaissance, the meeting of East and West usually resulted in tackiness and a crude kind of snobbery: Nehru's younger sister, who was educated by an English governess, looked down upon Nehru's wife, Kamla, mostly because the latter could not speak fluent English.

As his letters to this sister, Vijaylaxmi Pandit, reveal, Nehru was closer to her than to the woman his father had bullied him into marrying – he later gave her glamorous ambassadorial jobs in London, Moscow, and Washington. At a crucial moment in India's transition to independence in 1947, Nehru confided more in Lord Mountbatten, the pompous and incompetent last viceroy of India, than in many of his Indian colleagues, including Gandhi. But then Nehru's greater intimacy with English or Anglicized people, which Gandhi himself remarked upon, was hardly the result of his upbringing in Allahabad.

His intellectual and emotional outlook was formed by his early years in England, by the strain of liberalism in English life, of which the Fabians, whom he admired, were an obvious manifestation. This later made him a hero to Anglicized Indians. But in India he was restless and alienated, with a mystical longing for the Himalayas; and he was actually floundering until he met Gandhi. For it was Gandhi who set Nehru on the path to individual greatness first by alerting him to his world – the awakening Nehru later elaborated upon in such books as *A Discovery of India* – and then by anointing him, among many deserving aspirants, his political heir.

After independence, India became Nehru's private laboratory for the ideas, he had picked up from his reading and travels – a state-controlled economy, industrialization. It also forgave mistakes of the kind that would normally be expected to taint any political career. His refusal to share power with Muslim leaders made the partition of India inevitable, while his complacent belief in pan-Asian solidarity led to India's military humiliation by China in 1962.

*

Other postcolonial leaders were similarly unassailable. But unlike Nasser, Nkrumah, and Sukarno, Nehru was aware of the dangers in his situation. In 1937, the *Modern Review*, a prominent Indian magazine of the time, published the following anonymous analysis of Nehru. 'He has all the makings of a dictator in him – vast popularity . . . an intolerance of others and certain contempt for the weak and inefficient . . . His overmastering desire to get things done, to sweep away what he dislikes and build anew, will hardly brook for long the slow process of democracy . . .'

This remarkably acute description of a postcolonial leader in a hurry is more remarkable still when you learn that the author was Nehru himself. It was the kind of comment that probably made him appear to his daughter like 'a saint who strayed into politics'. Certainly, such self-awareness was absent from Indira's own life; the gap between father and daughter was wide. 'You are such a stranger to me,' Nehru once wrote to her, 'and perhaps you do not know much about me.'

Indira, in fact, liked to think of herself as a 'tough politician' – one of her more accurate self-descriptions. Interestingly, very little in her early life hinted at the toughness. Born in 1917, just as the freedom struggle switched into high gear, she grew up in a distracted household. Nehru was usually away, in prison or travelling across India. It was Indira who accompanied her perennially ill mother to various spas and sanatoriums in India and Europe, and, in the process, drifted through nine schools in Switzerland, England, and India, without distinguishing herself at any of them. Her star fellow pupil at Badminton School in England was the English novelist Iris Murdoch, who later remembered Indira as being 'very unhappy, very lonely'.

This unsettled upbringing probably only deepened the usual teenage insecurities. She was tall for her age and thin; she had a large nose and skin that she saw as too dark. Mrs Pandit, who didn't think Nehru's wife was good enough for him, also didn't much rate his daughter, Indira, whom she described as 'ugly and stupid', a remark that Indira overheard as an adolescent and took with her into her tormented old age, its wound still unhealed, or so she claimed to a close friend a few months before she was assassinated in 1984.

Indira later tried to inject some excitement and glamour into what had been a dull, anxiety-infested childhood and adolescence. In his biography, Dom Moraes reports her claim that from her house in Allahabad she saw the British police shooting dead Chandrashekhar Azad, an Indian revolutionary. This, though, is quite implausible, given the considerable distance between Anand Bhavan and the park where Azad was killed. And the most convincing rebuttal of her claim that she was ill-treated in a British prison comes from Mrs Pandit's daughter, Nayantara Sahgal, who, in a shrewd book about her ambitious cousin, excerpted letters written by her mother at the time from the same prison, all of which attest to the kid-glove treatment the Nehrus generally got from their British jailers.

'She lives in a world of dreams and vagaries,' Nehru had noted when Indira was seventeen years old. 'Extraordinarily self-centred . . . remarkably selfish,' he wrote to his sister. 'She must have depths.' Nehru hoped that his daughter would travel and learn languages, and then, 'with this background of mental training and a wider culture discover the fascinating place that is India', just as he himself had done. With this in mind, while in prison, Nehru dedicated a book of letters about world history to her – she didn't read it until several years later. After his wife Kamla's death in 1936, he arranged for Indira to study at Somerville College, Oxford, but she preferred to hang out with some fashionably left-wing Indian friends in London and failed her Latin exams twice.

He was probably most disappointed by his daughter's intention, soon after returning from England in early 1940, to marry one of the hangers-on at Anand Bhavan, a young Parsee man called Feroze Gandhi (no relation to Mahatma). He registered his own protest against the 'absurd haste of a marriage' and then brought much pressure to bear upon Indira through his friends and relatives. Mahatma Gandhi, worried that Indira might be getting swept away by her sexual feelings for Feroze, recommended a celibate marriage to her – a proposal Indira responded to with some obvious irritation. Surrounded by powerful men and their bullying advice, she wished to be, for once, her own person, and it is hard not to sympathize with her, even though the marriage was, as everyone expected, a disaster. Feroze was as unformed as she was, and although he eventually became a vigorous parliamentarian prior to his early death in 1960, Indira remained, much to his resentment, in thrall to her father's immeasurably greater power and style.

Harold Laski, whom Indira met in England, had noted her 'timid desire to submerge [her] personality in [her] father's', and warned that 'you'll just become an appendage'. This was exactly what she did become in the years after independence: Nehru's companion on his trips abroad, a housekeeper, and the host of official parties at her father's house in New Delhi – quite solemn occasions devoted to classical Indian dance and music, whose Gandhian austerity drove out at least one guest, W.H. Auden, who later complained to Nicolas Nabokov about the alcohol-free evening with the Nehrus.

In one of her letters to Dorothy Norman, a Manhattan socialite whom she had befriended during her visit to New York with Nehru in 1949, Indira confessed to not having found her 'métier'. She also confided in Norman her desire to retire to a small house in England with her two sons, Rajiv and Sanjay. She claimed to have little in common with the Indians who surrounded her and her father: 'They amuse me and they irritate me and sometimes I find myself observing them as if I were not of the same species at all.'

Nevertheless, for someone so much at odds with her environment, Indira was quick to accept, and then grow into, the responsibilities thrust upon her by the coarse politicians she complained about – the powerful regional bosses of the Congress who brokered the party's compact with the popular mass base created by the freedom movement, and who made her, in 1959, the president of the party. Just a few months later, the first ominous sign of her authoritarian ways appeared when she persuaded Nehru to dismiss, on spurious grounds of law and order, the communist government in the South Indian state of Kerala – it was the first democratically elected communist government anywhere in the world.

The ease and speed of Indira's ascent to the prime minister's office, two years after Nehru's death in 1964, surprised everyone at the time. It looks inevitable in retrospect. In the mid 1960s the Indian economy was crippled with food shortages, and there was much dissatisfaction with the way things had gone since independence.

Successive governments had remained preoccupied with Nehru's ambitious blueprint of an industrial and technical infrastructure for India: a strategy that, while creating thousands of exportable scientists and software engineers, doesn't directly address India's basic problems of poverty, disease, and illiteracy – problems that Indira spoke of constantly, but did little to solve. The vast, complicated administrative network the British had set up to retain their hold on India had remained intact, except that the civil bureaucrats, the unaccountable rulers of India during colonial times, had for the first time to accommodate the ambitions of elected politicians.

The state-controlled economy encouraged corruption as much as inefficiency, and the bureaucrats and politicians parcelled out its large and varied booty of big public projects, defence contracts, bribes from businessmen, jobs, foreign trips, telephone connections, etc – a serious steady internal plundering of the overcentralized state's resources that in the early nineties would expose India to the drastic therapies of the IMF and the World Bank. National politics became, and, beyond the excitement of new slogans and personalities, had remained, a set of transactions, with regional and caste leaders delivering votes to a broad-based national party like the Congress in exchange for a share of the power and resources at the centre.

There were regular elections – which, along with freedom of the press, are the major achievements of Indian democracy – and the Congress often lost at the state and local level. But these setbacks did not much weaken the party's stranglehold – quite like that of the PRI in Mexico – over the immensely powerful federal government in Delhi. Its supremacy wasn't successfully challenged by other parties until 1977, after a spell of dictatorship, and then, as it turned out, only for the sake of rewiring the network of patrons and clients the Congress had set up. Not surprisingly, despite universal suffrage, India has been very slow to develop a sense of citizenship or an awareness of the individual rights enshrined in the country's radically democratic constitution, beyond a small minority privileged by caste, class, and education – hence the Nehrus' own family servant futilely expecting to be favoured with a pension that was, after a lifetime of service, his by right.

The democracy Nehru wanted to create had barely thrown up any real challenges or potential political heirs to him. Indira's own long proximity to power had made her ambitious, despite all her fantasies about becoming a London house owner, and as a minister in the cabinet of Nehru's immediate successor, Lal Bahadur Shastri, she quickly showed a talent for the constant petty intriguing of Indian politics. She publicly disparaged the dhoti-clad Shastri, also a native of Allahabad but from a much humbler family. Some Anglicized admirers of Nehru in Delhi, who became Indira's advisers, strengthened her conviction that only someone from the Nehru family could provide enlightened leadership to India. As it happened, after Shastri's unexpected death in 1966, the party bosses found themselves unable to trust each other as supreme leader, and ended up elevating a pliant-seeming Indira as the prime minister of India.

Indira quickly outgrew her patrons, however. She was

offered a fresh start by the Congress Party's dismal performance in the national elections of 1967; she declared
herself a socialist, committed to destroying the sinister
influence she claimed big landlords and businessmen had
over the Congress and the Indian government. She nationalized banks and insurance companies, stopped all government privileges and payments due to the royal families of
India, and announced various programmes for eradicating
poverty. *Garibi hatao* ('Remove poverty') was the obvious
but effective slogan she used in the national elections of
1971 to win overwhelming support among traditionally
poor low-caste Hindus and Muslims who, weary of the
many middlemen and false promises since independence,
saw the daughter of Nehru as their true saviour.

Things briefly appeared to be working out for Indira.
The introduction, during Nehru's time, of high-yielding
crops had made India self-sufficient in food production in
the late 1960s; Indira encouraged this 'green revolution',
and also made herself popular among the relatively affluent class of cultivators by offering them state-subsidized
power, water, and fertilizers. Events outside India also
helped Indira to marginalize the Congress power-brokers.
In 1971, the Pakistani army responded to the disaffection
among Pakistan's eastern Bengali-speaking population
with a near genocide.

Millions of Bengali refugees arrived in India subsequently, straining an already shaky economy. Indira prepared India well for the war with Pakistan that began to
seem imminent as the Indian army trained and armed Bengali insurgents; she swiftly secured military and diplomatic
support from the Soviet Union after it became clear that
Richard Nixon, who suspected her of being an intellectual,

would 'tilt' toward Pakistan. India eventually fought and won a short war with Pakistan, and carved out a new nation. As the liberator of Bangladesh, Indira became, briefly, a universally celebrated figure. No longer the 'dumb doll' that a particularly bitter critic of the Nehru dynasty had dubbed her at the beginning of her time as prime minister, instead she embodied *Shakti*, the Hindu metaphysical concept for female energy and power.

Indira's speeches grew more confident, full of references to her family's prestige and self-sacrificing spirit. She also used the opportunity to banish all remaining and potential rivals within the Congress and to reward some of her lackeys with important positions in the executive, legislative, and the judiciary. The man she appointed as the president of the Congress Party soon devised the slogan 'Indira Is India, and India Indira'. The president of India during much of Indira's tenure in the early 1980s was Zail Singh, famous for claiming that at her command he was ready to wield a broom and become a lowly sweeper. But the sycophancy alone wasn't enough: some of the men Indira promoted were also required to put a fixed amount of money into her coffers.

This new ruthless and amoral side of Indira was almost all that India saw of her for the next decade. It bewildered and alienated even the few friends she had made during her insecure early years; the relatively frank letters to Dorothy Norman became dull rituals before ceasing altogether around the time of the Emergency. Indira's later years leave any potential biographer with little else to detail besides the intricacies of Indian politics. Indeed, much of Indira's life seems to show how a not particularly sensitive or intelligent woman was exalted by accident of birth and a callow political culture into the chieftancy of a continent-sized nation; and how a drab inner life came to be filled with an exaggerated sense of self and mission and an all-consuming quest for personal power.

The autocrat's search for unqualified loyalty usually ends within her own family. Indira's closest colleague in the seventies was her younger son, Sanjay Gandhi; while holding no official position, he had by the time the Emergency was declared in 1975 become the de facto ruler of India. Like many other undereducated scions of Third World dynasties, Sanjay had a weakness for cars. In the late sixties, he abandoned his apprenticeship at the Rolls-Royce factory in England, where he was regularly arrested for speeding, and came back to India with the ambition to make small cars for Indian consumers. Indira's government awarded his new company a licence despite competitive applications from Toyota, Renault, and Citroën. The nationalized banks advanced him generous loans; government officials bullied car dealers into placing large cash orders. No usable cars ever emerged from Sanjay's factory. Nevertheless, banks and industrialists continued to fund his company and Sanjay diversified into equally bogus 'consultancy services' in order to channel the incoming money into his personal accounts.

His little racket was one of the many instances of the crony capitalism that flourished alongside the rhetoric of socialism. Such brazen corruption, which had become commonplace in India by the early seventies, was made still more intolerable for the poor by rising inflation. Successive droughts and an inefficient and venal public distribution system had made food scarce. The Congress started doing badly in local elections. Large-scale protests by students and workers erupted across India in the run-up to the declaration of the Emergency in June 1975. Jayaprakash Narayan, an old Gandhian idealist, emerged from retirement to lead the growing opposition to Indira.

Indira, in turn, denounced the agitation for her removal as part of a broad CIA-backed conspiracy. She had already used the military and the police to crush a Mao-inspired insurgency in Bengal; and when a delayed court judgement invalidated her election to the Indian parliament and made it imperative that she resign, she decided to do away with the fast-unravelling facade of democracy.

In the anonymous self-analysis he published in 1937, Nehru had seen himself as 'too much of an aristocrat for the crudity and vulgarity of fascism'. Sanjay Gandhi, an admirer of Ferdinand Marcos and a devoted reader of Archie Comics, had no such aesthetic inhibitions. On the day before the declaration of the Emergency, he went about cutting off the power supply to newspaper offices in Delhi and drawing up lists of opposition leaders to be arrested. Later, Sanjay personally vetted the daily content of the media, which quickly turned to highlighting his speeches, and passed over in silence – what V.S. Naipaul described as the 'great silence' of the eighteen-month-long Emergency – the detention without trial of more than 110,000 people and the deaths of hundreds of protesters in police shootings all across India.

Lumpen young men gathered around Sanjay. They extorted money from small and big businessmen and apparently also dabbled in murders and kidnappings. But Sanjay had larger aspirations: 'I firmly believe', he claimed, 'that the best ideology for the people is my ideology.' He wanted to 'beautify' India's cities; to make the country 'ultra modern'; he wanted India to be a First World player, not just a backward Third World country; and his aggressive nostrums – overpopulation? forcibly sterilize and give the poor vasectomies; ugly cities? bulldoze the slums – had much support among middle-class Indians, who were as impatient as Sanjay with the stubbornly destitute majority of India's population.

With her son fully if unofficially in charge, Indira retreated into her own world; the extraordinary self-centredness Nehru had noticed now kept all reality at bay. 'There is no show of force whatsoever anywhere in the country,' she stated repeatedly. 'My family has been very much maligned,' she told a British journalist, 'and of course my son is not in politics at all.' Nayantara Sahgal attributes the falsehoods to Indira's profound craving to be seen as the truest and most principled leader of the Indian masses. This explains why she expected to win, and therefore held, the national elections in 1977, in which the unprotected poor who suffered most from the violent evictions and the terroristic 'family planning' schemes of the Emergency voted her out of office.

Difficult times might have then seemed inevitable for Indira. But the coalition of opposition parties began to collapse soon after it ended one-party rule over India. Its leaders, greedy after their long exclusion from the perks of high office, squabbled among themselves. They tried intermittently to arraign Indira for her various excesses during the Emergency, but their clumsiness only made her seem a victim – a role she took to passionately as she toured around the poorer parts of the country, asking for forgiveness and sympathy.

Soon after she was voted back to power in 1980, Sanjay Gandhi died while attempting some stunts in a light airplane above Delhi. The freak accident – 'the best thing that could happen to India', as one of Indira's own cousins tactlessly but truthfully remarked – seems to have deepened Indira's delusions. Throughout her remaining four years in office, she travelled, on government helicopters and planes, from one Hindu guru and temple to another, pleading for divine protection from her 'enemies' – the CIA, Sikh militants, the leaders of the opposition, and even Sanjay's widow, Maneka – who seemed to her to be everywhere, undermining her self as much as the 'national interest'.

In 1982, Indira expelled Maneka from the prime ministerial residence in New Delhi; her assistant tried to search Maneka's luggage as she left and Indira herself tried to hold on to Sanjay's young son, Varun. In Kashmir, in 1984, Indira engineered, through bribes paid to legislators, the collapse of a democratically elected government: it was the first of a series of events that forced Kashmiri Muslims into a full-scale anti-India insurgency in 1990. In Punjab, Sanjay and the Congress Party had promoted an extremist Sikh preacher called Bhindranwale in order to undermine the principal Sikh party, the Akali. In the early eighties, Bhindranwale turned against his sponsors and declared war on India. The random killings of Hindus by Bhindranwale's men in Punjab provided an opportunity for Mrs Gandhi to stoke up nationwide hysteria about the various threats to India's 'unity and integrity'.

Much of the media echoed her insinuations about the 'anti-national' tendencies of the Sikhs and Kashmiri Muslims. I remember from my own small-town childhood the abruptness with which many lower-middle-class Hindus began to distrust and scorn the Sikh neighbours they had previously lived alongside in perfect amity for decades. The Hindu nationalists owe their rapid, blood-strewn progress partly to this anti-minority frenzy Indira worked up during her last years in office.

In June 1984, Indira ordered the army to force Bhindranwale and other Sikh militants from the Golden Temple in Amritsar. The ill-conceived assault upon the Mecca of Sikhism resulted in the massacre of hundreds of innocent pilgrims as well as the desecration of many sacred sites. Barely four months later, on 31 October 1984, Indira was assassinated by two of her own bodyguards; both men were Sikhs seeking revenge for the brutalities in Amritsar.

But the bigger outrage occurred during the following three days, when mobs led by the Congress 'hit men' that Sanjay had once nurtured went around Delhi with electoral rolls that listed Sikh-owned houses. The police stood idly by as over three thousand Sikhs were murdered in Delhi. Altogether five thousand Sikhs were killed across India and as a whole generation of enraged young Sikhs took up arms against the Indian state, thousands more died in Punjab during the next decade.

'I do not want to be remembered for anything,' Indira told an interviewer in one of those fits of imperial pique that became more common towards her death. It is not a desire that posterity can honour. The hard-edged realpolitik with which Indira and her son replaced Nehru's impatient but benign patriarchy seems tailor-made for the BJP and its middle-class constituency. In a 2001 poll in *India Today*, India's highest-circulation news magazine, a majority of the middle-class respondents made plain their yearning for a 'strong leader' like Indira Gandhi.

The fascistic undertones are unsettling. But this is also what Indira helped create: a widely shared mood among the Indian middle class, compounded equally of fear, aggressiveness, contempt, and apathy; a climate of opinion in which India's various encircling cruelties – the uprooting of hundreds of thousands of tribal families by big dam projects, the suicides of hundreds of farmers victimized by the economic policies of the last decade – feel far away, in which the deaths of more than 50,000 people in Kashmir in the last decade incite little debate beyond the narrow parameters of 'national interest', and the pogroms against the minorities can go unpunished. This national mood, Indira's truest legacy, now seems almost crucial to the building of a new Indian identity, of which Hinduism, nuclear bombs, beauty queens, and information technology tycoons have, in recent years, become essential, if conflicting, components.

3 Bourgeois Anxieties

Most middle-class people I talked to in Allahabad had to think hard when asked about the chances of the four main candidates, and were often unable to remember their names; they worried more about the uncollected garbage on the streets of Allahabad, the lack of drainage, the pot-holed roads, the power and water breakdowns. They talked about growing corruption and crime in the city, about the recent murder of a young female doctor, the rise of mafia dons, the deteriorating environment outside their homes, and the general atmosphere of insecurity. They did not think that the elections would make much of a difference. Some of them denounced politicians, described democratic politics as being 'ill-suited' to India, and wished that the army could take over. They said they lived with large fears about their property, their family, and sometimes their lives.

This subdued fear and foreboding was a curious fate for the middle class which, created during colonial times, had inherited the British instinct for law and order. After 1859, while the British grew increasingly self-absorbed, a small group of Indians had begun to embrace some of the benefits the British had brought to India while colonizing it. In 1887, the year Kipling arrived in Allahabad, the network of English-style universities was extended to the city. The general British policy was to consolidate their rule over India by exposing an elite class of Indians to European civilization. This elite class of Indians grew fast, each generation building upon the achievement of the preceding one; and for at least six decades after the establishment of the first college in 1873 (where the father of Pandit Nehru was a student), Allahabad was to witness a political and intellectual awakening without precedent or parallel in North India. The Congress Party did not only find a base in the Nehru family mansion; it also recruited many important members in the city. There were literary associations and clubs, new magazines and newspapers, libraries and reading rooms.

Few traces of this sudden flowering now survive. It seems more and more like a freakish episode that nationalist passion and the British, relatively benevolent in their last years, had together brought about – something which eventually worked against, but also required, the order and certainties of colonial rule, and which couldn't have withstood the pressures of poverty and population arising from even a minimally democratic India.

The scramble for basic livelihood has now undermined colonial institutions built for very different purposes. The most prominent example in Allahabad is the university I went to. It was once known as the 'Oxford of the East', where much of the intellectual fervour of the colonial period had originated. Soon after independence, it was overwhelmed with students from nearby poverty-stricken areas who came not for the higher learning the university offered but to improve their prospects for government jobs. However, there weren't that many government jobs available (opportunities in business and private industry had been further limited by Nehru's decision to adopt a socialistic economy for India) and most of these students, adrift after acquiring several useless degrees, became part of the floating reserve army of the unemployed who ultimately found subsistence in the related vocations of crime and politics.

There had been a police raid on one of the hostels just before I arrived in Allahabad. During my time, Hindu Hostel, as it was known, had been much feared for the large population of criminals who had taken refuge there, encouraged by old laws that forbade the police to enter the premises without authorization from the university. Over the years, the criminals had driven out most of the students, and had come to rely on pure terror to establish their right over the hostel. When the electricity board cut off the power supply after bills remained unpaid for several years, they went in a mob and burnt down the local power station. Power was duly restored, and after a student leader from the hostel arranged for the digging of a tube-well on the hostel's grounds, the residents became fully self-sufficient. The hostel was no longer connected to the university, its reputation repulsing even ordinary visitors to the nearby Alfred Park, its very presence suggesting an extreme kind of secession from the city.

Finally, the university administration, headed by a new man, acted. The local police, bolstered by additions from outside the district, surrounded the hostel early one morning. Roads leading to it were sealed off before the police stormed the building and took the residents by surprise. These elaborate preparations were necessary: the residents, armed with crude country pistols and bombs, had thwarted an earlier police attempt to enter the hostel.

The police raid on the hostel didn't excite any fresh hopes for the university or the city. The yellow-painted trucks and dirty canvas tents of the police standing on the hostel grounds were seen as temporary; as soon as the policemen were gone the criminals were expected to return and throw out any students the university might assign to the hostel in the new academic year.

Middle-class people learnt to live with these little set-backs, which they saw as commonplace, secretly hoping that they would move on without being sucked into the violent world around them – something possible at any time, as I myself found out.

After a week of living in an empty hotel in Allahabad, I had become used to its silence, and was surprised to be woken up one night by noises coming from next door. I checked the time: it was two in the morning. The man at reception said he would 'do some enquiries'; he never called back. I waited for the noises – mobile phone tinkles, hectic shiftings of furniture, room-service orders, hollow television baritones – to cease, but they only grew louder. They went on for about half an hour. I wondered if I should call reception again or get up and ask the new arrivals to pipe down. In the end, laziness kept me in bed, and at some point, I drifted back into sleep.

In the morning, the elevator and lobby were full of young aspiring politicians – recognizable by their white cotton kurta pyjamas, mobile phones, and keen-eyed look; three things that often went together, like the distinguishing signs of some tainted priesthood. They had come to meet someone – probably, I thought, the Bombay film star, Shatrughan Sinha, who had been campaigning on behalf of the BJP's candidate, and whose arrival in the city prompted several people to phone me, wanting to know if I was Mr Sinha's secretary.

Silence was restored in the adjacent room the next night, and I didn't think any more of it. Three days later, I was introduced to Piyush, who worked as a local correspondent for the *Times of India*. He came up to my room, and the first thing he said was that he had met Raja Bhaiyya at the room adjacent to mine three days before. I was startled. Raja Bhaiyya: I knew the name. One of the feudal lords of the region, he belonged to one of the many landed families, whose control of various small principalities, mostly by means of terror, had been tolerated by the British as long as the revenues came in on time, and was now sustained in independent India through electoral politics.

With several cases of murder, kidnapping, extortion and

gunrunning still pending against him, Raja Bhaiyya, like many other scions of pseudo-royal families, had become a politician, and secured his victory in elections to the state legislature not by hard-selling good intentions or promises, but by the simple expedient of 'booth-capturing', whereby armed men took over voting booths, drove away all legitimate voters, and then filled the ballot boxes at their leisure.

Unaffiliated at first, Raja Bhaiyya had joined the Hindu nationalists after they promised to make him a minister in the state government. Soon after assuming power, he arranged for the transfer of a police officer who had shown unusual zeal in pursuing criminal cases against him (it had always been hard to prosecute Raja Bhaiyya, for no one dared take the witness stand against him and he had secured several acquittals in the courts).

It was then the national press had suddenly taken notice of him. There were accounts of his brutality, a trait he had inherited from his father, who, according to one story, used to feed his opponents to the crocodiles in a nearby lake. The story was probably apocryphal; but the legend had held, and then there were the stories that couldn't be dismissed. Piyush had researched Raja Bhaiyya's criminal background, and seen the lake whose large fish population Raja Bhaiyya claimed as his legitimate source of income. He said that it was good I hadn't knocked on his door that night in my irritated state. Apparently, Raja Bhaiyya didn't take well to criticism. A Muslim shopowner who had spoken against him had recently been hacked to pieces in the middle of a crowded bazaar by one of his henchmen. (The murderer was arrested but as always there were no witnesses, and later I was to see pictures of decayed unclaimed corpses on the police station noticeboards in Raju Bhaiyya's region.)

Piyush said, 'The responsibility of high office has mellowed him only slightly. Perhaps, he now thinks a bit before ordering someone's murder.'

Piyush, shy and talkative at the same time, detailed Raja Bhaiyya's excesses with sarcastic energy. But behind his eagerness lay boredom. Later, when the talk turned to his own work as a journalist in Allahabad, he asked me about jobs on the Delhi papers. Researching spectacular crime and corruption, chasing after provincial politicians, interviewing minor celebrities from the metropolises – he had done all this for two years, and he now wished to get out of Allahabad.

I recognized that urge. It was what I had myself felt, as a student in Allahabad, when the stories of Raja Bhaiyya, and people like him, weighed upon me oppressively, and I longed constantly for a life beyond them.

That life lay for most people in the British-created refuge from the threatening chaos of India – Civil Lines, whose prestige and glamour after independence were to grow in Allahabad and in hundreds of other towns and small cities across British-ruled India, all with their own Civil Lines. For hundreds of thousands of educated Indians who had just emerged from a background of poverty, a job with the colonial bureaucracy, kept more or less intact after independence, was the chief way to get to Civil Lines. Once there, you inherited the lifestyle of the British almost instinctively. Eighty-five years after Kipling, Arvind Krishna Mehrotra, one of India's finest poets in English, remembered his childhood in the Civil Lines of the 1950s, with Indians by then fully installed in the bungalows vacated by the British, and found that same faux colonial world of clubs and new respectability that Kipling wrote about:

> At seven-thirty we are sent home
> From the Cosmopolitan Club
> My father says, 'No bid,'
> My mother forgets her hand
> In a deck of cards.
> I sit on the railing till midnight,
> Above a worn sign
> That advertises a dentist.
> I go to sleep after I hear him
> Snore like a school bell.
> I am standing alone in a back alley
> And a face I can never recollect is removing
> The hubcaps of our dull brown Ford.
> The first words I mumble are the names of roads,
> Thornhill, Hastings, Lytton . . .

Although the roads, Mehrotra writes, were later renamed after Hindu nationalists or provincial leaders, the old life of Civil Lines went on for a while. But there had to come a time when it felt the weight of the anarchic world just outside. When I visited Allahabad, a different and ominous resident had just begun to appear in Civil Lines. It was the wife of a judge at Allahabad High Court who spoke of this to me one evening at her bungalow, her tone alternating between impatience and sudden gloom. There was no power, and we sat, perspiring, in her candle-lit living room, surrounded by framed pictures of her children, one of whom had just got married in Boston, while two servants outside on the dark verandah carefully wiped golf clubs. One bungalow away, a local mafia don had forced out the original landowners and started building a commercial complex called 'Mak Tower'. The building was only four storeys high; to the judge's wife the word 'tower' was a menacing sign of the man's vanity and ambition, a menace she felt extended to the whole of Civil Lines. She said, 'There is no opposition from the residents, who in any case fear the mafia man and what he might do to them.'

I had met the man she mentioned. His name was Atiq Ahmed. He was a Muslim politician who had just resigned from the Samajwadi party over its failure to back Sonia Gandhi in her attempts to form a coalition government after the BJP government's collapse. He lived in the warren of narrow lanes with overhanging two- or three-storey houses and small shops, which made up the old quarter across the tracks from Civil Lines. It had rained heavily on the evening I went with a friend to see him. A stench from uncollected mounds of garbage hung in the humid air; the unlit road was all large water-filled craters, treacherous and almost impossible to negotiate in the dark. Mr Ahmed is famously alleged to have shot his greatest rival in one of the more public squares of the old city. By living where he did, he had made it difficult for his own would-be murderer to reach his house. The walled compound was patrolled by armed men and ferocious-looking Dobermans, and packed with gleaming new Toyotas and Hondas and Tata Sumo jeeps. Tall stocky men walked around the verandah of the house, speaking into mobile phones; a row of sofas with frayed blue-satin upholstery lined the wall, several rooms beyond which probably were – though hard to imagine in this rough masculine atmosphere – the living quarters for women.

Mr Ahmed's thick curling moustache, his burly frame

and brisk waddle, suggested a brute panache. But he dressed simply in white kurta pyjamas, a long scarf wound around his head, Bedouin-style, and he received us in a small bare room, where a singlet hung limply from the lone hook on the yellow walls, and a wrinkled sheet with a faded red-roses print covered the bed in one corner, under a glossy calendar picture of Mecca at night.

Ostentation in general wasn't Mr Ahmed's style. His power seemed to partly lie in remaining, or at least appearing to be, a man of the people. He had begun his career by stealing tar from road-construction sites; had become a contractor for the railways; successfully contested the elections to the state legislature, and then after an alleged series of strategic murders of potential rivals, had emerged as the unchallenged authority in a part of the old quarter populated largely by poor Muslims: thin, gaunt, angular-featured men in prayer caps who stood idle before lightless shops and gazed warily at the passing cars.

For local politicians in need of Muslim votes, Mr Ahmed was the person to talk to; and the phone rang constantly, with callers from Benares, Mirzapur, Pratapgarh, and Fatehpur entreating him to visit these neighbouring constituencies and work his special persuasive magic on the Muslim voters, who formed up to 20 per cent of the electorate of the region. Mr Ahmed usually pleaded busyness, uncancellable engagements. He was gruffly matter-of-fact: while I was with him he received many telephone calls informing him that an associate of his had been shot, and after ascertaining that the man was still alive and arranging for him to be taken to a 'nursing home', Mr Ahmed became increasingly brusque in his replies. Putting the phone down, he would assume a friendly demeanour, and with the graciousness that is the politician's acquired skill, he would urge us to take more pistachios from the bowl on the table before us.

In between phone rings, he talked, seriously and engagingly; he spoke like a man who had moved on, after the petty crimes and murders, to a higher idea of himself. He worried about the Brahmin vote-bank in Allahabad. He feared that most of it would go to BJP's Brahmin candidate, the incumbent Mr Joshi, even though the Congress had also put up a Brahmin candidate. He thought the Brahmins weren't ready to accept Sonia Gandhi's leadership. He worried, too, about the 'fascist' tactics of the BJP: the Hindu nationalists had no respect for democracy, he said. They had staffed the district administration with their upper-caste sympathizers – this was something I heard often – and were going to rig the elections in their favour.

It wasn't just his expressed concern for democracy that made judgement on Mr Ahmed difficult. In his area, almost a ghetto with its boxed houses and cramped lanes and restricted lives, among a minority made insecure and fearful by the rise of the Hindu nationalists, Mr Ahmed with his wealth and political power offered certain guarantees to otherwise unprotected people. His power, though often asserted in violent and arbitrary ways, kept at bay the violence and arbitrariness of other men in other ghettos: the Raja Bhaiyyas, the Hindu nationalists, the corrupt policemen.

Now he was extending his suzerainty to the city across the tracks; and he made the inhabitants of Civil Lines nervous. The judge's wife spoke to me of the general turning-away from the city, a retreat that appeared more extensive than that of the British after the shock of the mutiny in 1857, but without the power and security of the latter. 'People living here in Civil Lines,' she said, 'long ago stopped taking any kind of interest or pleasure in their city; they want to have as little to do with it as possible. They send their children out of the city for studies; sometimes they, too, move out.'

The idea that she may have been speaking out of a more private worry was given to me by a journalist who knew about a recent burglary at her house, in which she had suffered some minor injuries after confronting the intruders. The journalist, who knew her husband well and respected his probity, was convinced that the burglary was connected to something the judge possessed, and foolishly kept at home: a video tape of a marriage ceremony at a corrupt fellow-judge's home, in which all of the twenty-five guests accompanying the bridegroom had been presented with brand-new cars. The journalist said that the burglars had struck soon after the tape was shown to the Chief Justice.

4 *The Reclaiming of India*

The middle class that had depended for a long time on its close affiliations with the executive and legislative branches of the administration – and on its class loyalties, now weakened at a time when every man was for himself – the middle class in small towns and cities sees itself as besieged. In this you could detect the beginning of the end of an India that thought itself safe in the cocoon of colonial privilege; an India that with all its inherited advantages had failed to create a democratic and egalitarian society, and was instead forced to accommodate people like Mr Ahmed.

It could all seem fated from the time, soon after independence, when the new bourgeois self-confidence that had once contributed to the making of modern India decayed into a desire for colonial forms of self-assertion and authority: the high-placed job with the government, the big bungalow, the gravelled driveway, the servants in the kitchen, the uniformed sentinel at the gate. Many more Indians seek to enter that world. The reclaiming of India by Indians – the logical result of independence from colonial rule – often appears only just to have begun.

This process is inevitably hardest and longest for people whom the caste system and poverty had previously kept in darkness. Rama Dular Singh Patel, the candidate in Allahabad of the Bahujan Samaj Party, which claimed to represent the interests of the Dalits (the all-inclusive term for all formerly untouchable and oppressed castes), thought politics could short-circuit the process. Dalits form roughly 20 per cent of India's population. By using their vote effectively they could be a force for instability, and instability was good, Mr Patel said, looking searchingly at me, since 'it confuses and bewilders Brahmanical forces and hastens their break-up'.

The leaders of Mr Patel's party had been known to begin their press conferences by asking all Brahmin journalists to leave. It was a kind of reverse humiliation, a small retribution for centuries of oppression, and my initial nervousness about contacting Mr Patel had grown after he failed to return my calls. I had then gone to his house early one morning with the hope that he would be more receptive to a visitor at home. He lived in Allahapur, a residential area built on sloping ground near the Ganges, where the broad straight streets of Civil Lines suddenly shrink, and turn into a maze of narrow, often unpaved lanes with pot-holes and open gutters and piles of filth. When I was there last, the houses were no more than two or three square or rectangular boxes of brick and cement stacked on top of, or next to, each other. They formed unbroken walls on both sides of the lane, their facades mouldy and grimy after three months of monsoon rains – some of these were boarding houses and lodges where many students from the region around Allahabad lived. The lanes were choked with cows and pigs, which seemed unusually big in that constricted space, and street vendors selling vegetables and fruits and fried snacks on open stalls, but a steady stream of rickshaws, scooters, and motorcycles still managed to wend past them. Before a hand-pump, a man furiously soaped his swarthy torso, as two men waited behind him, brushing their teeth. A tangle of electric cables hung loosely and dangerously from electric poles at every corner – illegal power connections you could acquire by bribing the local electricity staff.

Mr Patel's house, a white two-storeyed building, was separated from the main lane by a stretch of bare ground that heavy rains had scored into a miniature mountain valley of gullies and mounds. My shoes left a trail of mud as I walked up a staircase at the back of the house to a room where bleary-eyed young men in undervests and pyjamas sat cross-legged under fast-spinning fans. There was no furniture apart from a wooden cot and an old sofa with its straw stuffing exposed; some rumpled and frayed sari-like sheets on the rough floor indicated the place where the men would have slept. The walls were bare except for a poster with the words, 'God loves you', and an oil painting in garish colours of Dr B.R. Ambedkar, Gandhi's rival and the original leader of the Dalits.

The men in the room, dark and thin and subdued-looking, shot quick glances at my clothes and shoes, and it occurred to me that I was the only fully dressed person there. One of the men introduced himself, ordered tea, and then informed Mr Patel, dressing for the day in an inner room, of my arrival. The man's name was Sandip. A thick beard covered his round, rather jovial face. His undervest had tiny holes in it; but the upright way in which he sat suggested authority. He told me – speaking with the practised fluency of a public speaker – that the other young men, most of them Dalits, were student volunteers for Mr Patel's campaign. Some of them were from villages outside Allahabad; others lived nearby, in the dingy boarding houses I had just passed.

They stared at me as Sandip spoke, still sitting where I had surprised them, and I wondered if, after the first burst of caste-loyalty and enthusiasm that had taken them to Mr Patel's home, they had found themselves at a loose end, unsure of what they were supposed to do.

Mr Patel soon appeared. He was tall and lean, with thick hair and pencil-thin moustache, and a mole in the middle of his forehead that looked incongruously like the caste mark of the devout Brahmin; in his crisp white kurta and dhoti he stood out in the bare room full of shabbily dressed students who, passive until this point, immediately clustered around him. He was at first surprised, and then pleased, to see me: it turned out that there hadn't been any press coverage so far of his campaign. But he didn't have much time: he was on his way to address meetings in the rural areas south of the Yamuna river. The leaders of his party were soon arriving in Allahabad to lend support to his campaign, and they were coming by helicopter. Mr Patel himself planned to travel in the helicopter with them – a resonant fact for him; he kept repeating it, to the extent that it seemed that the helicopter had become, like the expulsion of Brahmins from press conferences, another small way of experiencing a long-denied power.

The students looked impressed; and after his first moment of surprise, Mr Patel spoke to me slightly mockingly, dismissing my questions in his slow deliberate voice, inviting smiles from the students who watched his face intently.

The real issue in this election, Mr Patel said, wasn't one that anyone outside his party had taken up. It was this: how can Dalits live in India with dignity and self-respect and receive equal opportunities in education and employment? Fifty years after independence, most Dalits were victims of the worst kind of exploitation: they were worked into the ground and underpaid; in villages they were not allowed to draw water from the communal well; they were killed at random, and their wives and daughters raped. There was only one way of stopping all that: by welding the Dalits into a solid political unit. Mr Patel clenched and unclenched his fist to illustrate his point. It was an unsettling gesture after the softness of his voice. The combined strength of the Dalits, Mr Patel continued, would then hold the balance of power against 'Brahmanical forces' who after all were just 20 per cent of the population as opposed to 20 per cent Dalits, 30 per cent other backward castes, and 15 per cent Muslims and other minorities.

And then after this swift reckoning Mr Patel left,

quickly pattering down the stairs, a small retinue of party men with flags and banners running to keep pace with him. The students dispersed and became idle again. Sandip, who had been standing next to Mr Patel, suddenly laughed embarrassedly and said that he himself was a 'student leader', the first Dalit to have won an election to his college's student union, which the upper castes had previously monopolized. His ambition now – and here Sandip's voice suddenly became full of passion – was to help elect Mr Patel as the first Dalit member of Parliament from Allahabad, where duplicitous Brahmins from various political parties had managed to fool the Dalit masses with false promises for over fifty years.

Later that afternoon, I was at a tea-shack in Civil Lines when a Tata Sumo jeep flying the BJP flag – saffron-coloured, with a lotus in the middle – stopped before it. Two students emerged, identically plump in tight jeans and T-shirts with mobile phones strapped to their trouser belts. The jeep was new, with plastic covers still draped across the seats. It was probably a temporary gift, along with the mobile phones, from the party. It emerged that the students had been going from door to door in the middle-class parts of the city, campaigning for Dr Murli Manohar Joshi, the BJP's Brahmin candidate for Allahabad. Despite this, the two saw themselves not as active politicians but as members of the Sangh Parivar – the family of both extreme and moderate Hindu nationalist groups who, since they do not take part in electoral politics, are free to make unpopular gestures of Hindu assertion, such as the recent attacks on Christians across India that the BJP's sister outfit, the Bajrang Dal, organized.

They were trying, they said, to present the issues before the people, such as whether India was to be ruled once again by a foreigner, an 'agent of the Vatican' (the Italian-born Sonia Gandhi); whether India was to defeat attempts by Islamic fundamentalists to destroy it; whether India was to regain its past glory as a strong self-sufficient Hindu nation.

They looked confused when I asked them how the BJP proposed to achieve the last-mentioned aim. One of them began to say something about India's nuclear tests, and then stopped. When I asked them about the Dalits and Mr Patel, they were scornful. They said that the politics of hate and animosity Mr Patel and his party practised would weaken Hinduism and India. The Dalits were welcome to join the mainstream of Hindu society, but their current demands for more reservation in government jobs was going to lead to civil war. As it was – and here they became agitated – India faced all kinds of challenges from abroad. Did I know that Osama bin Laden had issued a call for jihad against India? The Pope already had a dangerous agent in India: Sonia Gandhi. And now America had declared war through its missionaries who were bribing innocent Hindus to convert to Christianity. Had I heard about the beating-up of the missionaries last winter in Allahabad? They knew the man responsible for it. It was the right thing to do; it had sent a clear message to America: that Hindu India would fiercely rebuff any attempts to undermine it.

Raised from ordinariness by the elections, and given a slightly glamorous identity by the jeep and mobile phones, the students hadn't really bothered to think through their rhetoric. They found it easier to work with a sense of the enemy: bin Laden, Sonia, the Pope. I hadn't asked, but I knew they were Brahmins; their political affiliations and opinions were enough of a hint. Most of the educated upper castes were with the BJP; the rest of the parties fought over the 'backward caste' and Dalit and Muslim votes in the intensely competitive politics based on group identity that had emerged in India after the politically torpid years under the Congress.

Just fifteen years ago, I couldn't have encountered people like Sandip or the BJP's supporters; the Dalit students wouldn't have been clustering reverently around Mr Patel. The Congress then had a brute majority in the parliament. For much of the time since independence, it had managed to keep the lid on most of the bewildering social and political contradictions of India; it had appeared to address all the different claims made by rich and poor, Hindu and Muslim, Brahmin and Dalit, North Indian and South Indian.

This elastic appeal was the party's legacy, along with its nationwide organization, and its association with the great names of Gandhi and Nehru. It had been sustained as much by the glamour of its dynasty as it had by the ineptitude of opposition parties or by the monopoly it came to have over the institutions of the colonial state – the system of rewards and punishments it created within the civil bureaucracy and the newly opened state-controlled industries. The Congress's unchallenged dominance had made for a simple political and intellectual life in the country. Academics and journalists looked for shelter in the great network of state patronage created by the Congress. Small talk and gossip crowded out political discussion in the newspapers. It was rare for the politicians and journalists who used to cluster at the old coffee house in Allahabad to do more than speculate about who was in or out of favour with the big bosses of the Congress.

In the end, the Congress had been undermined by its own inner complexity. The peace it maintained between antagonistic groups began to crumble, and this was as much due to an ossified leadership as to the fact that individuals as well as special-interest caste and regional groupings had become more conscious of what was owed to them. This was a the self-awareness that the stability of colonial and then Congress rule – a sterile stability with no end but itself – had managed for the most part to suppress. Provincial party bosses challenged the leadership and were, in turn, themselves challenged by newly emergent activists from below. India had now reverted to being a nation of many minorities, each with their own grievances.

The Congress, weighed down with self-serving coteries and lobbyists, and dulled by its years in power, had been late to wake up to the fact that it could no longer meet the conflicting needs of Brahmins and Dalits, rich and poor, Hindu and Muslim. It tried to appease everyone, and sought renewal through the few surviving members of the Nehru–Gandhi dynasty.

Some measure of the Congress's confusion was revealed by an election meeting at the university student union. It was to be addressed by Rita Bahuguna, the Congress's candidate from Allahabad. She had been elected mayor of Allahabad three years ago but this wasn't going to help her defeat Mr Joshi, the BJP MP. She was blamed for the deteriorating civic condition in the city; but she was, in effect, powerless since the municipal corporation spent most of the little money it had on staff salaries. The hall was packed, a mixed crowd of students and teachers perspiring under slow fans. Mrs Bahuguna was late and a series of student leaders appeared on the platform, assured the audience of her imminent arrival and then proceeded to harangue those waiting. Their oratorical style was fierce: broad loudspeakers squatting under tall portraits of freedom fighters boomed and clanged as the students clasped the microphone close to their faces and shouted into it at the very top of their voices. The passion in these leaders, who looked so much like other students: thin-limbed, dressed in ill-fitting shirt and pants and plastic sandals, was oddly disturbing. One by one they came and after expressing their frenzy retired sheepishly to the side of the platform, where they sat half-listening to other speeches, their sweat-glistening faces blank.

They spoke of many things – the BJP's failure in Kashmir, the arrogance of Mr Joshi, the sitting MP from Allahabad, whose commando bodyguards had physically evicted from Mr Joshi's house the father of a man who had been drowned in a boat accident. But they never strayed far from their chief target: the police and university administration that had 'conspired' to force students out of their hostel.

The speeches stopped as more leaders arrived: not students, but middle-aged men, large paunches showing under loose white kurta pyjamas, many-ringed fingers clutching mobile phones. These were the local Congress's senior people. Small garlands of stringy sunflowers and roses mysteriously appeared in the hands of the student leaders as they lined up to greet the newcomers.

A tall long-faced man with gold-rimmed glasses hung around his neck received the most garlands, all of which he immediately took off and handed to his pretty young daughter. He didn't look like a politician and in fact he was a former admiral of the Indian navy; his arrival in the city had been reported in the morning papers. He had been recently sacked by the BJP government for not very clear reasons, and he had subsequently taken to touring the country on behalf of the Congress, denouncing the government, particularly the defence minister, who was responsible for sacking him.

Cut off from the easeful life of high office and navy clubs, the man appeared to be struggling to know his new audiences. Hailed by the preceding speaker as a national hero, he started off his speech with an exhortation to the students to emulate Stanford University.

This provoked no titters, just puzzlement: few students in that hall would even have heard of Stanford. His daughter looked anxious, but he improved as he went on, his sentences composed of as many English words as Hindi, as he spoke about the fascist tactics of the Hindu nationalists, their attempt in particular to 'saffronize' (saffron being the Hindu colour) the armed forces. Then, while discussing parallels in Nazi history, he asked the students if they had read the chapter entitled 'Triumph and Consolidation' in William L. Shirer's history of the Third Reich. The students, now massed around the doors, looked on mystified.

Rita Bahuguna finally arrived. Fresh garlands appeared – perhaps the same ones, I couldn't tell – as the town leaders queued up before Mrs Bahuguna. In the new hierarchy that sprang up, the student leaders had to vacate their places, and even the Admiral was ignored for a while.

Mrs Bahuguna, sitting in her blue sari among burly white-clad men on the platform, was small and frail. A few rose petals clung to her hair when she rose to give a strangely brusque speech. She didn't need to establish her 'credentials' (she used the English word) before students, she said. She was their teacher after all (even though she was the elected Mayor of Allahabad, Mrs Bahuguna still taught medieval Indian history at the university). She said she knew all about their problems, none of which had been solved by Mr Joshi, also a former teacher, of physics, at the university. She ended by denouncing the police raid on the hostel, and promised to ensure, if elected, a safe environment for students inside the university.

The crowd had grown suddenly quiet. The police action had been popular with the students. Vinod, a young men sitting next to me, had smiled wryly when the student leaders spoke, in loud sentimental tones, of the poverty of parents who sent their children to the university in the hope they would pass the civil service exams and help them in their old age. Vinod himself was one of the countless students from poor families at the university preparing for the civil services exams, and fortunate enough to live in a bare tiny hostel room, much like the one I had once lived in, where thick books on general knowledge and the Indian economy stood in a tall pile on the solitary table, next to a rusty hotplate on which he made tea and warmed omelettes bought from a stall outside the hostel gates. But he approved of the police operation, and so, he said, did most of the students who couldn't find cheap accommodation anywhere outside the hostels. He said that Mrs Bahuguna had been wrongly advised by the city leaders, several of whom were close to the criminals residing at Hindu Hostel. It was another instance of the Congress protecting only its own interests, and being out of touch with general feeling; it was now going to cost them votes among the students.

Vinod felt that Mrs Bahuguna, who was the daughter of an influential Brahmin politician in the city, should have known better. She had come late to politics herself, several years after the death of her father, but she hadn't played her moves too badly until that point (although she lost the first parliamentary election she contested from a neigh-bouring constituency; she had opposed the Congress in that instance, mocking it for choosing Sonia Gandhi, a foreign woman, as its president. A few weeks before the present elections, she had managed to get Sonia Gandhi's backing for the contest in Allahabad).

The Congress leaders in Delhi had chosen Mrs Bahuguna for her father's name, a Brahmin name that it expected would put a dent in Brahmin support for the BJP, while attracting Muslims, among whom her father had been popular. She already had some support among the small group, not more than 2 per cent of the electorate, of liberal, educated people in the city – teachers, lawyers, journalists – who, though not always political, felt com-fortable with her and saw her as a bulwark against the Hindu nationalists. The student union hall she spoke from was full of teachers from the university, many of them women in stylish saris. The next morning at her house, there were more women, door-to-door campaigners wear-ing fresh lipstick and smelling of deodorant. Some were part of a study-group called *Chetna* (Consciousness) and also ran a private organization called *Sahyog* (Assistance), which supervised shelters for bonded child labour and battered women.

There was much that was admirable about these

women. It was they who seemed to affirm a sense of a shared society otherwise absent in small cities like Allahabad. But generating middle-class support within the city wasn't going to be enough to elect Mrs Bahuguna. I accompanied her to the villages south of the Yamuna river where she had to work hard to win the Dalit and Muslim votes for the Congress. Driving out of Allahabad, the city rapidly receding after the bridge over the swollen and muddy Yamuna, she seemed a bit out of her element. She held the end of her sari over her nose to block the diesel fumes from passing trucks and tractors, as she talked to me of the conferences she had attended in European and American cities as Mayor of Allahabad.

At the small roadside settlements of half-built brick houses and shops we passed, men holding Congress flags ran up to her: these were local party workers, who were to 'deliver' their villages' uncommitted voters, mostly illiterate, to the Congress. Important men, many of them old enough to have known her father, they would have been paid a small price for this support: employment for their sons or brothers, the expediting of housing and agricultural loans after the election

A heavily built man with a Hindu, stereotypically sage-like white beard and long hair sat behind Mrs Bahuguna in her large new jeep. Dal Bahadur was the Congress candidate from Allahabad in the previous election – and prompted her as soon as he saw the party workers. He knew all their names; he knew the caste they belonged to, and introduced them to Mrs Bahuguna with gruff familiarity. She exhorted them to work harder for her victory, her bookish Hindi strikingly different from the dialect Dal Bahadur spoke. She turned back, slightly flushed, and then as the jeep moved on, she returned to chatting with me. 'I had a good time in New York,' she told me at the gas station where we had stopped to refuel, and then suddenly started to wave at someone behind me. I turned to find a couple of slightly amused petrol station attendants. 'Will you remember me on election day?' she shouted at them. There was a fluency to her speech, and an ability to change register that she couldn't have acquired during her long career as an academic. It matched the sudden silences in the jeep, and it seemed as if, coming late to politics, she had been surprised by the inherited politician's skills rising to the surface; as if she had only recently tapped into some new elastic part of herself.

But her family background had also burdened her with a sense of entitlement: this was what made her so abrupt with the students; this was what that afternoon made her work her way through a series of poor low-caste villages, offering little more than her father's faded good works and the talismanic name of the Nehrus and Gandhis.

At one of the roadside settlements, a small crowd was waiting under a string of paper Congress flags hung between two mango trees. Mrs Bahuguna mounted a wooden cot that served as a platform and gave a speech that was barely audible. She spoke of Sonia Gandhi's bereavement, and the sacrifices of the Nehru–Gandhi family. The crowd watched her, not hearing much, but still agog. Many of them had walked a long way through the surrounding fields to see her. They were like the people Sonia Gandhi and the then prime minister Vajpayee would address in Allahabad a few days later. The celebrity speakers were hardly visible to a majority of the audience, and the speeches were all lost in the bewildering echoes from loudspeakers, but it was the seeing that seemed important, the contact with the powerful and privileged.

I saw a number of light-eyed boys with sharp features in the crowd: it turned out that they belonged to a Muslim community of horse-riders from Rajasthan that had migrated to this part of India two generations ago. This community of 3,000 lived in the mud huts lining the road; most were unemployed and survived by skinning cows killed in road accidents. Nearly all were illiterate. An old Hindu man from the adjacent tea-shack, himself only slightly better off, was sympathetic to their plight. He told me, '*Yeh bilkul zero hain*' ('These people are completely zero'). Some of the boys came over as he talked and stared at me, frank appraisal on their raw young faces. They nodded with unexpected vehemence when the man said that it was a school, above all, they wanted their Member of Parliament to provide.

A few miles ahead – open fields of wheat and rice on both sides, an occasional hut in the distance – a freshly painted signboard announced a girls' school. I saw a small shack with just one long room, dark, the mud walls without windows, the only light coming from between the stacked bundles of straw on the roof. The roof would have leaked during the finest drizzle and the ground around the jute mat where the children would sit was damp. There were simple sums scrawled on the blackboard on one of the walls.

A couple of young men appeared as I stood there. They were the two teachers; they cycled in from nearby villages every morning and then cycled on to a local college where they studied for postgraduate degrees and also 'prepared' for the civil service. They were paid a monthly salary of

Rs 400 by the school's owner, a local contractor for gravel, for whom the school was only one business among many.

At the talk of teachers' salaries, Mrs Bahuguna's secretary, a plump, friendly young man with glasses, who had followed me into the room, perked up. He had been travelling in my car after the jeep had filled up with local Congress leaders, and a little while before he had been explaining to me why Mrs Bahuguna would win. There was no question about the areas we were travelling through: her father had done so much work here, they all remembered him. Teachers all across the state (and there were 60,000 in Allahabad constituency alone), he said, were going to vote against the BJP and for the Congress. They had been on strike protesting their low salaries, but the BJP-run government had done nothing. And now a senior leader of the teachers' association had been murdered in Lucknow. (I had seen the newspaper reports that morning. A week later, there was a report of a police 'encounter' in which the alleged killer of the leader had been shot dead, 'police encounter' being the all-Indian word for summary execution. A journalist from the *Times of India* arrived to see the bullet-riddled body lying next to a police inspector who was still on the radio to his headquarters, shouting excitedly, for the official record, about bullets flying everywhere. There were allegations from the teachers' association that the police had murdered the so-called killer of their leader in order to close the case quickly.)

By the afternoon, dark clouds had gathered in the big sky as we drove along a muddy river, more cars now following Mrs Bahuguna's jeep on the narrow road. For the next many miles it rained, a fierce blinding rain, from which cyclists and bullock-cart drivers sheltered in wet cowering groups under massive mango trees, or under the leaking corrugated-iron roofs of tea-shacks and paan-stalls. The windows began to fog up; the cars, jolted from side to side by large potholes, proceeded warily. Barefoot children in rags, their wet hair plastered to their skulls, ran after the bouncing rocking cars and pounced upon the propaganda leaflets thrown from their windows.

There was no welcoming party at the next riverside village, and no one seemed to know much about the place, except Dal Bahadur, the sage-like man, who now disappeared, leaving the rest of the party standing on a rain-soaked knoll.

I walked behind him on the muddy lane squelchy with rainwater and sheep and cow droppings. In front yards messy with straw and dung, women sifting wheat stopped to stare at me, their pink and purple saris bright against the pale mud-yellow of the houses. Naked children with distended bellies shrank to one side as I passed them. An old man slumped on a string cot gestured at me from inside his hut; and when I went in, he wanted to know if I was from the government.

It was cool and fragrant inside the hut, the smell of cow-dung almost turned into something heady and intoxicating by the rain. Two boys in their early teens came in: both thin, with stick-like legs, their large eyes glowering in the dark room. Their father was a rice farmer and fisherman, like most people in the village. Rice and fish was what they ate – the food cooked on the chulha fire in a little alcove off the room, cakes of cow-dung stacked to one side of it. They had never been to school, and they had no other clothes than what they wore – clothes their father had bought from the nearby bazaar two years ago. The over-sized polyester pants and shirts torn at the armpits and around the collar were adequate for ten months of the year, and when winter arrived, they tied straw to the insides of the shirts.

It took the boys some time to get used to my presence, and even then they spoke with difficulty; they did not understand the simplest words. Their sparse vocabulary reflected the bareness of the room that, apart from the string cot, had no furniture or personal possessions, words and things both absent and making for a kind of all-enveloping vacancy.

Back where the cars had stopped, Dal Bahadur had emerged with a few old women timidly trailing behind him. They stood speechless, their wizened, toothless faces half hidden by sari veils pulled down to nose level, as Mrs Bahuguna asked them about their 'problems'. Still they said nothing, and so Mrs Bahuguna began to describe Sonia Gandhi's presidency of the Congress, and how women were best placed to understand other women's problems. They looked on, puzzlement appearing in eyes that held great anxiety and patience. And now an embarrassed Dal Bahadur prompted them, in his gruff voice, 'Don't you know who this is? Don't you remember how her father once distributed lai chana?'

Lai chana! the puffed rice and chickpeas that was the poor man's snack, stuffed in rusty tin containers in the gloomy one-room shops in shanty markets we had passed. It was hard not to feel the pathos of the situation. Decades after it had been made, the old women were being asked to remember a meaningless offering from a long-dead politician, in a village which near-total destitution had taken beyond the simple deprivation of the rural poor elsewhere, beyond lack of water, electricity, primary schools, and hospitals to the earliest, most elemental form of human community, where the outside world intruded only in the form of election-time visitors and the propaganda leaflets the ragged children had pounced upon.

The more you examine the reclaiming of India by Indians, the more uneven the whole process looks. It is never very clear who is reclaiming what. Mr Patel, the candidate of the Bahujan Samaj party, had presented himself as a Dalit to me. I had been nervous about going to his house and possibly facing expulsion. I had been relieved to find him a friendly figure, eager for attention from the press. It now turned out that he wasn't a Dalit at all. He was a Kurmi, which – so important, these differences – made him a member of a technically 'backward' caste, much better placed, socially and financially, than the Dalits.

Accordingly, Mr Patel also turned out to be the owner of a large agricultural estate outside Allahabad. He was also a very recent member of the Dalit party whose strategy for instability he had explained to me – the party whose leaders in their few months in power in the state of Uttar Pradesh had emptied the state exchequer and had created little empires for themselves in addition to building grandiose monuments to Dalit leaders.

Mr Patel had joined the party just a few weeks before the elections. It was Sandip, himself a Kurmi, who told me this, a trifle sheepishly. We were driving south of Allahabad, into the poor districts of Meja and Karchana where there was a large Dalit population. Mr Patel sat in the front

seat and was unusually quiet. Party flags fluttered on top
of houses and shops. Few of them were of Mr Patel's party.
At places where meetings had been arranged, and microphones and platform set up, hardly anyone, apart from a
couple of party workers, waited to greet him, and Mr Patel
had to move on without giving his speech.

It was in the embarrassing silences that descended inside
the jeep after every aborted meeting that Sandip started
talking about his own family. Proudly, he told me about
the number of relatives he had in the state and central civil
services. Why did he join politics, then, I asked. He immediately said, 'I wanted to explore other options.' There was
no irony; he spoke in earnest. Later, attempting clarifi-
cation, he added: 'It is not enough for Dalits to join the
civil service. They have to enter the arena of politics and
take on the Brahmanical forces there. It is Dalit assertion
that will expose the BJP's self-serving rhetoric about the
terrorism and the threats to India's integrity.'

Brahmanical forces, Dalit assertion, India's integrity:
the words stood for certain recognizable realities. But it
was possible to see too much in them, and to forget the
simple intentions of the politicians using them, people who
weren't always sure what they meant, and who, despite
the difference in rhetoric, spoke for themselves alone, and
in the end were fighting for the same things. Misused by
politicians, the words had acquired the neutrality of math-
ematical figures; you could fit them anywhere in the hectic
accounting of electoral politics, which in a socially and
economically restricted society had become an increasingly
attractive means for upward mobility.

To the mass of peasantry and workers, and the middle
class of lawyers, doctors, engineers, bureaucrats, teachers

and businessmen, a new class of professional politicians has been steadily added since 1947. Thousands of men have emerged from amongst the general mass of deprived people and taken important positions within central and state legislatures. These are men with no special training or skills, sometimes not even those of basic literacy and oratory. A large number of them are criminals. Few of them offer anything apart from their caste and religious identity. Most of them are content to plunder the state's resources, and sometimes share the loot with members of their family or caste group. They all seek the power that in societies degraded by colonialism often comes without a redeeming idea of what it is to be used for – the kind of power that, in most cases, amounts to little more than an opportunity to rise above the rest of the population and savour the richness of the world: junkets to New York, helicopter rides, free railway passes and gas connections and 'commando' bodyguards and chauffeur-driven cars and crowds of supplicants outside one's door.

Behind the rhetoric of caste and religious redemption, the defections and betrayals, the collapse of governments and fresh elections, the constant intrigues in Delhi and state capitals, behind all the endless drama of politics in India, there lies the fear these men exalted above their station feel: that at any moment the richness of the world might be withdrawn and they might be returned to the small house in the dingy lane, the meanness and insignificance from which the profession of politics had rescued them.

With this fear often comes a contempt for the electorate, an impatience with the process of appeasing and wooing people you have left behind. The people, in turn,

aren't slow in developing their own contempt for the up-
starts among them. A lot of people in Allahabad claimed
to have known Mr Joshi, the incumbent MP for Allahabad,
during the time when he lived in a two-room house,
dressed in khaki shorts, and hitched rides on scooter
pillions to the university where he taught physics – un-
memorably, people said. But Mr Joshi, living now in a
well-marbled house, travelling in a bulletproof Ambassador with tinted windows, and with ferocious-looking
commandos dressed in black and carrying carbines and
AK-47s framing his small white dhoti-clad figure (the commandos were not really required except as badges of status;
there was no danger to Mr Joshi's life, at least in his own
town) – Mr Joshi, beginning to appear now in the society
columns of the Delhi papers, had managed to place himself well above small-town envy and resentment.

The reference to Mr Joshi's humble past was usually
followed by some example of his new-found arrogance,
which was in fact the irritable manner of a man prevented
from rising even higher. For over a decade, he had been
considered the third most important leader of the BJP, and
during his tenure as Minister for Human Resources and
Development, he had tried but failed to improve that seemingly perennial third-placeness. He had sought to impose a
new educational curriculum that drastically revised Indian
history as a continuous battle against idol-breaking Muslims; but was stopped by his own prime minister. He had
come up with a new slogan for the economic nationalists
within the BJP: 'Computer chips, not potato chips'. He had
played up his reputation as a man of science among the
urban middle classes. Among rural Brahmins, he did not
fail to mention his campaign against cow-slaughter. 'Hindu

civilization,' he lectured me, 'couldn't have existed without cows, without their milk, curd, manure. They are at the basis of our national identity.'

But it was a different basis for national identity – nuclear bombs – that he spoke of to the small crowd of peasants and menial workers outside a small technical institute in Allahabad three days before polling day. He had arrived four hours late, and until then most people, many of whom had been paid to attend, had just stood there, wearing bright orange BJP visors, punished by the harsh sun, among mounds of garbage and black rain-dried filth from overflowing gutters and piles of junked rusty machinery. The tone was set by the first speakers, local politicians, who scrambled to touch his feet, tore garlands out of the full arms of a boy wearing a grimy sleeveless singlet and draped them around Mr Joshi's neck, before applying a few more layers to the vermilion caste marks on his forehead. In a long rambling speech, one reported a conversation with a visiting 'lady' from Paris: she had exclaimed at the mention of Allahabad: 'Isn't that where the great son of India, Mr Joshi, lives?' Mr Joshi, sitting hunched on the floor, marigold petals sticking to his well-oiled hair, his legs dangling from the stage, looked impatient as speaker after speaker went on in this vein. When his turn came, he started by mentioning the great boost given to India's prestige by the nuclear tests, and added that the disapproval of the international community could not deter India. 'How many bombs should we build?' he asked the audience in the interactive style I was told he had developed after being criticized for his uninspiring oratory. A few feeble voices went up. 'Twenty!' 'Fifty!' 'A thousand!' Mr Joshi nodded at the last figure.

He mentioned the battles in Kashmir. He said he had told Pakistan, 'If you provoke us one more time, we'll smash you to pieces.' There was a smattering of applause from among the harried perspiring faces in the crowd. He mentioned the water sports complex he was planning to build on the Ganges. He boasted of how he had got rid of all the 'communists' working in the government-funded Indian Council for Historical Research.

And then he was through, and quick to leave, a small brisk figure walking in the narrow corridor the commandos created for him by pushing and shoving blindly at the pressing crowds, back to the white Ambassador where he was once again inscrutable behind tinted-glass windows as the cars raced off, sirens blaring hysterically, past the auto-repair shops and tea-shacks and the bewildered men in rags squatting on ground turned by diesel oil and rainwater into black paste.

Mr Joshi's next stop that day was a new mansion of grey marble and fake Spanish tiles in a high-walled compound several miles out of Allahabad. It was where the Jaiswals – a merchant caste – had arranged an election meeting. Paunchy men in baseball caps, dark glasses, broad-band gold watches and rings and chains sat on plastic chairs before a stage where the banner proclaimed: 'All fellow caste-brothers are welcome'. This was Mr Joshi's constituency: upper-caste men with money, part of the strong network of Hindu nationalist sympathizers and volunteers, whose complaints about his aloofness and arrogance had grown louder as the elections approached. He had no choice but to sit through the banal comedy of speeches and introductions and garlandings that began all over again.

Almost all of the speakers talked of how the Jaiswals through their success as shopkeepers had forced the rest of Hindu society to treat them with respect. But they had been deprived of affirmative action in government jobs – a great injustice, which they expected Mr Joshi to rectify as 'honourable minister' in the new government. Mr Joshi sat on the edge of the stage, his legs dangling, as they had at the previous meeting, looking impatient. In his speech, he dealt with this request in the same way he had dealt with a similar request a few days earlier at another upper-caste conclave, where speaker after speaker had told of their exploitation by the Brahmins as well as, astoundingly, by the Dalits: he promised to give the matter his 'most sympathetic consideration'.

There was a swimming-pool lunch afterwards. Mr Joshi sat in the middle of the table and ate quickly from his leaf plate. One of the more persistent speakers – a plump safari-suited man, the owner of the mansion – sat next to him and kept shouting at the serving boys to refill Mr Joshi's plate. Mr Joshi had to keep waving the boys away as, dressed in red livery and rubber flip-flops, they hovered over his shoulders with glinting steel bowls of dhal and kheer.

His lunch finished, Mr Joshi looked ready to leave. But various people approached him and whispered in his ear; he nodded and nodded. The commandos ate in another corner of the pool; they looked surprisingly relaxed. One rinsed his oily fingers in the swimming pool. There were others who had done so, but it was the commando that the safari-suited owner saw, and, wrenched away from Mr Joshi's conversation, his face suddenly filled with horror.

It rained early in the morning on polling day. But the voting booths in the city – set up in schools and colleges and small parks – remained empty long into the afternoon. An unusually low 30 per cent of the electorate had bothered to show up before 4 p.m., an hour before voting officially ended. Bored policemen played cards, their truncheons and rifles resting on the ground, and polling agents from the contesting parties sat looking morose behind small children's desks as a thin trickle of voters shuffled through the voting procedures, past the polling officials stern behind rough wooden tables piled with voting lists. The streets in the old quarter were deserted; and in the strangely unrestricted vistas, the old houses of the rich merchants and traders – often built adventurously, with Art Deco and Mogul and Rajput motifs – looked worn down by time, heat, rain, as well as the constant friction of passing tongas, scooters, rickshaws, cars, and motorcycles, of the yells of the fruit and vegetable vendors and haggling housewives and the music blaring from tiny electronics shops.

Shutters covered all the one-room shops. I went to see the brothel standing on the site of the oldest ancestral home of the Nehrus. Young girls from Nepal, wearing white saris, fresh jasmine in their hair and thick lipstick on their small mouths, sat gossiping in small cool dark rooms facing an empty lane.

The only noticeable crowd was in the Muslim quarters. The vote here was going in the Congress's favour. It was what Mr Ahmed had asked of his fellow Muslims; and the burka-clad women walked silently to the booths in small determined groups. But they weren't the only reason that the polling agents of the BJP looked nervous. Most of the Hindu middle class on which the BJP had depended in past elections had decided to stay away, and this was a setback to Mr Joshi's chances. There weren't even enough people to cast fake votes, an easier process this time due to the introduction of electronic machines.

Early expectations of Mr Joshi's defeat after the low turnout were cancelled later on polling day when the fabled network of the Hindu nationalists went into action, and the voting percentages rose abruptly to 45 and sometimes 50 per cent. An election agent for the BJP – the headmaster of a local school – told Piyush, the journalist from the *Times of India*, with anxious satisfaction, how he had to bring in students from his own school and persuade the local polling official to let them cast 15–20 votes each in Mr Joshi's favour. (The Socialist Party candidate, Reoti Raman Singh, organized a sit-down protest outside the district collectorate against the rigging, which was allegedly widespread, but it was too late.)

At a polling booth a few miles out of Allahabad, there had been a fight among party workers from the BJP and Samajwadi (Socialist) Party. A new Tata Sumo jeep stood on the road, its windshield and windows broken, its tyres slashed. A small crowd of local villagers stood still around it, as though wondering at the swift destruction of something so apparently solid and expensive. A few miles away, in a shanty town, one of the victims, beaten with iron rods, was in a half-built hospital. His bed had no sheets, only a torn mattress with its straw stuffing exposed, and he lay, moaning softly, not in one of the empty rooms, but the dusty corridor, blood-soaked bandages around his head and ribs, blood-transfusion tubes attached to his thin arm, surrounded by white-clad BJP men busily summoning press photographers on their mobile phones.

But away from the main roads, and deeper into the countryside, the polling was uneventful, and the turnout was up to 60 and 70 per cent. There were no surprises. Most people affirmed their caste solidarities, and the undecided or the weak and ignorant followed decrees issued by the local chieftains. An old man walking to the polling booth, his peasant face immemorially creased and wrinkled, said he had been ordered by the government to vote for the BJP. There were others who weren't quite sure who they were voting for; most recognized the parties only by their symbols: bicycle, lotus, the palm of hand. But there were crowds everywhere – even at a primary school where you had to wade through knee-deep rainwater in the front yard to get to the voting booth – and they brought a holiday atmosphere to the proceedings.

The huts looked freshly cleaned and paved with dung. The women had put on their most colourful saris; the men had well-oiled moustaches and turbans and starched kurtas. At village after village that afternoon, people waited patiently in long queues, under the harsh monsoon sun, their normally impassive faces brimming with excitement – images stereotypical of Indian elections and democracy, which ignored so much of what was not seen: the caste consolidations, the regimented votes, the feudal decrees, the ignorance and brutality. And yet it was hard not to feel the strength of the hopes and desires of the people lining up to vote; hard not to see poignance in the care and devotion they brought to their only and very limited intervention in the unknown outside world; hard not to be moved by the eagerness with which they embraced their chance to alter the world that wielded such arbitrary power over their lives.

The monsoons had retreated by the time the votes were counted, almost three weeks after polling day. The counting took place in a sprawling *mandi*, a local trade centre, six miles outside Allahabad. Police jeeps and trucks choked the broken lanes between large halls, beneath corrugated-iron roofs where thousands of men sat before a chaos of paper and big grey metal trunks, while echoing loud-speakers announced the results after each round of counting.

Mr Joshi was, as expected, well ahead of the rest. Mr Singh, solidly supported by the rural poor, was coming in at second place, and Mrs Bahuguna, despite the Muslim and liberal votes in her favour, was placed third.

Mr Patel of the Dalit party was a distant fourth. I ran into him at one of the counting sites. He had reasons for his poor performance: the Brahmanical parties had bribed voters with cheap country liquor, and Brahmanical forces in the district administration had subverted democracy – and he was serene in his expectation of defeat. His party was doing well in the rest of the state; it would have enough seats in the parliament to play its desired role of destabilizer. Mr Patel himself had done his share of desta-bilizing in Allahabad: he had taken away 'backward' caste and Dalit votes from the Congress and Socialist party, thus making it easier for the BJP, with just 34 per cent of the votes, to win.

But didn't that help the Brahmanical BJP, I asked. Yes, he said, but it was important for the BJP to be in power; it was the political force most likely to cause instability and disorder in the country, which was the long-term plan of his party and Dalits in general.

There were other long-terms plans being put into action

in the hall where Mr Joshi sat watching the national results come in on TV, the air thick with the excited voices of analysts and pundits in the Delhi studios. The BJP and its allies were going to win a safe majority in the parliament. The district officials, who sat at a formal distance from Mr Joshi, and who had previously appeared to me to be under some slight pressure because of the rigging accusations, now looked more relieved with every passing moment. They were solicitous towards Mr Joshi, who was certain to be a minister again in the new government; they were quick to leave their sofas and red-sashed attendants as he summoned them with the crook of his finger; standing half-bent before him, they gave him the latest news about the increasing margin of his victory.

Wearing a blue embroidered silk scarf, his Brahmanical topknot well-oiled, Mr Joshi watched, with the restless air of a man being left out of big things, the interviews with senior politicians in Delhi studios. When a phone call came from the local radio station, he expressed, with a solemn expression, measured tone and well-rehearsed words, his utter lack of surprise at having won.

Later that evening – the results declared, the shops in the city again open, Civil Lines once more bustling with shoppers and promenaders, the elections almost forgotten – I saw his victory procession. The sirens could be heard in the far distance; people stopped to stare as the first Ambassadors came into view, moving fast and recklessly on the narrow road crammed with rickshaws and cars and scooters and motorcycles. There was a continuous hooting of horns from the vehicles in the motorcade. Commandos in black, their AK-47 muzzles poking out of open windows, shouted abuse at rickshaw-wallahs slowing down their progress, and the startled and frightened men thrust their thin naked legs at the pedals and slid timidly out of the way. Jeep after jeep full of slogan-shouting young men in saffron shawls went past before Mr Joshi's bullet-proof Ambassador appeared, piles of rose garlands draped around the crazily revolving blue light. Surprisingly, at this moment of public celebration Mr Joshi hadn't put himself on show, but sat partly hidden behind tinted windows, remote in his soundless cabin from the frenzied sloganeering, safe from the clouds of dust launched by his swift-moving motorcade. Behind his blank face he showed relief – the relief of the man finally allowed, after a brief scare, to continue a private journey that had already taken him from the scooter pillion to a bulletproof Ambassador.

Ayodhya:
The Modernity of Hinduism

1 History as Myth

AYODHYA IS THE CITY of Rama, the most virtuous and austere of Hindu gods. Travelling to it in January 2002 from Benares, across a wintry North Indian landscape of mustard-bright fields, hectic roadside bazaars, and lonely columns of smoke, I felt myself moving between two very different Hindu myths, or visions of life. Shiva, the god of perpetual destruction and creation, rules Benares, where temple compounds secrete internet cafes and children fly kites next to open funeral pyres by the river. But the city's aggressive affluence and chaos seem far away in Ayodhya, which is small and drab, its alleys full of the dust of the surrounding flat fields. The peasants with unwieldy bundles under their arms brought to mind the pilgrims of medieval Indian miniature painting; and sitting by the Saryu river at dusk, watching the devout tenderly set afloat tiny earthen lamps in the slow-moving water, I felt the endurance and continuity of Hindu India.

After that vision of eternal Hinduism, the numerous mosques and Mogul buildings in Ayodhya came as a surprise.

Most of them are in ruins, especially the older ones built during the sixteenth and seventeenth centuries, when Ayodhya was the administrative centre of a major province of the Mogul Empire, Awadh. All but two were destroyed as recently as 6 December 1992: the day, epochal now in India's history, on which a crowd led by politicians from the Hindu nationalist BJP demolished the mosque they claimed the sixteenth-century Mogul emperor Babur had built, as an act of contempt, on the site of the god Rama's birthplace.

None of the mosques are likely to be repaired any time soon; the Muslim presence in the town seems at an end for the first time in eight centuries. This was the impression I got even in January 2002, a month before anti-Muslim rage exploded in the western Indian state of Gujarat, at Digambar Akhara, the large, straw-littered compound of the militant Sadhu sect presided over by Ramchandra Paramhans. In 1949, Paramhans initiated the legal battle to reclaim Babur's mosque, or the Babri Masjid, for the Hindu community; in December 1992, he exuberantly directed the demolition squad.

The sect, Paramhans told me, was established four centuries ago in order to fight the Muslim invaders who had ravaged India since the tenth century AD, and who erected mosques over temples in the holy cities of Ayodhya, Benares and Mathura. The Sadhus had been involved, he added, in the seventy-six wars for possession of the site of the mosque in Ayodhya, in which more than 200,000 Hindus had been martyred.

Two bodyguards nervously watched my face as Paramhans described this history. More armed men stood over the thin-bricked wall of the compound. The security seemed excessive in what was an exclusively Hindu environment. But as Paramhans explained, caressing the tufts of white hair on the tip of his nose, the previous year, he had been attacked by home-made bombs delivered by what he called 'Muslim terrorists'.

Paramhans, who died in 2004 at the age of ninety-three, headed the trust in charge of building the temple, which the leaders of the BJP had vowed to build on the site of Babur's mosque. When I spoke to Paramhans in late January 2002, he expected up to a million Hindu volunteers to reach Ayodhya by 15 March, defying a supreme court ban on construction at the site of the mosque, and to present another fait accompli to the world in the form of a half-built temple.

Thousands of Hindu activists from across India travelled to Ayodhya through the first few weeks of February. Many of them were from the prosperous western state of Gujarat, whose entrepreneurial Hindus, often found living in Europe and the United States, have formed a loyal constituency of the Hindu nationalists since the 1980s. On 27 February, some of these activists were returning on the train from Ayodhya, when a crowd of Muslims attacked and set fire to two of the cars just outside the town of Godhra in Gujarat. Fifty-eight Hindus, many of them women and children, were burnt alive.

Murderous crowds of Hindu nationalists seeking to avenge the attack in Godhra rampaged across Gujarat for the next few weeks. Wearing the saffron scarves and khaki shorts of Hindu nationalists, they were often armed with swords, *trishuls* (a sort of trident), sophisticated explosives and gas cylinders. They had the addresses of various Muslim families and businesses, which they attacked systematically. The police did nothing to stop them, and even led the charge against Muslims. A BJP minister sat in police control rooms while pleas for assistance from Muslims were routinely disregarded. Hindu-owned newspapers printed fabricated stories about Muslim atrocities and incited Hindus to avenge the killings of Hindu pilgrims.

In the end, more than 2,000 people, mostly Muslims, were killed. About 230 mosques and shrines, including a 500-year-old mosque, were razed to the ground; some were replaced with Hindu temples. Close to 100,000 Muslims found themselves in relief camps. Corpses filled mass grave sites; they often arrived there mangled beyond recognition, with foetuses missing from the bellies of pregnant women that had been cut open.

The chief minister of Gujarat, a young, up-and-coming leader of the Hindu nationalists called Narendra Modi, quoted Isaac Newton to explain the killings of Muslims: 'Every action,' he said, 'has an equal and opposite reaction.' The Indian prime minister at the time, Atal Behari Vajpayee, who visited the site of the massacres a whole month after they began, expressed shame and lamented that India's image had been spoiled. 'What face will I now show to the world?' he asked, referring to his forthcoming trip to Singapore. Later, at a BJP meeting, he rejected demands from the opposition and the press for Modi's sacking and proposed early elections in Gujarat. In a public speech, he seemed to blame Muslims. 'Wherever they are,' he said, 'they don't want to live in peace.' He added, referring to Muslims and Christians, 'We have allowed them to do their prayers and follow their religion. No one should teach us about secularism.' A resolution passed by the RSS (National Volunteers' Organization), the parent group of Hindu nationalists, from which have emerged almost all the leaders of the BJP, the VHP and the Bajrang Dal, and whose mission is to create a Hindu state, described the retaliatory killings as 'spontaneous', stating that 'the entire Hindu society had reacted', and even making the following declaration. 'Let Muslims understand,' the RSS said, 'that their real safety lies in the goodwill of the majority.' Both Vajpayee and his seniormost colleague, L.K. Advani, are members of the RSS, which was involved in the assassination of Mahatma Gandhi in 1948.

In Ayodhya in January, Paramhans had told me, 'Before we take on Pakistani terrorists, we have to take care of the offspring Babur left behind in India; these 130 million Muslims of India have to be shown their place.' This message seems to have been taken to heart in Gujarat, where the Hindu nationalists displayed a high degree of administrative efficiency in the killing of Muslims. In Gujarat's cities, middle-class Hindu men drove up in new Japanese cars – the emblems of India's globalized economy – to cart off the loot from Muslim shops and businesses.

The rich young Hindus in Benetton T-shirts and Nike trainers appeared unlikely combatants in what Paramhans told me was a *dharma yudh*, a holy war, against the traitorous 12 per cent of India's population. Both wealth and education separated them from the unemployed, listless small-town Hindus I met in Ayodhya, one of whom was a local convener of the Bajrang Dal (Hanuman's Army), the stormtroopers of the Hindu nationalists, which has been implicated in several incidents of violence against Christians and Muslims across India, including the 1998 murder of a Australian missionary in the eastern state of Orissa. In response to a question about Muslims, he dramatically unsheathed his knife, and invited me to feel the sharpness of the triple-edged blade, in the form of the trident of the Hindu god Shiva.

But, despite their differences, the rich and unemployed Hindu Indians shared a particular world view. This was outlined most clearly for me, during my travels across North India in early 2002, by students at Saraswati Shishu Mandir, a primary school in Benares, one of the 15,000 such institutions run by the RSS. The themes of the morning assembly I attended were manliness and patriotism. In the gloomy hall, portraits of the more militant Hindu freedom fighters mingled with signboarded exhortations including, 'Give me blood and I'll give you freedom', 'India is a Hindu nation', and 'Say with pride that you are a Hindu'. For over an hour, boys and girls in matched uniforms of white and blue marched up and down in front of a stage where a plaster-of-Paris statue of Mother India stood on a map of South Asia, chanting speeches and songs about the perfidy of Pakistan, of Muslim invaders, and the gloriousness of India's past. The principal watched serenely. He later explained to me how Joshi-ji – the education minister – was making sure that the new history textbooks carried the important message of Hindu pride and Muslim cruelty to every school and child in the country.

This message clearly resonates at a level of caste and class privilege, flourishing in a society where deprivation always lies close at hand. But the school and most of its pupils and the surrounding area were firmly middle class; just beyond the gates, banners advertising computer courses hung from electric poles bristling with illegal connections. The out-of-work upper-caste advertising executive I met at

my hotel in Benares seemed to be speaking of his own insecurities when he suddenly said, after some wistful talk of
the latest iMac, 'Man, I am scared of these Mozzies. We
are a secular modern nation but we let them run these
madrasas, we let them breed like rabbits and one day they
are going to outstrip the Hindu population and will they
then treat us as well as we treat them?'

The Muslims of course have a different view of how
they have been treated in secular, modern India. In Madan-
pura, Benares's Muslim locality, a few minutes' walk from
Gyanvapi, one of two Mogul mosques the Hindu nationalists have threatened to destroy, I met Najam, a scholar of
Urdu and Persian literature. He is in his early thirties, and
grew up with some of the worst anti-Muslim violence of
post-independence India. In the slaughter in Benares in
1992, he saw Hindu policemen beat his doctor to death
with rifle butts.

'I don't think the Muslims are angry any more,' he said.
'There is no point. The people who demolished the mosque
at Ayodhya are now senior ministers in Delhi. We know
we will always be suspected of disloyalty no matter what
we say or do. Our madrasas will always be seen as producing fanatics and terrorists. We know we are helpless,
there is no one ready to listen to us and so we keep silent.
We expect nothing from the government and political parties. We now depend on the goodwill of the Hindus we live
with and all that we hope for is survival, with a little bit of
dignity.'

Hindu devotees throng the famous Viswanath temple
in Benares all day long, but few, if any, Muslims, dare to
negotiate their way through the scores of armed policemen
and sandbagged positions to offer *namaz* at the adjacent

Gyanvapi mosque. It is not easy for an outsider to enter the Indian Muslim's sense of isolation. There was certainly little in my own background that could have prepared me to understand the complicated history behind it. As Brahmins with little money, we perceived Muslims as another threat to our aspirations to security and dignity. My sisters attended an RSS-run primary school where pupils were encouraged to disfigure the sketches of Muslim rulers in their history textbooks. At the school I went to, where the medium of instruction was English, we were taught to think of ourselves as secular and modern citizens of India and to view religion as something one outgrows.

In the 1970s and 1980s when I heard about Hindu–Muslim riots, or the insurgencies in Punjab and Kashmir, it seemed to me that religion was the cause of most conflict and violence in India. The word used in the newspapers and in academic analyses was communalism – the antithesis of the secularism advocated by the founding fathers of India, Gandhi and Nehru, and also the antithesis of Hinduism itself, which was held to be innately tolerant and secular.

Living in Benares in the late 1980s, I was unaware that this ancient Hindu city was also holy for Muslims – unaware, too, of the seventeenth-century Sufi shrine just behind the tea-shack where I often spent my mornings. It was one of many in the city which both Hindus and Muslims visited, part of the flowering of Sufi culture in medieval North India. It was only in 2003, after talking to Najam, the young Persian scholar I met in Benares, that I discovered that one of the great Shia philosophers of Persia had sought refuge at the court of a Hindu ruler of Benares in the eighteenth century. And it was only after returning from my most recent trip to Ayodhya that I read that Rama's primacy in this pilgrimage centre was a recent development; that Ayodhya was for much of the medieval period the home of the much older and prestigious sects of Shaivites, or Shiva-worshippers (Rama is only one of the many incarnations of Vishnu, one of the gods in the Hindu trinity, in which Shiva is the most important); many of the temples and sects currently devoted to Rama actually emerged under the patronage of the Shia Muslims who had begun to rule Awadh in the early eighteenth century.

Ramchandra Paramhans in Ayodhya had been quick to offer me a history full of temple-destroying Muslims and brave Hindu nationalists. Yet Paramhans's own militant sect had originally been formed to fight not Muslims but Shiva-worshipping Hindus; and it had been favoured in this long and bloody conflict by the Muslim Nawabs who later gave generous grants of land to the victorious devotees of Rama. The Nawabs, whose administration and army were staffed by Hindus, kept a careful distance from Hindu–Muslim conflicts. One of the first such conflicts in Ayodhya occurred in 1855, when some Muslims accused Hindus of illegally constructing a temple over a mosque, and militant Hindu sadhus (mendicants) massacred seventy-five Muslims. The then Nawab of Awadh, Wajid Ali Shah, a distinguished poet and composer, refused to support the Muslim claim on the building, explaining:

> We are devoted to love; do not know of religion.
> So what if it is Kaaba or a house of idols?

Wajid Ali Shah, denounced as effeminate and inept – and deposed a year later – by British imperialists, was the last great exponent of the Indo–Persian culture that emerged in

Awadh towards the end of the Mogul empire, when India was one of the greatest centres of the Islamic world, along with the Ottoman and the Safavid empires. Islam in India lost some of its Arabian and Persian distinctiveness, blended with older cultures, but its legacy is still preserved – amid the squalor of a hundred small Indian towns, in the grace and elegance of Najam's Urdu, in the numerous songs and dances that accompany festivals and marriages, in the subtle cuisines of North India, and the fineness of the silk saris of Benares – but one could think of it, as I did, as something just there, without a history or tradition. The Indo–Islamic inheritance has formed very little part of – and is increasingly an embarrassment to – the idea of India that has been maintained by the modernizing Hindu elite over the last fifty years.

That idea first emerged in the early nineteenth century, as the British consolidated their hold over India, and found new allies among upper-caste Hindus. In India, as elsewhere in their empire, the British had largely supplanted, and encountered stiff resistance from, Muslim rulers. Accordingly, the British tended to demonize Muslims as fanatics and tyrants, and presented their conquest of India as at least partly a humanitarian intervention on behalf of the once-great Hindu nation that had been oppressed for centuries by Muslim despots and condemned to backwardness.

Most of these early British views of India were useful fictions at best since the Turks, Afghans, Central Asians, and Persians who together with upper-caste Hindu elites had ruled a variety of Indian states for over eight centuries were rather more than plunderers and zealots. The bewildering diversity of people that inhabited India before the arrival of the Muslims in the eleventh century hardly formed a community, much less a nation; and the word 'Hinduism' barely hinted at the almost infinite number of folk and elite cultures, religious sects, and philosophical traditions found in India.

But these novel British ideas were well received by educated upper-caste Hindus who had previously worked with Muslim rulers and then begun to see opportunities in the new imperial order. British discoveries of India's classical sculpture, painting and literature had given them a fresh invigorating sense of the pre-Islamic past of India. They found flattering and useful those British orientalist notions of India that identified Brahmanical scriptures and principles of tolerance as the core of Hinduism. In this view, such practices as widow-burning became proof of the degradation Hinduism had suffered during Muslim rule, and the cruelties of caste became an unfortunate consequence of Muslim tyranny.

A wide range of Hindu thinkers, social reformers and politicians followed the British in dismissing the centuries of Muslim domination as a time of darkness, and upholding imperial rule with all its social reforms and scientific advances as preparation for self-rule. Some denounced British imperialism as exploitative, but even they welcomed its redeeming modernity, and, above all, the European idea of the nation – a cohesive community with a common history, culture, values, and sense of purpose – which for many other colonized peoples appeared a way of duplicating the success of the powerful, all-conquering West.

Muslim leaders, on the other hand, were slow to

participate in the civilizing mission of imperialism; they saw little place for themselves in the idea of the nation as espoused by the Hindu elite. British imperialists followed their own strategies of divide and rule: the decision to partition Bengal in 1905 and to have separate electorates for Muslims further reinforced the sense among many upwardly mobile Indians that they belonged to distinct communities defined exclusively by religion.

It is true that Gandhi and Nehru worked hard to attract low-caste Hindus and Muslims; they wanted to give a mass base and wider legitimacy to the political demands for self-rule that intensified in the early twentieth century under the leadership of the Congress Party. But Gandhi's use of popular Hindu symbols, which made him a Mahatma among Hindu masses, caused many Muslims to distrust him. Also, many Congress leaders shared the views not of Gandhi, or the poet Rabindranath Tagore, who criticized western-style nationalism, but such upper-caste ideologues as Veer Savarkar and Guru Golwalkar, the spiritual and ideological parents of Hindu nationalists of today.

2 The Rashtriya Swayamsevak Sangh: Indian-Style Fascism

On the evening of 30 January 1948, five months after the independence and partition of India, Mahatma Gandhi was walking to a prayer meeting in the grounds of his temporary home in New Delhi when he was shot three times in the chest and abdomen. Gandhi was then seventy-nine years old, and a forlorn figure. He had been unable to prevent, and so was widely blamed by many Hindus for, the bloody creation of Pakistan as a separate homeland for Indian Muslims. The violent uprooting of millions of Hindus and Muslims across the hastily drawn borders of India and Pakistan had tainted the freedom from colonial rule that he had been so arduously working towards. When the bullets from an automatic pistol hit his frail body at point blank range, he collapsed and died instantly. His assassin made no attempt to escape, and even, as he would later claim, shouted for the police.

Millions of shocked Indians waited anxiously for further news that night, fearing unspeakable violence if Gandhi's murderer proved to be a Muslim. There was much relief, and also some puzzlement, the next morning when the assassin was revealed as Nathuram Godse, a Hindu Brahmin from western India, a region relatively untouched by the murderous passions of the Partition.

Born into a lower-middle-class family, Godse began his career in 1932 as a Hindu activist with the RSS, which had been founded by a Brahmin doctor called Hegdewar in the central Indian city of Nagpur seven years previously. The RSS was, and remains, dedicated to establishing a Hindu nation by uniting Hindus from all castes and sects and by forcing Muslims, Christians and other Indian minorities to embrace Hindu culture. Godse received both physical and ideological training from members of the RSS, and absorbed their ideas about the greatness of pre-Islamic India, and the havoc wrought upon Hindus by eight centuries of Muslim invasions and tyranny.

During his trial, Godse made a long and eloquent speech in English explaining his background and motives. He claimed that Gandhi's 'constant and consistent pandering to the Muslims', whom he described variously as fanatical, violent and anti-national, had left him with no choice. He blamed Gandhi for the 'vivisection of the country – our motherland', and denounced the latter's insistence upon non-violence, saying that it was 'absurd to expect [400 million] people to regulate their lives on such a lofty plane'. He claimed it was the terrorist methods of Hindu and Sikh freedom fighters, not Gandhi's non-violence, that had forced the British to leave India, and hoped that with Gandhi dead, 'Indian politics would surely be practical, able to retaliate', and the nation, he claimed, 'would be saved from the inroads of Pakistan'.

Godse requested that the judge at his trial show him no mercy, and he did not appeal against the death sentence passed on him. He went to the gallows in November 1949 shouting such slogans as 'Long live the undivided India' and singing paens to the 'Living motherland, the land of the Hindus'. The Indian government under Pandit Nehru banned the RSS a few days after Gandhi's murder, and arrested thousands of its members. The ban was lifted a year later, after the RSS agreed to have a written constitution and confine itself to 'cultural' activities – a promise it quickly broke. Not much is known about the RSS in the West, although both the former prime minister Atal Bihari Vajpayee and his deputy, L.K. Advani, belong to it, and have never repudiated its militant ideology – the ideology of Hindu nationalism that seeks aggressively to 'Hinduize' South Asia and has often threatened to plunge the region, which has the largest Muslim population in the world, and two nuclear-armed nations, into catastrophic war.

After 11 September 2001, the Hindu nationalists presented themselves to the West as reliable allies in the fight against Muslim fundamentalists. But in India their resemblance to the European fascist movements of the 1930s has been clear for a long time. In his manifesto, *We, or Our Nationhood Defined* (1938), Guru Golwalkar, director of the RSS from 1940 to 1973, during which time both Mr Vajpayee and Mr Advani joined the organization and rose to become senior leaders of its political wing, said that the Nazis had manifested 'race pride at its highest' by purging Germany of the Jews. According to Golwalkar, India was Hindustan, a land of Hindus where Jews and Parsis could only ever be 'guests', and to which Muslims and Christians came as 'invaders'. Golwalkar was clear about what he expected from both the guests and the invaders.

> The foreign races in Hindustan must either adopt the Hindu culture and language, must learn to respect and hold in reverence Hindu religion, must entertain no idea but those of the glorification of the Hindu race and culture, i.e. of the Hindu nation, and must lose their separate existence to merge in the Hindu race, or may stay in the country, wholly subordinated to the Hindu nation, claiming nothing, deserving no privileges, far less any preferential treatment – not even citizens' rights. There is, at least should be no other course for them to adopt.

Golwalkar and his disciples in the RSS and Congress saw India as the sacred indigenous nation of Hindus which had been divided and emasculated by Muslim invaders, and which could be revived only by uniting India's diverse population, recovering ancient Hindu traditions, and weeding out corrupting influences from Central Asia and Arabia. This meant forcing Indian Muslims to give up their allegiance to such alien lands and faiths as Mecca and Islam and to embrace the so-called 'Hindu ethos', or Hindutva, of India – an ethos that was, ironically, imagined into being with the help of British orientalist discoveries of India's past.

By the 1940s, the feudal and professional Muslim elite of India had grown extremely wary of the Hindu nationalist strain within the Congress. After many failed attempts at political rapprochement, this elite finally arrived at the demand for a separate homeland for Indian Muslims. The demand expressed the Muslim fear of being reduced to a perpetual minority in a Hindu majority state, and was, initially, a desire for a more federal polity for postcolonial India. But the leaders of the Congress chose to partition the Muslim-majority provinces in the west and east rather than share the centralized power of the colonial state that was their great inheritance from the British.

This led to the violent transfer of millions of Hindus, Sikhs, Muslims across hastily drawn artificial borders. The massacres, rapes, and kidnappings further hardened sectarian feelings: the RSS, which was temporarily banned after Gandhi's assassination, found its most dedicated volunteers among middle-class Hindu refugees from Pakistan, such as the former home minister, Lal Krishna Advani, who was born in Muslim-dominated Karachi and joined the RSS as early as 1942. The RSS floated a new party, the Jana Sangh, later to become the BJP, which in 1951 entered electoral politics in independent India with the renewed promise of a Hindu nation; although it worked for much of the next three decades in the gigantic shadow of the Congress Party, its sudden popularity in the 1980s now seems part of the great disaster of Partition, which locked the new nation-states of India and Pakistan into stances of mutual hostility.

In Pakistan, a shared faith failed to reconfigure the diverse regional and linguistic communities into a new nation. This was proved when the Bengali-speaking population of East Pakistan seceded, with Indian help, to form the new state of Bangladesh in 1971. Muslims in India continue to lack effective spokespersons, despite, or perhaps because of, the tokenist presence of Muslims at the highest levels of the government. Politically, they are significant only during elections, when they form a solid vote-bank for those Hindu politicians promising to protect them against discrimination and violence. Their representation in government jobs has steadily declined.

Secularism, the separation of religion from politics, was always going to be difficult to impose upon a country where religion has long shaped political and cultural identities. But it was the only useful basis on which the centralized government in Delhi could, in the name of modernity and progress, establish its authority over a poor and chaotically fractious country. However, when Sikh and Muslim minorities in the states of Punjab and Kashmir challenged the great arbitrary power of the Indian government, Nehru's heirs, his daughter, Indira, and grandson Rajiv, were quick to discard even the rhetoric of secularism and to turn Hindu majoritarianism into the official ideology of the Congress-run Central Indian government.

The uprisings in Punjab, and then Kashmir, were portrayed by the Indian government and the middle-class media as fundamentalist and terrorist assaults on secular democracy. In fact, although tainted by association with Pakistan and religious fanaticism, the Sikhs and Kashmiri Muslims expressed a long-simmering discontent with an anti-federalist state in Delhi: a state that had retained most of the power of the old colonial regime, and often wielded it more brutally than the British ever had. The uprisings were part of a larger crisis, one that has occurred elsewhere in post-colonial nations: the failure of a corrupt and self-serving political and bureaucratic elite to ensure social and economic justice for those it had claimed to represent in its anticolonial battles.

By the 1980s, when the Hindu nationalists abruptly rose to prominence, the Congress had disillusioned lower-caste Hindus, and looked incapable of preserving even the interests of its upper-caste Hindu constituency. It kept raising the bogey of national unity and external enemies. But the disturbances in the border states of Kashmir and Punjab only gave more substance to the Hindu nationalist allegation that the Congress with its 'pseudo-secularism' had turned India into a 'soft state', where Kashmiri Muslims could blithely conspire with Pakistan against Mother India.

It was in the 1980s, with the Congress rapidly declining and the pseudo-socialist economy close to bankruptcy, that the Hindu nationalists saw a chance to find new voters among upper-caste Hindus. Like the National Socialists in Germany in the early 1930s, they offered not so much clear economic policies as fantasies of national rebirth and power. In 1984, the VHP announced a national campaign to rebuild the grand temple at Ayodhya; the mosque the first Mogul emperor Babur had erected was, they said, a symbol of national shame; removing it and rebuilding the temple was a matter of national honour.

Both history and archaeology were travestied in this account of the fall and rise of the eternal Hindu nation.

There is no evidence that Babur had ever been to Ayodhya, or that this restless, melancholic conqueror from Samarkand, a connoisseur of architecture, could have built an ugly mosque over an existing Rama temple. Rama himself isn't known to recorded history; the cult of Rama-worship arrived in North India as late as the tenth century AD, and no persuasive evidence exists for the Rama temple that apparently once stood on the site of the mosque.

But the myths were useful in reinforcing the narrative of Muslim cruelty and contempt. At first, they found their keenest audience among wealthy expatriate Hindus in the UK and the US, who generously bankrolled a movement that in upholding a strong self-assertive Hinduism seemed to allay their sense of inferiority induced by western images of India as a miserably poor country. In India, the anxieties that persuaded many upper-caste Hindus to support the BJP were much deeper. In 1990, the government in Delhi, then headed by defectors from the Congress Party, decided to implement a long-standing proposal to reserve government jobs for poor 'backward-caste' Hindus. Upper-caste Hindus were enraged at this attack on their privilege. The BJP saw the plan for affirmative action as potentially destructive of its old goal of persuading lower-caste groups to accept a paternalistic upper-caste leadership as part of presenting a united Hindu front against Muslims.

Later that year, the leader of the BJP, L.K. Advani, decided to lead a ritual procession on a faux chariot – actually a Chevrolet – from Gujarat to Ayodhya, where he intended to start the construction of the Rama temple. Appropriately, he set out from the temple in Somnath, Gujarat, which, looted by a Turk conqueror in the eleventh century AD, was lavishly rebuilt in the early 1950s by devout Hindu leaders of the Congress Party. This wasn't just play-acting, however: more than 500 people, most of them Muslims, were killed in the rioting that accompanied Advani's progress across India. Hindu policemen were indifferent, and sometimes even participated in the violence. When I was in Benares recently, a friend casually pointed out a distant relative of his walking down the street. He was a retired police officer who liked to boast of how he had shot and killed fourteen Muslims during a riot in the city of Meerut.

It is strange to look back now and recall that just two decades ago the temple–mosque controversy was hardly heard of outside Ayodhya. Local Hindus first staked a claim on the mosque in the mid nineteenth century, and British officials allowed them to worship on a platform just outside the building. In 1949, two years after independence, a Hindu civil servant working together with local abbots surreptitiously placed idols of Rama inside the mosque. The story that Lord Rama himself had installed them there quickly spread. The local Muslims protested. Prime Minister Nehru sensed that nothing less than India's secular identity was threatened. He ordered the mosque to be locked and sacked the district official, who promptly joined the Hindu nationalists.

The idols, however, were not removed, and Muslims gradually gave up offering *namaz* at the mosque. During the three decades that followed, the courts were clogged with cases concerning Hindu and Muslim claims on the site. In 1984, the VHP began a campaign for the unlocking of the mosque. In 1986, a local judge allowed the Hindus to worship inside the building. A year later, Muslims held their largest protest demonstration since independence in Delhi.

Until 1984, however, Babur's mosque remained relatively unknown outside of a small circle of litigious and property-hungry abbots in Ayodhya. Religion was a fiercely competitive business in Ayodhya: the local abbots fought hard for their share of donations from millions of poor pilgrims, and, more recently, wealthy Indians in the US and the UK, and they were notorious for murder and pillage – the attack on Ramchandra Paramhans that he blamed on Muslim terrorists was probably the work of rival abbots. But, as the movement for the temple intensified, entrepreneurs of religiosity such as Paramhans were repackaged by Hindu nationalist politicians as sages and saints and turned into national celebrities. Rama himself suddenly evolved from the benign, almost feminine, calendar-art divinity of my childhood to the vengeful Rambo of Hindu nationalist posters.

The myths multiplied in October 1990 when Advani's Chevrolet-chariot procession was stopped and police in Ayodhya fired upon a crowd of Hindus attempting to assault the mosque. The largest-circulation Hindi paper in North India, *Dainik Jagaran*, spoke of 'indiscriminate police firing' and 'hundreds of dead devotees', and then reduced the death toll the next day to thirty-two. The rumours and exaggerations, part of a slick propaganda campaign, helped the BJP win the elections in four North Indian states in 1991. The mosque seemed doomed. When on 6 December 1992 Babur's mosque was demolished by a crowd of mostly upper-caste Hindus equipped with shovels, crowbars, pickaxes and sometimes just their bare hands, the police simply watched from a distance.

Uma Bharati, one of the more vocal Hindu nationalist politicians, cheer-led the crowd, shouting, 'Give one more push and break the Babri Masjid.' The president of the VHP announced the dawn of a 'Hindu rebellion' while a leader of the BJP said that for 'those who want to see the flag of Pakistan flutter over Kashmir, the process of showing them their right place has begun'.

That evening the crowd rampaged through Ayodhya, killing and burning thirteen Muslims, some of whom were children, and destroying scores of mosques, shrines and Muslim-owned shops and houses. Protests and riots then erupted across India. Altogether 2,000 people, mostly Muslims, were killed. Three months after the massacres, Muslim gangsters in Bombay retaliated with bomb attacks that killed more than 300 civilians.

In Delhi, the elderly Congress prime minister, Narasimha Rao, napped through the demolition. The next day he dismissed the BJP governments, banned the RSS and its sister organizations, and promised to rebuild the mosque. The leaders of the BJP tried to distance themselves from the demolition, saying that it was a spontaneous act of frustration, provoked by the anti-Hindu policies of the government. However, the Central Bureau of Investigation (CBI) concluded that such senior leaders of the BJP as L.K. Advani, subsequently home minister of India, had planned the demolition well in advance. As for the anti-Muslim violence, Advani claimed in an article in the *Times of India* that it would not have taken place had Muslims identified themselves with Hindutva: the same sentiment echoed after the riots in Gujarat.

Six years after the demolition, the BJP, benefiting from India's 'first past the post' electoral system, became the dominant party in the ruling National Democratic Alliance (NDA) in Delhi. Despite being forced to share power with more secular parties, the BJP's ideological fervour seemed undiminished, if ultimately unfulfilled. Certainly, the Hindu nationalists have tried hard to whip up Hindu passions. In early 1998, during their first few months in power, they conducted nuclear tests, explicitly aiming them against Pakistan, which responded with its own tests. The VHP and Bajrang Dal distributed radioactive earth from the nuclear tests site as sacred offerings; they were also responsible for an unprecedented series of mob attacks on Christians across India. About half of these occurred in Gujarat, but Advani claimed that there was 'no law and order problem in Gujarat', and at a meeting of Hindu nationalists shared the dais with the new chief of the RSS, K.S. Sudharshan. The latter spoke of 'an epic war between Hindus and anti-Hindus', asked Christians and Muslims to return to their 'Hindu roots', and also attacked secular intellectuals as 'that class of bastards which tries to implant an alien culture in their land' .

A clearer sense of the world view RSS members subscribe to from childhood can be had from a long discourse K.C. Sudharshan, the present supreme director of the RSS and a regular adviser to Mr Vajpayee and Mr Advani, delivered to RSS members in 1999. In this speech, later published in Hindi with the title of *Ek Aur Mahabharata* ('One More *Mahabharata*'), Sudharshan described how a new epic war would shortly commence between the demonic and divine powers that apparently forever contended for supremacy in the world. Sudharshan identified the United States as the biggest example of the 'rise of inhumanity' in the contemporary world. As he described it, violence was endemic in America, where the institution of the family lay shattered and where 'all the tender feelings of man' had died. Referring to the Monica Lewinsky affair, he asked, 'What can you say about a nation whose president itself is so crazed with lust?' He claimed that India exercised the 'greatest terror' over America, primarily because Indians were extremely intelligent and talented. He had touched on this theme in his praise of India's nuclear tests in 1998, when he said that, 'Our history has proved that we are a heroic, intelligent race capable of becoming world leaders but the one deficiency that we had was of weapons, good weapons.' America, he said, was trying to subjugate India through its multinationals. Sudharshan ended his speech by denouncing the international conspiracy hatched against India by the US alongside the World Trade Organization, the Pope, and Sonia Gandhi – a conspiracy he predicted would result in a 'final victory' of Hindu nationalism.

This mishmash of anti-American rhetoric, paranoia, moral arrogance, and ill-digested history brings to mind the rants of Osama bin Laden. But the comparison with al-Qaeda or other radical Islamists does not go very far. The RSS doesn't reject so much as seek an alternative route to western modernity. In fact, much like the Japanese nationalists of the 1930s, the RSS upholds modern science and technology as the essential way to national strength – four out of the five supreme directors of the RSS so far have held college degrees in medicine, nuclear physics, biology, chemistry, and engineering. Suffering from an inferiority complex vis-à-vis the modern West, Hindu nationalists are obsessed with beating the West at its own game.

During the six years the BJP held power in New Delhi, the RSS members I met exulted in private conversation about their well-placed colleagues in the Indian government. But the RSS does not aim at capturing state power alone. M.G. Vaidya, the RSS's official spokesman – an elderly man wearing a dandyish silk scarf and a rakishly tilted black cap – told me in his Delhi office in September 2002, 'Forming a state without building and unifying a nation doesn't work. Look at the Soviet Union. The communists had power, but the nation was not with them, and they collapsed.'

Golwalkar had hoped to reorganize India into a microcosm of the RSS, achieving the 'perfectly organized state of society wherein each individual has been moulded into a model of ideal Hindu manhood and made into a living limb of the corporate personality of society'.

Some part of this vision also motivated my father and uncles, who like hundreds of thousands of Brahmin men in the 1940s, became active members of the RSS – a couple of my uncles were in prison briefly after Gandhi's murder. These young educated Brahmins were anxious about how they would fare as a somewhat privileged minority in independent democratic India. The ideal Hindu manhood proposed by the RSS – to be both a Hindu man and to mould your world according to your image – was irresistible to them. The vision did require them to subjugate their will and intellect to a larger cause. But this was and is considered even now by some a small price to pay for security and identity in a poor chaotic country.

The RSS's large-scale schemes of moulding individuals

seem closer to the engineering of human souls that Stalin and Hitler attempted in their different ways. They mark the RSS as 'totalitarian'. Anxieties about the fascistic outlook and make-up of the RSS are not allayed by its strongly hierarchical and centralized organization, in which the word of the supreme director is final, and the members have little say in the shaping of policy.

There is also their reputation as a secretive, extra-constitutional force, which does not provide details about the size and spread of its membership. 'The RSS is not interested in publicity,' I was told by the brusque young man in charge of the RSS's media office in Delhi. Mr Sudharshan declined my request for an interview; neither did he reply to a letter seeking clarifications on some of his assertions. The then deputy prime minister L.K. Advani also declined to be interviewed on his connection with the RSS, which he joined in 1942 as a young student in what is now the Pakistani city of Karachi. Other members of the RSS bluntly refused to talk to someone they described as an 'anti-Hindu' writer. The few members I did manage to talk to suddenly became elusive after the first meeting.

'The Hindu nationalists are cautious at present, especially with the foreign press,' a senior Indian journalist told me. 'Their fascistic nature has been obscured so far in the West by the fact that India is a democracy, has regular elections, and has a potentially large consumer market. They have managed to speak with two voices, one for foreign consumption, and the other for local. But they know that religious extremists are under closer scrutiny worldwide after 9/11, and they know that they don't look too good after the killings of 2,000 Muslims in Gujarat.'

Tarun Vijay, the youngish editor of the RSS Hindi

weekly *Panchajanya*, who was represented to me by Delhi journalists as the 'modern face of Hindu nationalism', was, he confessed to me, 'wary'. He said he was 'very sceptical' about foreign media, and 'left-wing Indians and secularists'. 'Westerners don't understand,' he said, 'that the RSS is a patriotic organization working for the welfare of all Indians.' Mr Vijay's own career seems to prove this. Born in 1956 to a middle-class family in North India, Mr Vijay was educated eclectically at schools run by Gandhians and American Presbyterians. But he was impressed most by the 'selflessness' and 'patriotism' of the RSS members he met as a young man. They inspired him to leave home and work in western India, protecting tribal peoples from exploitation and discrimination. They had even helped arrange his marriage.

When I met him Mr Vijay had been working on *Panchajanya*, a magazine with a circulation of 90,000, for over a decade. The magazine's first editor, in the late 1940s, was Vajpayee – the dusty walls of Mr Vijay's office are covered with enlargements of Vajpayee's old editorials demanding that the then Indian government take an aggressive line with Pakistan over Kashmir. In the early 1990s the Hindu nationalists became the most powerful political group in India; and Mr Vijay was considered to have contributed to their success. The English-language news magazine *Outlook* described him as one of the closest confidants of deputy prime minister Advani. He would show up frequently on STAR TV, India's most prominent news channel. For some time he appeared to be destined for even higher things: a ministerial or advisory position with the federal government; an ambassador's job. But, when we met, his suave manner often broke to reveal impatience and restlessness.

'I was educated at a Christian school,' he said. 'Some of my best friends are Muslims. My wife wears jeans, and she wears her hair short, we eat meat at Muslim homes, we go to church on Christmas Day. There are reasonable people among Muslims, but they are afraid to speak out their minds. We are trying to have a dialogue with them. We are trying to talk with Christians also. After all, Jesus Christ is my greatest hero. But the left-wing and secular people are always portraying us as anti-Muslim and anti-Christian fanatics.'

An Indian journalist, who reported on the RSS regularly, later explained Mr Vijay's defensiveness as that of an ambitious man who recognizes the extreme aspects of Hindu nationalism as a disadvantage in the modern world. The journalist thought I should meet Uma Bharti, probably the most famous woman among the Hindu nationalists, and one of the senior leaders accused of demolishing the mosque in Ayodhya in 1992.

Power and responsibility – she was now the federal minister for sports and youth affairs – seemed to have tempered her nationalist zeal. I met her at her office, where her ochre robes – ochre, the Hindu colour of renunciation – stood out brilliantly against the bare blue-painted walls, and the bureaucrats running around in western-style trousers and shirts seemed the employees of a spiritual self-help corporation. Ms Bharti, then forty-two years old, and a self-declared sannyasin, someone who has renounced the world for the sake of spiritual wisdom, started her life in a poor low-caste village in central India. A decade ago, her tales of Muslim cruelty towards Hindus sent her vast audiences into a frenzy. But in her conversation with me, Ms Bharti seemed keen to distance herself from Hindu nationalism. In fact, her aides granted me an interview on the condition that I would only question her about her work among underprivileged Indians.

She brushed aside a question about the killings in Gujarat and instead told me that she had not forgotten what it meant to be poor, low-caste and a woman in a small village in the middle of nowhere. She was very young when her father, a communist activist fighting against local landlords, died. Her mother worked as a menial labourer in order to support her family. She was four when she saw her house burnt down and the family cattle destroyed by a vengeful landlord in her village. It was then she began to memorize the Hindu epics, mostly by listening to other people recite them. Devout Hindus invited her to their homes for religious discourses. She acquired a reputation as a divinely inspired speaker. Later, local leaders of the VHP saw her potential, and turned her into a performer before the large, intense Hindu audiences clamouring for a Rama temple.

It was a sense of injustice – why were Hindus not allowed to worship where Lord Rama was born? – that had provoked her into joining the campaign for the Rama temple in Ayodhya. But, she said, she now derived her 'ultimate satisfaction' from attacking poverty and social injustice. She felt herself inspired by not just Hanuman, the Hindu monkey god, and Shivaji, the seventeenth-century militant Hindu chieftain, but also Che Guevara, the Latin American revolutionary. For her religious past that she now wished to outgrow, Ms Bharti had a simple explanation.

She wanted to fight injustice, she had wanted power, and 'religion seemed the only way to have it'.

3 *Engineering Souls*

After a few days in Delhi, I travelled to the Central Indian city of Nagpur, where the RSS was established in 1925. At first, Nagpur seems an unlikely birthplace for the RSS. Its grand colonial buildings and broad avenues confirm its reputation as an educational and administrative centre. Its new shopping complexes and residential high-rises speak of the affluence the city has known since the Indian economy was liberalized in the early 1990s. Nagpur has few Muslims, and its largest community consists of Dalits, who have traditionally shied away from the RSS, which they consider, not unfairly, as dominated by, and serving the interests of, Brahmins. It was in Nagpur in 1956 that Dr B.R. Ambedkar, the Dalit leader who was a disciple of the American philosopher John Dewey and who drafted the Indian constitution, led a mass conversion of low-caste Hindus to Buddhism in protest against the inequities of Brahmanical Hinduism.

I went to see Shyam Pandharipande, who belongs to an old Brahmin family and now edits Nagpur's only monthly feature magazine in English. Mr Pandharipande's father was an early member of the RSS, and so was Mr Pandharipande himself, before his disillusionment with Hindu nationalist ideology led him towards Gandhi-inspired environmental organizations. His long experience of the RSS seems to have given him an acute insight into its workings. He told me that when Dr Hegdewar, a native of Nagpur, set up the RSS in 1925, his first recruits were all very young Brahmin men from educated middle-class families. He persuaded some of these Brahmins to travel to many different parts of India and set up RSS branches there. It was these missionaries who first brought most of the current leaders of the BJP – Vajpayee and Advani – into the RSS. The RSS really began, Mr Pandharipande said, as a rearguard action by privileged and insecure Brahmins who felt that they would have little place in a new democratic India where low-caste Hindus would grow assertive and demand their rights.

In 1926, the first *shakha* (assembly) was held in an open ground. Young RSS members dressed in khaki shorts, white shirts, and black caps did military-style drills, played traditional Indian team games, learnt to use the lathi (a thick bamboo stick) and were intellectually indoctrinated with ideas about Muslim invaders and the need for Hindu unity. In 2000, the RSS celebrated its seventy-fifth birthday with a giant *shakha* at its Nagpur headquarters of 60,000 uniformed men and boys.

The *shakha* quickly became the most important ritual in the life of an RSS member; it was also a recruiting ground for new members, mostly boys, attracted by the idea of open-air games. One evening, a couple of months ago, I went looking for a *shakha* in Nagpur. I was accompanied by Devendra, a young advertising executive in his mid twenties. He told me that he had attended RSS *shakhas* as a child much in love with the outdoors, but then, like most people of his generation, he had grown bored of the Indian games. He had wanted to play tennis, but the RSS men disapproved of western sports.

We drove through a sudden monsoon shower. The

streets were empty; so were the small parks within middle-class localities where the *shakhas* were usually held. We were about to give up when unexpectedly we found a crowd of middle-aged men in a leaky damp-stained room at the corner of one of the larger parks.

These were mostly retired Brahmin professionals, engineers, doctors, civil servants – the kind of middle-class people that had always formed the backbone of the RSS. They sat in neat rows on the damp cement floor, many of them dressed in the RSS uniform. Before them, on a small stage, were framed photographs of the RSS's founder Dr Hegdewar – his moustache in the photo almost as thick as the marigold garland that framed his face – and of the densely bearded Guru Golwalkar, Hegdewar's successor. An ochre flag hung listlessly over the photographs.

We had arrived during a *baudhik*, an intellectual session. A thin man in a black cap gave a long rambling speech, the principal, and perhaps overplayed, themes of which were the perfidy of Muslims, the cunning of Christian missionaries, and the need for Hindu unity. The elderly audience, which had listened to the same speech many times before, was attentive. As he spoke, blank white envelopes were passed around the assembled crowd, to be filled with rupee notes. When the talk ended, we walked in a brisk queue towards the stage, taking it in turns to pick up rose petals from an urn on the floor and throw them in the general direction of Dr Hegdewar's photograph, before dropping the envelopes in a little bag and walking back to our seats. The RSS prayer – '*Salutations to thee O loving motherland*' – and a slogan – '*Victory to Mother India*' – concluded the *shakha*.

I had been, I later discovered, to the annual ceremony

called *Guru dakshina* ('offering to the Guru'), where RSS members express their dedication to the aims of the organization in the form of a cash donation. The ceremony was repeated at roughly 45,000 *shakhas* the RSS now holds across India; and also, as reported by newspapers the next day, at the home of a senior minister in New Delhi, where Mr Vajpayee and Mr Advani joined other RSS members in affirming their allegiance to the elite order of Hindu nationalism.

The superior organization of the RSS, which until recently reached up to the highest levels of the Indian government, is its strength in a chaotic country like India. Its members run not just the biggest political party in India, but also educational institutions, trade unions, literary societies, and religious sects; they work to indoctrinate tribals and low-caste groups as well as affluent Indians living in the West. It is through what Guru Golwalkar called the 'untiring, silent endeavour of hundreds and thousands of dedicated missionaries' that the RSS hopes to create a Hindu nation.

The scale and diversity of this essentially evangelical effort is remarkable. I was startled when Tarun Vijay triumphantly showed me his magazine's headline about the patenting of cow urine in the United States. Western science, he said, had validated the ancient Hindu belief in the holiness of the cow; it was another proof of how the holistic Hindu way of life anticipated and indeed was superior to the discoveries of modern science, economics, ecology, and sociology. The cow had re-emerged as the key to self-sufficient, ecologically sustainable living.

This was more than rhetoric. Forty miles out of Nagpur,

at a clearing in a teak forest, I came across an RSS-run laboratory devoted to showcasing the multifarious benefits of cow urine. The supervisor, a middle-aged RSS member called Chandrashekhar Kundle, told me that this was a favourite project of Ashok Singhal, the president of the RSS affiliate, VHP. Most of the cows were out grazing in the forest, but there were a few frightened-looking calves in a large shed – 'rescued' recently, Mr Kundle said, from some nearby Muslim butchers. In one room, its whitewashed walls spattered with saffron-hued posters of Lord Rama, devout young Hindus with vermilion marks on their forehead stood before test tubes and beakers full of cow urine; they were distilling the holy liquid, it turned out, to get rid of the foul-smelling ammonia, and make it more palatable. In another room, tribal women in garishly coloured saris sat on the floor, before a small hill of white powder – dental powder, Mr Kundle explained, made from cow urine.

The nearest, and probably unwilling, consumers of the dental powder and other products made from cow urine were the poor tribal students in the RSS-funded primary school next to the lab. In gloomily dark rooms, where students both studied and slept, and where their frayed laundry hung from the iron bars of the windows, there were gleamingly clean portraits of militant Hindu freedom fighters. We sat in the small office of the headmaster, a thin excitable young man wearing polyester trousers. It was market day in the nearby town, and from the window, above which hung a large fantastical map of undivided India, I could see tribal women who had walked from their homes and now sat on the porch examining the sores and calluses on their bare feet, waiting to meet their children during recess.

The principal had his work cut out. His task was to make the students aware of the glorious Hindu culture from which tribal living had sundered them; he expected them to go home and educate their parents and relatives and alert them to the dangers of Christian missionaries who were disturbingly active in the tribal areas that the students came from. The message of the RSS, the principal said, was egalitarian and modern; it believed in raising low-caste people and tribals to a higher level of culture.

To prove this, he offered to summon a student – his brightest – and ask him to recite the Gayatri mantra, an invocation from Sanskrit scriptures, which for centuries only Brahmins could recite without fear of punishment. A boy in his early teens and wearing a vermilion mark on his forehead arrived. The headmaster looked on approvingly as the boy gave Mr Kundle the RSS salute by placing his right arm parallel to the ground and close to his chest, but grew nervous as he proceeded to stumble and bluff his way through the mantra.

John Dayal, the vice-president of the All India Catholic Union, told me that the RSS has spent millions of dollars in trying to convert tribal people to Hindu nationalism. Dayal, who monitors the missionary activities of the RSS very closely, claimed that in just over eighteen months, the RSS distributed 350,000 *trishuls* (tridents), in three contiguous tribal districts in Central India.

Dr B.L. Bhole, a political scientist I met at Nagpur University, saw a Brahmanical ploy in these attempts. He told me that the RSS had tried to turn not just Gandhi but also

Dr Ambedkar, the greatest leader of the Dalits, into a Hindu nationalist icon. K.S Sudharshan, the current supreme director of the RSS, had recently garlanded the statue of Dr Ambedkar at the park in Nagpur where the latter rejected Hinduism and converted to Buddhism in 1956. Dr Bhole thought this outrageous. He had joined local Dalit activists and intellectuals in ritually 'purifying' the statue after Sudharshan's visit.

Dr Bhole said, 'The RSS can't attract young middle-class people any more, so they hope for better luck among the poorest, socially disadvantaged people. But the basic values the RSS promotes among low-caste people and tribals are drawn from the high Sanskritic culture of Hinduism which considers the cow as holy, etc, and which seeks to maintain a social hierarchy with Brahmins at the very top. The united Hindu nation they keep talking about is one where basically low-caste Hindus and Muslims and Christians and other communities don't complain much while accepting the dominance of a Brahmin minority. But the problem for the RSS is that most of the low-caste Hindus and tribals don't want to learn any Brahmin mantras. They form an increasingly independent political group within India today; they no longer want any kind of Brahmin paternalist leadership. Even such low-caste leaders of the BJP as Uma Bharti want to focus on tangible rights for their community; they won't be fobbed off with nationalist ideology. Their assertiveness is really the greatest achievement of democratic politics in India, which has so far been dominated by upper-caste Hindus.'

Dr Bhole said, 'The RSS has been most successful in Gujarat, where low-caste Hindus and tribals were indoctrinated at the kind of schools you went to; they were in the mobs led by upper-caste Hindu nationalists that attacked Muslims and Christians. But the RSS still doesn't have much support among low-caste people outside Gujarat. For the RSS, this is a serious setback, and the only thing they can do to increase their mass base is keep stoking anti-Muslim and anti-Christian passions and hope they can get enough Hindus, both upper-caste and low-caste, behind them.'

The consistent demonizing of Muslims and Christians by Hindu nationalists may seem gratuitous – Christians in India are a tiny and scattered minority, and the Muslims are too poor, disorganized and fearful to pose any kind of threat to Hindus – but it is indispensable to the project of a Hindu nation. Hindu nationalists have always sought to redefine Hindu identity in opposition to a supposedly threatening 'other'. They hope to unite Hindu society by constantly invoking such real and imagined threats as are posed by the evangelical Christians and militant Muslims.

Visiting villages and towns across North India in the last few years, I found Muslims full of anxiety about their fate in India. They spoke to me of an insidious and regular violence: of the frequent threats and beatings they received from local Hindu politicians and policemen.

At one mosque in the countryside near Ayodhya, a young man broke into a conversation about police harassment, and loudly asserted that Muslims would not suffer injustice any more, and would retaliate. His elders shouted him down. An argument broke out – the young as usual accusing the old of suppressing the truth – and then a mullah gently led me out of the madrasa with one arm around my shoulders, assuring me that the Muslims were loyal to India, their homeland, where they had long lived in peace with their Hindu brothers.

Professor Saghir Ahmad Ansari, a Muslim social activist in Nagpur, told me that the Muslims he knew feel 'that the Hindu nationalists, who were implacably opposed to their existence in India, now controlled everything, the government, our rights, our future'. He said he worried about the Muslim response to Gujarat. 'When the government itself supervises the killing of 2,000 Muslims, when Hindu mobs rape Muslim girls with impunity, and force 100,000 Muslims into refugee camps, you can't hope that the victims won't dream of revenge. I fear,' he said, 'although I don't like saying or thinking about this, that the ideology of jihad and terrorist violence would find new takers among the 130 million Muslims of India. This will greatly please the Islamic fundamentalists of Pakistan and Afghanistan who are presently very downcast after the defeat of the Taliban and al-Qaeda.'

Mr Ansari's fears about vengeful Muslims were proved right a month after I spoke to him. In September 2002, Muslim terrorists from Pakistan murdered thirty-five Hindus at the famous Akshardham temple in Gujarat in ostensible retaliation for the mass killings of Muslims in the state earlier that year. It was the biggest attack by Muslim terrorists anywhere outside the Indian state of Kashmir; and the Hindu rage it provoked further ensured the victory of Hindu nationalist hardliners in elections held in Gujarat in December 2002.

In August 2003, two bomb explosions in Bombay killed more than fifty people – the sixth and most lethal in a recent series of similar blasts across the city. Soon after visiting the site, L.K. Advani, the then deputy prime minister, blamed terrorists based in Pakistan. This was to be expected. Hindu nationalists routinely describe India as besieged by Muslim terrorists backed by or based in Pakistan, especially in the disputed valley of Kashmir. This time, however, Mr Advani's accusation was qualified swiftly by the Bombay police. They revealed that the four persons arrested in connection with the attacks were Indian Muslims, part of a new group called the 'Gujarat Muslim Revenge Force'. They may have received logistical support from a Pakistani militant outfit with links to al-Qaeda, but they were Indian citizens.

The radical Islamist movements that spread quickly in the last decade in Pakistan, Bangladesh, and Afghanistan, had until now left largely untouched India's 130 million Muslims. Indian Muslims stayed away from the anti-India insurgency of their culturally distinct co-religionists in Kashmir. More remarkably, no Indian Muslim in the past seems to have heeded the many pied pipers of jihad in Afghanistan and Pakistan who lured Muslims from all parts of the world and who managed to delude even John Walker Lindh, a non-Muslim from California.

It may be that most Indian Muslims were and are too poor and depressed to join radical causes elsewhere. It is also true that they have an advantage denied to most Muslims in the world: they can participate in regular elections, and, since they comprise 13 to 14 per cent of India's population, choose their representatives, if not their rulers.

But this faith in democracy, which Indian Muslims have long expressed by voting tactically in large numbers, has been tested repeatedly in recent years. In 1996, an inquiry identified some of the Hindu police officers and politicians responsible for the killings of over 1,000 Muslims in

Bombay in 1992–3. To date no one has been tried and convicted. The perpetrators of the very public massacres in Gujarat are mostly known, but they are unlikely to face justice.

So the surprising issue, perhaps, is not that militant groups with international connections, such as the 'Gujarat Muslim Revenge Force', are emerging in India, but rather that it has taken them so long. The members of such organizations are educated, with degrees in business management, forensic science, chemical and aeronautical engineering. They have been radicalized in a geopolitical environment that has never been more highly fraught for the Muslim community at large. While the rage and resentment of these educated Muslims may have purely Indian origins – in Gujarat, or Bombay – such emotions are also inspired by international events – the wars in Afghanistan and Iraq, the car bombs in Bali, Casablanca, Riyadh, and Baghdad – that probably still seem remote to an older, impoverished generation of Indian Muslims.

The growth of religious militancy in South Asia is likely to enthuse many Hindus. As they see it, Gujarat proved to be a successful 'laboratory' of Hindu nationalism, in which carefully stoked anti-Muslim sentiments eventually brought about a pogrom, and a Muslim backlash seemed to lead to even greater Hindu 'unity'.

The victory of the BJP in Gujarat indicated that this plan was going well. It hinted that well-to-do Indians were likely to support the Hindu nationalists, even the extremists among them, as long as they continued to liberalize the Indian economy and help create a consumer revolution. But neither the BJP nor their supporters had reckoned with the larger, neglected majority of India's population, which expressed its scepticism about Hindu unity by voting out the BJP in the general elections in May 2004.

Opinion pollsters, political pundits, and journalists had predicted an easy victory for the ruling NDA (National Democratic Alliance), the coalition of BJP and its allies, which claimed in its advertising campaign to have created an 'India Shining' in the previous six years. But it was the opposition Congress that emerged as the single largest party in the 545-seat Indian parliament. These results surprised most middle-class Indians, for it was during the BJP's six years in power that India's urban prosperity, achieved by the economic reforms initiated in 1991, became most visible. The BJP had supported the reforms, which greatly benefited those who were best placed to take advantage of new opportunities in business and trade and the economy's fast-growing service sector (information technology, jobs offshored by Europe and America): the educated middle class, the BJP's primary constituency, which, despite growing fast in recent years, still makes up less than 20 per cent of India's population.

The reforms also attracted a generation of rich Indians who live in the US and the UK and were eager for cultural and economic links with their ancestral land – a desire that turned non-resident Indians into the BJP's most devoted followers and sponsors, and helped the BJP itself evolve rapidly, despite its Hindu nationalism, into a keen advocate of economic globalization. During its six years in power, new highways, shopping malls, brand-name boutiques, Starbucks-style coffee bars, and restaurants with exotic cuisine and London prices, transformed the cities of Bangalore, Hyderabad, Delhi, Chennai, and Bombay. New-found wealth created a heady mood among the middle class – what the leaders of the BJP called the 'feel-good factor' (so important that in March 2004 the BJP was initially reluctant to send the Indian cricket team to Pakistan out of the fear that it might lose and make the cricket-obsessed, nationalist middle class feel not so good any more). Most English-language newspapers began to print entire daily supplements in order to cover film premieres, fashion shows, champagne-tasting sessions in five-star hotels, and the lifestyles of beauty pageant winners, models, Bollywood actors, and other celebrities. The general air of celebration overwhelmed many formerly left-wing intellectuals, academics, and journalists. Convinced that the BJP would be in power for many years, they aligned themselves openly with the party, and lobbied for political and diplomatic posts. Some of the most influential TV news channels, newspapers, and magazines, including *India Today*, once India's best news magazine, were content to become an echo chamber for the BJP's views.

Not surprisingly, the BJP, and its supporters and advisers in the media, couldn't see beyond the 'India Shining' of the Hindu middle class, and turn their attention to the 70 per cent of Indians living in the countryside. They barely noticed the Indians that lived in slums or in equally degrading conditions in the big cities; the fact that while high-tech hospitals in the big cities cater to rich Indians and foreigners, or medical tourists, public health facilities in small towns and villages decline rapidly; that communicable diseases such as malaria, dengue, and encephalitis have revived; that half of all Indian children are undernourished and more than half a million of them die each year from diarrhoea; that an estimated five million Indians are infected with HIV/AIDS.

A powerful ideology often shaped the reforms the BJP espoused: that the free market can usurp the role of the state. This meant that government often withdrew from precisely those areas where its presence was indispensable. Though India had more than sufficient food grains in stock, the government's failure to distribute it effectively led in recent years to an unprecedented rise in the number of drought-affected villagers starving to death in many of the most populous states.

In this new India, preoccupied with life-or-death economic issues, the temple in Ayodhya may appear a dead issue; but it stands ready to be ignited by the BJP as it struggles to broaden its constituency beyond the affluent middle class. You reach Ramjanmabhoomi ('Rama's birthplace'), as it is now called, through a maze of narrow, barricaded paths. Armed men loom up abruptly with metal detectors and perform brisk body-searches. These are members of the Provincial Armed Constabulary (PAC), which is notorious for its pogroms of Muslims in North Indian towns; and they are particularly on the lookout for cameras. Pictures of the site have not been allowed by the government for the last decade.

A canvas canopy protects the platform built over the rubble of the mosque, on which stand the idols draped in garlands and sequinned cloth. A priest in a silk kurta and with caste marks on his forehead sits below the platform briskly dispensing *prasad* – tiny sugary balls – and squirrelling away the soiled and wrinkled rupee notes tentatively offered by peasant pilgrims.

As I groped for some small change one afternoon in February 2003, a PAC inspector wandered over, asked me if I was a journalist from Delhi, and attempted a little history. He told me that Lord Rama had placed the idols inside the mosque in 1949; it was his wish that a temple be built on his birthplace. My companion, a resident of Benares, challenged this, saying that the idols had been placed there by a district official. The inspector did not defend his story; he only smiled and replied that this proved that the official was a true Hindu.

Many such true Hindus looked the other way while the temple was prefabricated in Ayodhya and other cities across India. In a vast shed a short distance from the Ramjanmabhoomi lie stacks of carved stone pillars. Here, you can buy promotional literature – *The Blood-Soaked History of Ayodhya* and *Ayodhya: An Answer to Terrorism and Fundamentalism* are the bestselling titles – and also admire the miniature glass-cased model of the temple. Labour is cheap – £2 a day for craftsmen – but the temple, whose architect previously designed the Swaminarayan temple at Neasden, seems to have come out of a garish fantasy of marble and gold.

Local abbots are impatient with the slow pace of the construction; it is easy to see why. The offerings at the temple are likely to run into millions of dollars annually, and much money has already arrived from generous donors in India and abroad. No one knows where most of it has gone – rumours point to the opulent new buildings in Ayodhya and elsewhere.

As for the mosque – which appears now in memory as a melancholy symbol of a besieged secularism – there seems little hope it will ever be rebuilt. It has fallen victim not just to the ideologues but to less perceptible changes in India's general mood during the last decade. The talk of poverty and social justice; the official culture of frugality; the appeal, however rhetorical, to traditions of tolerance and dialogue – all these seem to belong to the past, to the early decades of idealism. A decade of pro-globalization policies has created a new aggressive middle class, whose concerns dominate public life in India. This class is growing – the current numbers are between 150 and 200 million. There are also millions of rich Indians living outside India. In America, they constitute the richest minority. It is these affluent, upper-caste Indians in India and abroad who largely bankrolled the rise to power of Hindu nationalists. In the global context, middle-class Hindus are no less ambitious than the class which in the Roman Empire embraced Christianity and made it an effective mechanism with which to secure worldly power. Hinduism in the hands of these Indians has never looked more like the Christianity and Islam of popes and mullahs, and less like the multiplicity of unselfconsciously tolerant faiths it still is for most Indians.

Gujarat in 2002 provided a glimpse of this modernized Hinduism, as Benetton-clad young Hindus carted off the loot of digital cameras and DVD players in their new Japanese cars. Ayodhya presents both a miniature image and a sinister portent of this Hinduism, with its syncretic past now irrevocably falsified, its mosques destroyed, its minorities suppressed: an Ayodhya where well-placed local abbots helped by elected politicians wait for new lucrative connections to the global economy, and prove, along with much else, the profound modernity of religious nationalism.

Bollywood:
India Shining

IN BOMBAY IN DECEMBER 2003 I met Mahesh Bhatt, one of India's most famous and successful film-makers. He told me, 'Bollywood is part of what our culture has become. We are lying to ourselves all the time.'

It wasn't what I expected to hear from Mahesh when I emailed him from London, explaining that I wanted to explore the world of Bombay films, or Bollywood, and requesting an interview. I had seen and liked some of his forty-odd films, the autobiographical ones about his illegitimate birth, his unhappy childhood with his Muslim mother, and his extramarital affair with a mentally ill actress that had made his reputation in the 1980s. Though he had stopped directing films five years earlier, he still wrote screenplays and supervised his daughter's and brother's production companies. He had published a book about his philosopher friend, U.G. Krishnamurthy. He made documentaries, but was also increasingly known for his denunciations in the press and on television of Hindu nationalists, sexual puritans, and US foreign policy.

I saw him often on television, where he was a striking figure in his loose black shirt, which set off the white hair remaining on his shiny pate. I had once seen him shout during a debate with a Hindu nationalist leader, 'I insist on my right to watch pornography!' 'Mark my words,' he said on another occasion, 'Hindu fundamentalism will destroy this nation.' More recently, he had turned down an invitation to a breakfast prayer meeting at the White House, and described George W. Bush as the 'worst villain in the world'.

Drama was clearly important to Mahesh. 'My God died young,' he told me, and then went on to describe how – angered by a God who kept apart his Muslim mother and Hindu Brahmin father – he had one day immersed his small statue of Ganesha in the Arabian Sea off Bombay. When I first met him in Bombay, on the set of *Murder*, a film he had written for his brother, he had just returned from his first visit to Pakistan. It had been, he said, a profound emotional experience. He had felt his buried Muslim self come alive in Pakistan. The visit had also stirred up memories of his long-suffering Muslim mother.

Though only fifty-five years old, he remembered his life as a long journey with clear-cut stages. In his twenties, he had taken a lot of LSD and gone 'shopping in the spiritual supermarket'. In his thirties, when he finally made it as a film-maker, he had come to know a 'great inner emptiness', feeling only sadness as his fax machine spun out box-office figures from across India. It was in Los Angeles, the 'capital of materialism', that he had decided to renounce the 'pursuit of success'. He had rejected his one-time guru, 'Osho' Rajneesh, by flushing his rosary beads down the toilet. He spoke with passion and conviction, and I didn't feel I could ask him if the water pressure in his Bombay toilet had been strong enough to flush away the beads.

*

His outspoken views had made him unpopular in Bollywood. 'He is a self-publicist,' one film journalist told me. 'Ask him why he helps his brother and daughter make B-grade films. Or, why he rips off Hollywood plots for his scripts?'

But Mahesh was frank about his own work. 'I have made a lot of trashy films. Recycling old formulas, which is what Bollywood does most of the time. I guess one has to keep working.' He said he regarded film-making without illusions, as a business like any other. 'Don't wait for the ideal offer, there is no such thing,' he told a young actor, a part-time model with a gym-toned body who had come to seek his advice. 'What will you do at home anyway, apart from bodybuilding?'

After the actor left, he turned back to me. 'These young people probably want to hear something else. They come to me, they think I am in the business, doing a lot of work, and will encourage them. But I can't. I can't make Bollywood bigger than it is.'

He said that his own films, even those that had made him rich and famous, had left him 'deeply unfulfilled'. He added, 'But I know that there is no fulfilment awaiting me anywhere. My friend U.G. Krishnamurthy says that there is no other reality apart from the one you live with every day.'

There seemed something too neat and packaged about Mahesh's self-awareness. But, while in Bombay, I found myself travelling often to his office in the suburb of Juhu. I walked straight past the reception to his small room, where I usually found him lying on a long sofa, under a broad window with a view of shanties cowering under grimy buildings. Two mobile phones rested on his ample stomach. One of them rang more often than the other; but Mahesh picked up both at the sound and then raising his neck from the sofa squinted at their screens for what seemed a long time before deciding to answer.

He was brusque on the phone, except to his wife and daughter. 'Who is this?' he would often ask and then start repeating, 'Bye, bye, bye,' in rapid succession before ending the conversation. The door opened to admit Nirmal, his personal attendant, with tea and coffee, or some of the young, trendy people working at the office. Occasionally, there would be someone Mahesh had arranged to see: a Pakistani actress hoping to work in Bollywood; a Parsee musician and ballet dancer wishing to try her hand at films; a tall, arrogant-looking actor wearing a Superman T-shirt, who, I learned, was the grandson of a notorious Bombay politician, and had acted in *Murder*. Soni, Mahesh's wife, came once: a petite, shy woman, she had acted in many art-house films in the eighties and was now trying to direct a film.

The door opened less often for the aspiring actors, directors, musicians, distributors, and publicists who waited at reception, hoping to waylay Mahesh or his brother, Mukesh. They grew animated as Mahesh emerged from his room. A couple of them often trailed him, with pleading voices, all the way to the building's compound, and spoke rapidly and uninterruptedly until he got into his car.

There were more young men at the gate to the walled compound. I saw them every day, chatting with the *chowkidar* (watchman), and the drivers of the cars parked inside, breaking off only to gaze expectantly into cars entering into the compound. Mohammed, the driver of my hired car, said that they were 'aspirers' who had travelled to Bombay from various parts of India, hoping for a 'break' in Bollywood. They were often found outside producers' offices, waiting to catch the attention of the important or powerful people there.

This was how most people tried to gain a foothold in what was a very crowded and self-contained world. India produces more films annually than any country – up to a thousand in several Indian languages, made in Bombay as well as Madras, Hyderabad, Trivandrum and Calcutta. Bombay, or Bollywood, is the biggest and best known of the Indian film industries, and has the biggest audience. Releasing up to two hundred films per year, it faces little competition from Hollywood, which has never garnered more than 6 per cent of the film market in India.

In 1896, the Lumière brothers brought moving images to India, shortly after introducing them to Europe. The first Indian feature film was released in 1913 in Bombay. By the 1930s, a film industry of sorts was in place in Bombay, with studios and independent production companies and stars, and films that borrowed or adopted narrative styles as varied as village folk theatre, Victorian fiction, the *Ramayana* and the *Mahabharata*, and Hollywood comedies and melodramas.

The film industries in India now employ up to six million people, mostly on a contractual basis. There are 12,000 cinema theatres in India with an average capacity of 700 seats, priced anywhere between 30 cents and 3 dollars. Since the finance for films comes from outside the legal economy, no one knows what the actual turnover of Bollywood, or of any other film industry in India, is. Films are often made for less than a million dollars. Although some of Bollywood's recent films have cost as much as $30m., much of the money is spent on music composers, shooting stints in Europe and America, and the stars, who are now more powerful than anyone else in the business.

Not surprisingly, most of the aspirers wanted to be stars, not technicians. Occasionally, one of them succeeded and gave fresh currency to the dream of success. Mallika, a young actress I met at Mahesh's office, was an aspirer when two years ago she left her conservative family in a small town near Delhi in order to seek a career in Bollywood. Long queues of 'gorgeous women', she said, preceded her at every producer's office she went to. After a few model-ling assignments and casting-couch offers, she had finally found some 'decent work'. But then her father ostracized her after her first film in which she kissed the male lead seventeen times – a record of sorts in prudish Bollywood.

Mallika thought that he was unlikely to respond well to her next film, *Murder*, in which she had played an adul-terous wife.

She said, 'The film is very bold – although I hate the word. People abuse it so much in Bollywood, which is full of dishonest tight-asses. How long are they going to show sex by bringing two flowers together on the screen? India has the second largest population in the world. Do they think it came about by bringing flowers together?'

I met Mallika at the end of what had been a long day of shooting for her. But she came into Mahesh's office looking very excited, wearing a small white T-shirt and low-slung blue jeans over very high heels. A preview, or what she called 'promo', of *Murder* had just begun to appear on many of India's film-based television channels.

I had seen an unedited version of this promo at Mahesh's office earlier that afternoon, accompanied by a film 'broker'. A rapid succession of scenes shot in India and Thailand showed Mallika being undressed by invisible hands, making love, and walking provocatively on a beach, the camera firmly focused on her hips. The broker had pronounced the film 'very bold'. It was likely to get an Adults certificate from the censor board. But this did not much bother the distributors who were convinced that *Murder* was going to be a 'big hit'.

Mallika said, 'I have been getting lots of SMS about the promo. It is very hot. Lots of skin show. But you tell me. You must have seen lots of films in London: what's so bold about showing a housewife feeling passionate and saying she wants to make love? What is a bored housewife to do when she is feeling horny?'

Mallika told me that film-makers from South India constantly approached her, wishing to cast her in soft-porn films. They appalled and depressed her; as did most filmmakers in Bollywood. She really wanted to work abroad, in Europe or America, where 'real' films were made. She spoke of the work of Pedro Almodóvar and Roberto Rodriguez.

As she spoke, she kept brushing back thick, wavy hair from her full-lipped, oval face. On that Sunday evening, Mahesh's office was deserted, with only a *chowkidar* waiting four floors down along with Mohammed, the driver of my hired car. Mallika and I sat on a sofa, separated by a few inches – the narrow space into which she suddenly dropped, while still speaking of Almodóvar, two glossy photos.

They were publicity stills from *Murder* and showed her pouting in a bikini and sarong. When Mallika asked me if I had seen the promo for *Murder*, I had lied, mostly because I couldn't work up a response. But now the photos lay on the sofa and as I looked at them I felt Mallika's eyes on my lowered face.

She said, 'I want you to look at them. I want you to tell me if men are going to drool over me or not in this film. I want you to give me an honest opinion.'

English in India can be a deceptive medium. Even when the language is used well, as it is by an elite minority among the country's 200-million-strong middle class, the under-tones can be confusing. Moods and gestures are hard to figure out. Irony and humour are often perceived but rarely intended.

'You should meet Mallika,' Mahesh had said. 'She is the next sex-bomb of Bollywood. It would be an interesting story for you.' Mahesh had many such stories for me. But, although grateful, I wasn't always sure what *he* made of them, or what his true relationship with Bollywood was.

One evening, as we were leaving his office, Mahesh paused before entering his car and gestured to one of the young 'aspirers' standing near the gate to the compound.

The man Mahesh had signalled to was a tall, rather handsome man wearing a black bandanna. He walked towards us, his broad shoulders stooped, until he stood half-bowed in a silent *namaste* before Mahesh.

Mahesh said, 'This is Pritam. He has been coming to my office every day for eight years now, hoping to get a role in my films. I have often offered him money for the return fare to his town in Bengal, but he has always refused. Would you like to talk to him?'

I felt Pritam lift his head slightly to look at me. I felt a small crowd at the gate watching us. I nodded.

Mahesh told Pritam while slowly getting into his car, 'OK. Be here at two-thirty tomorrow.'

Driving back to my hotel, Mohammed was frantic with curiosity. He knew about Pritam, who was apparently famous in these parts. He had indeed been coming to the office for eight years but had not managed to speak to Mahesh sahib for the last three. And he had never gone up to his office. Was he now finally being given a 'break'?

I said I didn't know. When I arrived at the office the next day – late, around four – Pritam was standing with the drivers. As my car slid past the gate, his face appeared in the window. Half-bent, he accompanied the car until it stopped and then held my door open. I saw his beseeching eyes, and the sweat patches on his ironed blue shirt. I said I was sorry to be late. He didn't seem to understand. I said that I was sure Mahesh would call for him soon.

Upstairs, Mahesh was lying on his sofa, bubbling with news. He got up as I came through the door. He said he was travelling to Delhi the next day to see Sonia Gandhi, the Italian-born leader of both the Congress Party and the then opposition in the Indian parliament. Some Muslim theologians had arranged the meeting. They felt that Mahesh was best placed to convey their frustration with the Congress's failure to fight the anti-Muslim programme of the Hindu nationalist government.

Mahesh said, 'It is a sad reflection on our politics that they can't find anyone to approach her except Mahesh

Bhatt.' He showed me a folder of photographs sent to him from the western Indian state of Gujarat. The pictures were of Muslims attacked, some by Hindu policemen, in recent months: close-ups of bloody wounds on skulls, backs, and legs, or of shattered car windscreens, television sets, and dressing-table mirrors. Each photo had the date and time of the attack written on the back. The accompanying letter from a Muslim described how his daughter had been 'beaten like a dog'.

We talked about politics for a while. Mahesh's mobile phones kept ringing. A journalist wanted Mahesh's opinion on the Oscars. 'To hell with the Oscars,' Mahesh said. 'I am not interested in it. Bye, bye, bye.' Another journalist asked about the film Mahesh planned to make about the real-life conman caught conspiring with the police commissioner of Bombay. His daughter called. Her first film was due for release. Mahesh said that she was very nervous about it.

Nirmal brought us fresh coffee in styrofoam cups. A publicist from Lucknow arrived. 'An important man,' Mahesh explained. He was there to talk about Mahesh's upcoming visit to North India.

Around five or so, Mahesh told Nirmal to summon Pritam.

Mahesh said, 'He told me once that he had committed a murder – his uncle, I think. I think he wanted to impress me. I want to ask him about that.'

When Pritam came through the door, his face glistening with sweat, Mahesh said, pointing to the bathroom behind him, 'Go and wash your face.'

Water dripped from his face and on to his shirt when he came out. Mahesh said, 'Sit down.'

He looked awkward on the small, high-backed chair, his long legs jutting out.

Mahesh gestured towards me. 'He is a writer, wanting to know about Bollywood. What can you tell him?'

This was how Mahesh introduced me to actors, producers, distributors, and others in the film industry, often exhorting them to take me behind the 'glossy surface' of Bollywood and reveal its 'harder reality'.

As it turned out, Pritam couldn't tell me much about Bollywood, partly because he had spent eight years hoping that Mahesh would introduce him to it. He hadn't gone to any other film-maker, convinced that Mahesh would give him his 'break'.

'Why do you think that?' Mahesh asked.

Pritam smiled uncertainly and said in slow but precise English, 'Because I know that in my heart, sir. I know that you will take me to the summit of success. I have believed this for the last eight years and I will believe this for the rest of my life.'

Mahesh said, in Hindi, 'But why did you tell me that you had killed your uncle?'

Pritam wiped his mouth, and leaned forward on his chair. 'It is true, sir. I wanted to tell you that I can be very serious about anything, even murder. I only have to put my mind to it.'

He described how he had been provoked into murdering his uncle. He seemed to have worked on the story, which came out smoothly. His father had died when he was very young. Soon afterwards, his uncles had appropriated his mother's land and house. One of Pritam's uncles had been particularly vicious. Pritam had seen him repeatedly assault his mother. At seventeen, he had first thought of murdering him. He spent a year planning the murder before finally stabbing the uncle in question. As part of his meticulous preparation, he had left no clues for the police; they were still baffled by the murder.

His mother, Pritam said, was a *devi*, a goddess. He couldn't bear anyone being cruel to her, and wanted above all to look after her.

Mahesh said, 'In that case, what are you doing in Bollywood? You have come to the wrong place. You come to Mahesh Bhatt thinking he will make you a star. Mahesh Bhatt is telling you that you are chasing illusions, that you should go home, and look after your mother. Do you want money for the train fare?'

Pritam shook his head. 'I want you to give me a chance, sir. I won't go home without having worked with you.'

Someone opened the door to announce that the publicist from Lucknow was leaving. Mahesh said to me in English, 'Why don't you talk to Pritam while I meet the publicist in my brother's room?'

Without Mahesh in the room, Pritam relaxed. I wanted to know where and how he had lived in Bombay for the last eight years. He replied, looking distracted, slightly puzzled perhaps, by the bareness of the room he had wanted for so long to enter, that he lived like an ascetic, did not drink or smoke, and ate very little. He stole whatever money he needed.

How? I asked. But Mahesh returned to his room just then, and Pritam produced a letter in Bengali from his mother; evidence, he said, of his mother's good heart.

Mahesh asked him to translate it aloud.

'My dear son,' Pritam began slowly, his eyes darting

from Mahesh's face to mine, 'I have not heard from you for a long time and you have not sent me any money. I don't worry much, because I know that your faith in Mahesh sahib will be rewarded one day . . .'

The letter spoke of her continued suffering at the hands of her greedy relatives. When it ended, Pritam looked up hopefully at Mahesh. One of Mahesh's phones rang just then. He picked both up and, while squinting at them, said to Pritam, 'I think you should go home and help her.'

Pritam stayed on for a few more minutes, drinking tea, surveying the room, while Mahesh spoke on the phone. I was relieved when Mahesh told him as he left that he would 'try him out before the camera'. Outside, Pritam immediately conveyed the news to the crowd of chauffeurs and aspirers. Mohammed was very pleased on his behalf – it was the kind of break he hoped for himself.

I wondered later if Pritam had written the letter himself, just as he had made up the story about the murder, in order to impress Mahesh. In its extreme, raw emotions, his story sounded too much like a Bollywood film.

I didn't suggest this to Mahesh, however. I wanted Pritam to have his 'break'. Also, I knew a little about Mahesh's background, and he seemed unlikely to doubt a story just because it was too melodramatic. His own father, also a famous producer and director in his time, had lived with his Hindu wife while maintaining a Muslim mistress, Mahesh's mother, in another part of Bombay. He came irregularly to his second home, and didn't stay long. As a child Mahesh had spent many hours waiting for his father, and then when he did not turn up, consoling his mother.

Mahesh said, 'My mother loved him intensely until her

death. I always remained slightly in awe of this aloof man who would come and go away, and who had such a hold over my mother. When she died a few years back, he came to our house chanting Hindu scriptures and holding *gangajal* [Ganges water]. He saw my mother's corpse and said, "Put some *sindoor* [vermilion, the cherished symbol of matrimony for Hindu women] in her hair. She was always asking me, 'Put some *sindoor* in my hair.' I want this done now."'

The extent of Mahesh's father's love for his mistress was made clear, Mahesh explained, when his father himself died. 'I used to ask my mother, "Where will his corpse go?" As it turned out, he had left explicit wishes that he be cremated in our part of town. My mother's sisters knew what this meant. He was publicly acknowledging his devotion to the woman who loved him. My aunts showed up at the cremation. I saw them whispering, and stealing a fistful of ashes. I asked them what they had done with the ashes. They said they had sprinkled them over my mother's grave. They were wishing for some kind of union. Critics accused me of melodrama when I put some of my background in my film *Zakham*. I felt with that gesture that I had made my peace with him. This is what melodrama does: it reconciles people. This is what the best Bollywood films achieve.'

My own memory of Bollywood films was different. As a child in small railway towns, and then as an undergraduate in Allahabad, I had watched them frequently. For weeks, I would gaze longingly at the posters suspended atop electricity poles, or draped on the sides of the tonga (horse-cart) that clattered down dusty narrow streets with understocked shops and faded signboards, the driver announcing, through a megaphone, the latest arrival at the local cinema.

I was particularly struck by the posters of new films. They often featured men gnashing their teeth and pointing outsized guns at each other against a backdrop of exploding skyscrapers, and women showing bare arms and sometimes, more daringly, legs. My parents did not allow me to watch these films, claiming that they were too violent. They spoke fondly of the tragic or flamboyantly romantic male actors of a previous era – Dilip Kumar, Raj Kapoor, Guru Dutt, Dev Anand. They happily let me go to films from the 1950s and 1960s, some of which enjoyed re-runs in small-town cinemas, and whose mostly melancholy songs, leaking out of a hundred transistors in our Railway Colony, filled the long afternoons of my childhood.

But I wasn't much interested in the stories, where love, timidly expressed, was usually thwarted, worldly success proved an illusion, and whose songs rendered sweet the cruellest disappointment. Like many young men in India – and, unknown to me, also in Africa and the Middle East – I was fascinated by Amitabh Bachchan, although I watched most of his films after I left home and was pursuing an undergraduate degree in Allahabad.

Bachchan, a gawkily tall actor with a baritone voice, often played the role of the poor, resentful young man pitted against venal politicians, businessmen, and policemen. Women, apart from tearful mothers, played minor roles in his films and were often treated ungallantly. There was little in Bachchan's own background that hinted at political discontent. Before seeking a career in films in

Bombay, he had held a well-paid corporate job in Calcutta. His father, a distinguished poet in Hindi, had friends among the Nehrus and the Gandhis. But on screen Bachchan was the 'angry young man' and he spoke directly to an audience that was no longer moved by the gentle self-pity of the actors that my parents liked.

For many Indians, there was much to be angry about in the 1970s and 1980s. Freedom from British rule in 1947, and the proclamations of socialism and democracy, seemed to have benefited only a small minority of the country's population, mostly politicians, big businessmen, and civil servants – people who plundered the state-controlled economy, and protected their power and privilege almost as fiercely as the British had once dealt with challenges from the natives.

Bachchan first became famous around 1975, the year that Indira Gandhi responded to a mass political movement protesting against corruption and inflation by suspending India's democratic constitution and imprisoning many people opposed to her. In several of his films, Bachchan expressed the cynicism and despair that was particularly acute among unemployed, lower-middle-class men in small towns. He usually sought to avenge himself on an unjust society. Pure exhilaration rippled across the (always frankly expressive) cinema audience when, after successive humiliations, he finally exploded into violence.

This was an especially gratifying moment in Allahabad. For some years before I arrived, the university, once known as the Oxford of the East, had been a setting for battles between unemployed, and probably unemployable, young men seeking to make a career in state – or national level – politics. The student groups they belonged to were usually

caste-based and supported by national-level political parties such as the Congress and the BJP. The rewards were
few – at best, a party nomination in elections to the state
or central legislature – and competition was fierce. Crude
bombs and guns often went off in the middle of the
campus. People like myself, who were there to acquire a
degree and then apply for a job with the government, felt
small and anxious and scared most of the time.

Bachchan empowered us briefly. I remember watching
one of his films in Allahabad: how the audience roared its
approval as he, playing a chief minister, first eloquently
denounced his cabinet and then machine-gunned all its
members.

A more intractable world began just outside the cinema,
where the police constables waved their iron-tipped lathis
and exacted bribes from rickshaw drivers and streetside
vendors. Corrupt men ruled here through a long invisible
hierarchy – the money passed all the way to the police
officers at the top – and the best way to deal with them was
to join them. But to spend three hours in the cinema – on
the bare wooden seats, amid the peanut shells on the floor,
the cigarette and bidi smoke languidly rising through the
rays from the projector – was to partially fulfil all the fantasies the posters had nurtured. It was to shed, however
briefly, our deprivations, and to embrace the heady conviction that if the world failed to yield its richness – sex,
wealth, power – it would be severely punished.

As it turned out, I rarely went to the cinema after I left
Allahabad and moved to Delhi. The older I got, the more
Bollywood films began to seem long and unreal. Occa-
sionally, late at night in Indian hotel rooms, I would come

across previews of Bollywood's offerings on television. A few glimpses of songs and dances in Swiss meadows or at opulent weddings, Muslim terrorists in Kashmir and Pakistani villains plotting against India, and plump action heroes saving their motherland, and I felt I'd had enough.

I couldn't enter these films as unselfconsciously as I had before. Yet neither was I distant enough from them to enjoy them as kitsch. And there were always enough unread books on the shelves staring plaintively at me.

It was years later, while spending part of my time in London, that I became interested again in Bollywood films. Popular among a younger generation of British Asians, they were shown frequently on television. In the late 1990s, new Bollywood films had begun to appear in the UK box-office charts. Academics published monographs on them, arguing for their sociological import and neglected artistic quality. In 1999, Amitabh Bachchan – his name still unknown to most people in Europe and America – was elected ahead of Laurence Olivier as the 'Star of the millennium' in a BBC online poll.

Articles and profiles of Bollywood stars appeared even in the mainstream English newspapers following the success of the West End musical *Bombay Dreams*, which Andrew Lloyd-Webber produced in collaboration with A.R. Rahman, a Bollywood music composer. These articles usually portrayed Bollywood films as an exotic, somewhat amusing novelty. They rarely tried to explain why these films had been popular in many places – the former Soviet Union, Eastern Europe, the Middle East, China, and the Far East – where Hollywood had little or no influence; nor how they had penetrated countries with such strong indigenous cultures as Egypt and Indonesia.

After many years, I saw a new Hindi film in London. *Kal Ho Na Ho* (Tomorrow May Never Come), better known as *KHNH*, was a worldwide hit, especially popular among South Asians in Britain and America. Its male lead was Shah Rukh Khan, one of three superstar Khans who are apparently as bankable in Bollywood as Tom Cruise and Tom Hanks in Hollywood. Part of a new 'youth movement', its producers had turned their backs on the formulaic films made throughout the 1980s and 1990s – sterile years, I had read, for Bollywood, and very different from the current climate since, according to various websites and magazines I looked up, there were now in Bollywood people with the talent and the courage to be *hat ke* (literally 'different from'). *KHNH*, for instance, was *hat ke*. So was its young director, Karan Johar. The *hat ke* generation was bringing about as much of a revolution in Bollywood as young film-makers, inspired by European cinema, had briefly achieved in Hollywood in the late 1960s and 1970s. They were the counter-culture, connecting to a new, sophisticated audience.

KHNH was unlike any Bollywood film I had ever seen, mostly because it was set entirely in New York City and its characters were almost all Indian-Americans. But it also featured many songs, and its plot traced a romantic triangle much used in Bollywood. A woman meets two boys, loves one and is loved hopelessly by the other. Together they sing and dance for a bit along with a gregarious cast of brothers, sisters, parents, grandmothers and grandfathers before the young man she fancies is revealed to be fatally ill. Many tears later (the film is almost four hours long), he dies, but only after bravely singing and dancing through the lavish wedding of his heartbroken survivors.

The next day I looked up DVDs of Johar's previous two films, both of which had been equally successful among middle-class and expatriate Indians. Their titles also beginning with the letter K, they were known as *KKHH* and *KKKG* respectively. They were set in London and in an India greatly resembling a cross between England and America. One film was, the subtitle claimed, 'all about loving your parents'. The parents in this instance headed a corporate family that lived in an English-style country house and travelled in helicopters. Their son lived in London – not in any of the modest suburbs where most of the Indian immigrant communities live, but in posh Hampstead – and he drove a red Ferrari.

Johar's other film, *KKHH*, was partly set in a college modelled on Riverdale, the American high school depicted in Archie Comics, and the main characters were based on the high-spirited teenagers, Archie, Veronica, and Betty. They played basketball instead of cricket, and eventually secured highly paid jobs in an India made up almost entirely of equally affluent and charming relatives.

I saw other new films. I read books and fanzines and online interviews with Bollywood stars. In December, I finally travelled to Bombay, where I met Karan Johar. 'My films,' he told me, 'reflect my own reality. I love my parents, they love me. No matter where we are in the world, we are Indians and at home. I write out of my experience.'

Johar was upbeat about Bollywood, which he said was entering another era of film-making. Another young film-maker, Ram Gopal Varma, much praised for his films about the Bombay mafia, said, 'There is no point in patting ourselves on our backs. Our best films are not much better than an average film from Hollywood. I feel we have much more to learn from even B-grade Hollywood films. I have learned a lot from *The Exorcist*.'

Was this true? I couldn't tell. In Bombay, I became more aware that Bollywood was a world unto itself, in which the criteria normally used for judging films and their makers were only partly valid.

'Pictures,' F. Scott Fitzgerald once wrote, 'have a private grammar, like politics or automobile production or society.' Fitzgerald thought that people merely watching and commenting on films could not understand how Hollywood studios actually worked, the peculiar pressures they brought to bear upon screenwriters, directors, and actors. Bollywood too seems to have its own peculiar grammar. The songwriter or lyricist, music composer, dance director, and costume designer are frequently more crucial to a film's success than the script, which is often improvised on the set.

Bollywood's economic workings are more mysterious. It still exists in what was known as the 'informal and high-risk sector' of the Indian economy. Banks rarely invest in Bollywood, where moneylenders are rampant, demanding up to 35 per cent interest. The big corporate houses seem no less keen to stay away from film-making. A senior executive with the Tatas, one of India's prominent business families, told me, 'We went into Bollywood, made one film, lost a lot of money, and got out of it very fast,' adding that 'the place works in ways we couldn't begin to explain to our shareholders'.

Since only six of seven of the two hundred films made

each year earn a profit the industry generates little capital of its own. The great studios of the early years of the industry are now defunct. It is outsiders – regular moneylenders, small and big businessmen, real estate people, and, sometimes, mafia dons – who continue to finance new films, and their turnover, given the losses, is rapid. Their motives are mixed: sex, glamour, money-laundering, and, more optimistically, profit. They rarely have much to do with the desire to make original, or even competent, films.

Sometimes, shooting schedules drag on for years as the producer struggles to make interest payments to his various creditors. The delays are often caused by actors working in several films at once. The actual process of film-making seems equally arduous. For instance, actors record their dialogue not during but after the shooting, which can cause their voices to seem out of sync with their facial expressions, thus heightening the impression of artificiality. It is rare that an actor working without a proper script turns in a good performance.

In any case, not much by way of acting – as distinct from dancing and fight stunts – seems to be required of Bollywood stars. Even in real life, they tend to act out fantasies nearly as extreme as those they help create on screen. The most famous of them was recently caught hunting deer in contravention of wildlife laws. A few months before I arrived in Bombay, Salman Khan, one of the three superstar Khans, had been accused of running over and killing or wounding four men sleeping on a pavement while speeding late at night in his Land Cruiser – Mohammed pointed out the alleged spot of the accident to me every time we passed it and told the story of how Khan had managed to bribe the witnesses to change their accounts of the event.

Bachchan, whom I had once idolized, seemed disappointingly unaware of what he represented to millions of Indians, or what he could do with his enormous influence. In interviews he deflected questions about his political friends and spoke instead of his new intimacy with his son, Abhishek: he said he talked to him every day about girls and they exchanged dirty jokes. In recent years, he had lost millions of pounds in ill-advised business ventures, including the Miss World contest. Helped by politicians and businessmen, with whom he was frequently photographed, and the popular Indian version of *Who Wants To Be A Millionaire*, which he had anchored, he had recently managed to emerge from debt, and returned to making mediocre but well-paying films.

It wasn't easy, as I had discovered in London, to sit through most of Bachchan's films again. I found I preferred the older films my parents had admired: the films about love and loss, in which male as well as female characters faced adversity with strength and dignity, and did not confuse revenge with justice. I liked, too, the more contemporary films made by Mahesh Bhatt, Gulzar, and Rama Gopal Varma. I did not like remembering the self that had once been stirred by Bachchan's films, by their visions of private, bloody revenge.

I was not surprised to learn that these films had been made during a particularly low moment in Bollywood's history. Watching them again made me think that a small-town audience of today was probably better served by new films with multi-syllable titles, even if it felt bemused by their pseudo-Indian setting and characters and their detachment from issues of poverty and corruption.

But, as I quickly learned in Bombay, the small-town audiences with their cut-price tickets and long queues of eager young fans don't matter as much as they used to. The rapid spread of television in the late 1980s and early 1990s forced many cinemas to close down. The big profits now come from the multiple cinema complexes, or multiplexes, of the big cities such as Delhi, Bombay, Madras, Calcutta, Hyderabad, Pune, and Bangalore, and what was known as the 'NRI (non-resident Indian) circuit'.

Karan Johar was one of the shrewd *auteurs* making films for the growing upper middle class of the larger Indian cities as well as for the millions of Indians living in England and America – the Indians, who according to Shah Rukh Khan, 'seem to like love stories, pretty things, yellow flowers, high-speed action, women in saris, opulence'. Excited by the success in 2002 of a film called *Lagaan*, nominated for the best foreign film category at the Oscars, many people in Bollywood are aiming even higher, at Hollywood, the American and the British market. But even those who scoff at such ambitions – arguing correctly that most Americans are likely to find Bollywood wholly alienating – have little time for audiences outside the big cities.

'Frankly, I couldn't give a fuck for the villages,' Ram Gopal Varma was quoted as saying in *Time*. When we met, he denied having said this, but then went on to stress that he was content to make small-budget films for educated people in the cities. Sitting serenely in his office high above Nariman Point, miles away from the dusty northern suburbs of Bombay where most film people live and work, Pritish Nandy, once a poet and journalist and now a film producer, told me, 'I don't want to make films for people I don't know.' Karan Johar, made defensive by my suggestion that his films spoke primarily to affluent Indians, asserted, 'No one now can make a film for an all-Indian audience.'

People still try, however. *LOC Kargil*, the biggest film of the winter of 2003, was defiantly non-*hat ke*, a throwback to such big-budget multi-starrers as *Sholay*, the all-time Indian hit. Four hours long, it features almost all of Bollywood's established and rising stars, including Amitabh Bachchan's son, Abhishek. Its success seemingly assured, it deals with an event that has aroused much passion in India: the deaths of over 500 soldiers in the summer of 1999 during the desperate Indian effort to regain the hills in Indian-held Kashmir, seized by a group of Pakistan-backed Muslim militants.

The day before the film was released across India, I went to a preview with Khalid Mohammed. I first met him when he was a writer with the *Times of India*, famous for his slash-and-burn reviews of Hindi films. He still reviews new releases scathingly in the evening daily, *Midday*. But he offends more people in the industry now that he is a film-maker himself. 'He should make up his mind about what he wants to be,' one director had complained to me.

I liked Khalid. He seemed a solitary man in the bare, curtained-off rooms of his apartment, where he had lived with his grandmother, and where he had written scripts for films about his Muslim family – the mother who, abandoned by her Pakistani husband, married a Hindu prince from Rajasthan, only to die with him shortly thereafter in a plane crash; the aunt who shuttled for years between India and Pakistan, wanted in neither country. Mohammed was especially happy to drive me to Khalid's home. He and his family had twice seen Khalid's film about the survivors of the anti-Muslim pogrom in Bombay in the early 1990s.

When I met Khalid in Bombay in late 2003, his new film had just been released. It was unlike anything he had done, a drama inspired by Ingmar Bergman's *Autumn Sonata*, about mothers and daughters. Mostly panned by other reviewers, it had disappeared from most cinemas, and was playing at a resoundingly empty thousand-seater in Bombay. A friend of Khalid's told me, 'He was lucky to make the film he wanted – even very distinguished film-makers can't get sponsors for their projects – but now he has blown his chance.'

Khalid felt the failure keenly. 'I am reeling,' he said, only half-jokingly, on the phone. He blamed the distributors. It was a 'multiplex film' but they had released it in the big halls. He was writing a novel about Iranian restaurant owners in Bombay, and updating his coffee-table biography of Amitabh Bachchan.

We drove to the preview of *LOC Kargil* in Film City, a few miles out of Bombay. Khalid said that the Bachchans were anxious about their son's career. It was Jaya, Amitabh Bachchan's wife, who had arranged the preview.

I had heard about other anxious parents in Bollywood. Many of the new actors had little to recommend them apart from their famous film families; to the 'aspirers' they appeared to be blocking their way. Mallika had complained, 'Abhishek Bachchan has had *fifteen* flops but he still gets great offers.'

Abhishek wasn't present at the preview, but the audience, arriving in new, imported cars, mostly comprised his friends in the industry. A few minutes into the screening, it became clear that the film wasn't going to boost young Bachchan's, or anyone else's, career. Although, in reality, the United States government had forced the Pakistani government to withdraw the armed infiltrators from Indian-held Kashmir, Hindu nationalists in India had claimed a military victory over what they described as a perfidious enemy. *LOC Kargil* attempted to elaborate this myth and to justify and commemorate the martyrdom of Indian soldiers.

For the first hour, the soldiers tearfully took leave of their wives, lovers, sisters, and mothers. Thrown into battle, they uttered invocations to the goddess Durga as they clambered up steep stony hillsides. They sang patriotic songs as they died; and shouted crude profanities as they plunged their bayonets into the hapless Pakistanis. I left the hall after three hours of this, and paced the deserted foyer until with final patriotic song the film ended, and all the chauffeurs standing at the back emerged and hurried to their cars.

In the car on the way back to Bombay, Khalid's mobile phone rang continuously. There had been other previews across Bombay. The reviewer of *Midday*'s rival, the *Afternoon Dispatch & Courier*, rang to say that the film was 'major trauma'. Karan Johar called to say he was watching and hating it. Someone from the preview said that he had seen Abhishek's mother, Jaya, weeping copiously as the flag-draped coffins of Indian soldiers appeared on the screen. Khalid himself was cautious, wondering only if the film had come at the wrong moment. Relations between India and Pakistan had dramatically improved. There was talk of the Indian cricket team travelling to Pakistan for a series of matches. But no one could tell how the audience might react.

Khalid was more severe in his review three days later. Titled 'Out of Control', it described the film as a 'four-hour-plus bullet-o-rama'. It mocked the film's 'umpteen flashbacks to the beauteous, tearful and suffering fiancées and wives waiting back home'. Then, in a more serious tone, it deplored the 'disturbing religio-political sub-text' and the fact that none of the principal actors portrayed an Indian soldier from the Muslim community.

When I returned to Bombay after seven weeks, the Indian cricket tour to Pakistan had been announced. The verdict on *LOC Kargil* was also in. The Indian army had gone out of its way to help its director, J.P. Dutta, who had already made a successful war film. Hindu nationalist leaders had organized special screenings in Delhi, and exempted film exhibitors from sales tax. But they had not managed to save the film from sinking rapidly at the box office.

Its failure did not seem to have affected Abhishek's career very much, however. I saw him at a dinner party at the J.W. Marriott Hotel, a favourite haunt of young Bolly-wood stars. Almost as tall as his father, but with a fuller face and smile, he sat surrounded by his friends, young directors, writers, and actresses, and entertained them with an account of his visit to a film festival in Morocco. He recounted a long story about a famous Irish actor and his unsuccessful pursuit of a Bollywood starlet at the festival.

Khalid was among the guests seated farther away from Abhishek, and exempt from joining in the slightly forced laughter. He said he still felt hurt by the failure of his recent film. He had abandoned his novel. A producer had given him money to write and direct a thriller set in London. If all went well, he would start shooting later in the year. He wanted to wipe out the 'stigma of a flop'.

This stigma of failure seemed to weigh slightly more heavily on J.P. Dutta, the maker of *LOC Kargil*. He seemed surprised when I rang him from Mahesh's office and told him that I would like to meet him. 'Can you come right now?' he asked.

Mahesh said, 'He is probably surprised anyone wants to see him.' Mahesh had told me earlier that his daughter's film had done badly. 'She is now learning what failure means, especially in the film industry, where only success counts. She is entering the real world.'

Sitting in his office – all sleek white marble and black leather swivel chairs and statues of Ganesha – J.P. Dutta seemed disinclined to enter the real world. A small man wearing a grey beard and thick silver chain around his neck, he spoke in monosyllables until I asked him why *KHNH* had succeeded and *LOC Kargil* hadn't.

It was an unfair question, but it set him off. He spoke at length, interrupting his monologue with short, bitter laughs.

'I will tell you. Because we are not making films anymore. We are marketing them. Please understand what I am saying. People are making films for the metros [metropolitan cities], and claiming that they are hits. But India is not confined to the metros. Our cinema must come out of Indian culture. The films of the fifties and sixties were also city-based. But people outside cities identified with them. It is because they had meaning and depth. What has happened now? Our values have degenerated. The idealism of independence is gone. We are not reflecting our times. Where is the human angle in our cinema? I knew I was not making a commercial film with *LOC Kargil*. It was a tribute to our soldiers who risk their lives to defend their nation. My brother was an air force officer who died in a MiG-21 crash. I know what my film means to our nation's soldiers. I was not concerned whether it sinks or swims with the general public. But you know it is doing great business outside the metros. There are big queues outside the cinemas in UP and Orissa . . .'

'They all say that,' Tishu said when I reported Dutta's remarks to him, 'particularly the old, feudal-style filmmakers who feel left behind by the new kids on the block. But he has a point about the new films lacking roots in India.'

I had known Tishu when he was a student at the university in Allahabad. In Bombay last winter, I sought him out after discovering a film about student politics in Allahabad that he had written and directed. The film's characters and settings conveyed accurately the violence and cynicism through which most people at the university picked their way. Its lively dialogue employed well the Hindi dialect of the region. It seemed to me more like a *hat ke* film than any I had previously seen.

But it also had songs and dances, which disrupted the narrative and its carefully built-up mood, and rendered a good film more or less unwatchable for an audience outside India.

Tishu didn't disagree with me. He simply said he couldn't have raised the money for a film without songs.

It had been hard enough anyway to make something that reflected the world he lived in. He had 'struggled' for ten years in Bombay, writing scripts or working as assistant director for very little money, before he could dream of making his own film. The student leaders in Allahabad had protested against their depiction in the film. The university authorities had accused him of showing the university in a 'bad light' and had cancelled his permission for shooting on the campus. Then, the producers had delayed distributing the film for more than a year.

Things had worked out in the end. The film had made a profit; it had also got good reviews. Tishu had just finished shooting his second film about drugs and foreign tourists in Manali, and was already planning his third venture.

However, despite his success, he wasn't happy in Bombay. It was expensive to live in; the weather was oppressive; the work hard; he hadn't had a holiday with his family for over fourteen years. Worse, he couldn't escape the sense of being only slightly better than the mediocre people around him.

He knew how his work compared to the contemporary cinema of Britain, France, or even Iran and Egypt. A friend of his, an established writer-director, claimed that he was successful only because Bollywood had never had a George Cukor.

Bollywood is in crisis, Tishu said, financially as well as intellectually. The overwhelming majority of films failed at the box office, partly because the people making these films did not know India outside of Bombay. They barely knew anything about the experiences of ordinary people in Bombay. The audience couldn't be fooled forever. After all, it now had satellite television, other modes of fantasy to choose from. Not surprisingly, Bollywood had lost much of its traditional audience not just in India but also places like China, North Africa, and the Middle East.

There were young, talented people around, but it was absurd to think of them as forming a counter-culture as yet, for there were still relatively few opportunities for them to flower. The money went to established names working with old formulas, and the lessons of their repeated failure were not learned. There were more expensive miscalculations like *LOC Kargil* on the way, and more talentless sons and daughters of rich people waiting in the wings.

It isn't just outsiders like Tishu who chafe at the inadequacies of Bollywood. One evening in Bombay, I went to see Shashi Kapoor, a member of Bollywood's first film dynasty, and one of the few Indian actors known internationally, primarily for his roles in such films as *Shakespeare Wallah*, *Heat and Dust*, and *My Beautiful Launderette*. Unhappy with his work in Bollywood – there was no film of his, he said, that he felt proud of – Kapoor had set up his own production company in the 1970s and made a series of much-admired films, including the award-winning *36 Chowringhee Lane*. But the 'financial news' remained bad – there were no audiences for the films in India – and, in the early nineties, Kapoor had found himself in the courts with his creditors. He said, 'The same people who used to call me the, "Messiah of Good Films", sued me for very small amounts.'

'Shashi,' Mahesh had told me, 'has seen the dark side of the industry.' But he appeared content to be out of the business: 'I was a failure; I knew I couldn't make money, and I decided to leave. I am sixty-six years old. I have had a good life. Why complain?'

The younger film-makers trying to work their way out of the mainstream didn't, and perhaps couldn't, share Kapoor's equanimity. Aditya Bhattacharya, the grandson of Bimal Roy, one of the greatest film-makers of Bollywood's golden era, had recently returned to India after several years in Italy, attracted by the news that things were changing in Bollywood. He had then discovered that they were not changing fast enough for him. Some weeks before we met in the new Taj hotel in the suburb of Bandra he had published a letter in *Midday* to the creator of *Boom*, the biggest flop of the season. 'What happened to the story, bro?' he had written. 'Things like script, editing, story-telling, the movie? What was this magnum-pocus about? What exactly did you want to share?'

When I saw Aditya he was full of rage at the people who had financed the film. 'This clever boy arrives in Bombay,' he said, 'talking of what he has done in London and New York. They give him seventeen crores (£2.5m.) to play with, he signs up Amitabh Bachchan and other big stars and then produces a turkey.

'I saw the script. It had disaster written all over it. But people here didn't have a clue. Most actors and actresses don't know how to assess a script. They are happier if someone narrates them the story. No wonder that they still don't work with scripts and improvise the dialogue on the sets.'

We left the hotel and walked down the promenade beside the sea. It was very late, but a few families still lingered around the peanut and popcorn stalls. Aditya pointed out to me the bungalows of Bollywood's famous stars. He then suddenly began to denounce them.

They did nothing, he said, when their own city burnt during the anti-Muslim pogroms in 1993, and instead, prostrated themselves before Bal Thackeray, the chief of the Shiv Sena, the Hindu extremist organization, which then ran the city's government. He spoke of the stars' close friendship with the mafia and their hypocritical refusal to support Bharat Shah, a popular financier arrested for his alleged links to the mafia. Bollywood celebrities, he said, still lined up to appease Bal Thackeray, whose daughter-in-law had become a powerful fixer in the industry.

'No one,' Aditya said, 'should be fooled by the success of films like *KHNH*. It is like the big party the feudal land-lord throws before he goes bankrupt. People might make a little money by promoting the regressive values of these confused Indians living abroad. They are like salesmen who have persuaded people to buy a defective lighter. But sooner or later people are going to realize that the lighter doesn't work, and they need a better one.'

Aditya went on to describe the growing financial nexus between politicians, film stars, and the mafia. He spoke of the illegal and illogical ways in which films were financed. There were probably personal reasons for his bitterness – he had financed his own new film with difficulty. But I saw little reason to dispute his account.

In London, I had gone to see *KHNH* with Sally Potter, a British film-maker known for her experimental style. She gasped when after two very long hours the intermission sign came up. But she appeared to be enjoying the film, especially the songs, which effortlessly appropriated and mixed the rhythms of disco, rap, and gospel. When I saw her a few days later, she said that she wanted to explore the musical form in her next project. It was capable of speaking a universal emotional language that was no longer possible for cinema in its more rational European or American forms.

This seems right, and probably explains why Bollywood films managed to reach a very large and diverse audience in the Third World. With their songs and dances, and their unabashed love of glamour and escapism, they offer to Western audiences what Hollywood films have rarely attempted since the end of the 1950s and the beginning of the counterculture. Their formulaic plots seem refreshingly artless to people who have grown weary of the irony, cynicism and pessimism of European and American films. This partly explains the success in the West of the musical *Bombay Dreams* and, to a lesser extent, the Bollywood-influenced *Moulin Rouge*.

But – and I didn't tell Sally Potter this – *KHNH* baffled me. For a *hat ke* film, it barely acknowledged the peculiar dilemmas of people living between cultures – a theme that gives much literary fiction about Indian-Americans its emotional richness. And *KHNH* was, as I discovered, typical of many new Bollywood films set abroad or in a purely notional India. Their character seems to be fazed by neither Indian tradition nor Western modernity, neither home nor abroad. In *KKHH*, a miniskirted Indian student from London breaks into a devotional song after being taunted for her lack of cultural roots by the other students at the Archie Comics school. In *KKKG*, an Indian child manages to get all the white British people present at her school in Hampstead to sing the Indian national anthem.

These films seem to me to use a different idiom from the

one that once gave Bollywood a devoted following in underdeveloped countries. It was in Bombay that I began to understand something of their emotional language. I began to see that they were rooted in something after all, and that their amiable visions of a world that existed for Indians to painlessly inhabit, and perhaps dominate, had a potentially vast audience.

'I write out of my experience,' Karan Johar had told me. This experience seemed limited – like many young *hat ke* film-makers, Johar was, I discovered, the son of a rich producer. But it was more widely shared than I had imagined.

After ten years of economic liberalization, a small but growing number of Indians live as well as middle-class Europeans and Americans. During this time, many Indians in Britain and America have begun to see their ancestral country as an investment opportunity and a cultural resource. These rich but insecure Indians have bankrolled generously the Hindu nationalists' rise to power, and now support the assertion of Indian military and economic power. They also form the newest and most lucrative market for Bollywood films.

'India is shining,' the Hindu nationalist government claimed in a series of poster and newspaper advertisements in late 2003. The prime minister and his deputy repeatedly cited the growing prominence of Indians around the world and asserted that the twenty-first century was going to be the 'Indian century'. Many of the new Bollywood films increasingly came out of, and stroked, the same Indian fantasy of wealth, political power, and cultural confidence.

The fantasy isn't without basis. The gap between the 200-million-strong middle class and the other 800 million

Indians has widened, but the consumer economy has grown steadily, along with India's foreign exchange reserves. And so in Bombay, the stylish hoardings for *KHNH*, the baby-faced actors on it dressed as if for a wedding, seemed rightly indistinguishable from the 'India Shining' ads – the government's pictures of happy-looking Hindus, Muslims, and Sikhs – as well as the giant posters of Amitabh Bachchan and other Bollywood superstars cheerfully promoting Swedish cellphones, Swiss watches, and American colas.

Film posters in my childhood hadn't been so slick. Nor were the government's ads for family planning, *Hum Do, Hamare Do* ('Two of us, two we have'). The austere culture of underdevelopment of which those badly painted images spoke now exists out of sight, in the villages and towns where the country's poor majority still live, or in the slums, almost entirely concealed by giant hoardings along many Bombay streets. And Bollywood films set in the West or in a westernized, unrecognizable India seem to have become yet another echo chamber of upwardly mobile Indians.

In Bombay, I often found myself gazing at the many pictures of Bachchan in a grey beard and smart Western suit looming over the stagnant traffic. The angry young man of the 1970s seemed as iconic as ever in the ad where he said, with a reassuring smile, 'Don't worry, be happy.'

Mahesh told me, 'People attribute greatness to Bachchan. They have a statue of him at Madame Tussaud's. But I find him an empty figure. There is not much there. Many people feel this. But no one wants to say it in public. It is part of what our culture has become.'

He added, 'We are lying to ourselves all the time.'

This was what he had written about in the *Times of India* that morning. His friend Vijay Anand, who made many of the acclaimed films of the 1960s, had died the previous day. Mahesh wrote that he had been 'revolted' to see the news of a distinguished film-maker's death conveyed by ticker at the bottom of the screen on television while a reporter breathlessly described how the crockery for a leading actress's wedding was being imported all the way from Paris. He had accused the media of 'trying to create a world in which we hope to eliminate life's most unbearable features and replace them with those which conform with our own wishes.'

I had grown used to these pronouncements from Mahesh. They appeared in the *Times of India* on an almost daily basis, usually sharing the page with reports of opulent weddings and wild parties. I often agreed with them. But their frequency and intensity made me wonder.

I met many people in Bollywood who doubted Mahesh's intentions, and described him as a publicity-seeker. He also had many admirers. The actors he has worked with spoke well of him. Tishu had said, 'That man has talent. He is connected with an emotional reality outside Bombay. This is rare in a place where people lose sense of who they are and what they can do after just a little bit of success. That is why these people from small towns flock to him.'

I still wasn't sure. Had Mahesh been sincere when he told Pritam that he would like to try him out? At his office, Pritam still tried to catch my eye whenever my car passed him. Mohammed asked me almost continually if anything had happened. When I asked Mahesh, he said that he was waiting for his brother's next film to move ahead.

'I have never identified with Bollywood,' Mahesh had told me. And now he was, he claimed, looking at life beyond it. He couldn't see himself in politics, which had turned into a circus – he mocked the reports and photographs in the newspaper of film stars joining the BJP or Congress. He said, 'But I do want to speak for the Muslims in this country. Two thousand Muslims were killed in Bombay in 1992–3 and now two thousand of them have been killed in Gujarat. But no one gets punished; the killers are free and flourishing. I fear we are breeding a generation of terrorists.'

His meeting with Sonia Gandhi had gone well. He had spoken frankly, telling her of the desperation of Muslims in Gujarat. She had listened carefully and thanked him afterwards.

There had been a moment of uncertainty when the Muslim theologians accompanying him had asked him to button up his shirt at the chest. He said he had complied, but only after some hesitation. He didn't want to defer to politicians. There were enough film people already doing that.

The day before I left Bombay, the newspapers were full of reports of a row at an awards ceremony in Dubai – one of Bollywood's versions of the Oscars – between the reigning superstar Shah Rukh Khan and Amar Singh, the powerful politician accompanying Amitabh Bachchan. Apparently, Singh had shouted at the businessmen-organizers of the event after discovering that they had placed Bachchan and him in the eleventh row. It was an insult, he said, to the great artist who ought to have been in the front row. Shah Rukh Khan had intervened on the organizer's behalf, and there had been enough angry words for journalists to feast on.

Asked to comment by the *Times of India*, Mahesh attacked Amar Singh. 'When will our power-drunk politicians realize that with power comes responsibility?' he wrote. 'What was the need to use brute force in a matter as trivial as seat arrangement?' He also criticized Bachchan: 'No one in the world can insult you without your permission.'

Two days later I was in the Simla hills, preparing to leave for London, when Mahesh rang me from Lucknow. 'You missed the excitement,' he said. 'My piece created an uproar. I have just had the wife of a senior police officer on the phone. She told me that I should get out of Lucknow. It is Amar Singh's territory and he is out to get me – but I am staying where I am. I am not scared of Amar Singh.' He added: 'Such is the inner rot of Bollywood.'

Apparently, the businessman-organizer who had stood up to Amar Singh had lost a contract worth £12m. in India. Feeling himself under intense pressure, Shah Rukh Khan had apologized to Singh. But his pride had been hurt, and he was reconsidering his position. He had sent an SMS to Mahesh, saluting his courage and honesty.

In London, I read of a dispute between Mahesh and Mallika. The latter had not only refused to do a nude scene in *Murder*, but had also rejected the option of a body-double. Mahesh had been quoted as saying, 'My only grouse is that she agreed to the nude scene in the first place.

She remains a small-town girl with a conservative heart. What is the point of pretending otherwise?'

But when I rang Mallika from London, two days before *Murder* was due to be released, she had forgotten about the nude scene. She had apparently forgotten, too, her wish to work abroad.

She said she was flooded with new offers. 'The initial reports of *Murder* are just great,' she told me. 'The distributors are over the moon. The producer is receiving over-flow checks . . .'

'What are those?' I asked.

'I don't know. Probably something good. But you must be here to see it. The movie has created a big hoopla, you know. It is everywhere, the promos were a sensation, the TV channels, the press, everyone is talking about it . . .'

She faltered briefly when I asked why this was so. 'Oh, you know . . .' she began. 'It is probably because of the skin show, the promos, lots of hot shots, bold scenes, adultery . . .'

'But you know,' she added, 'there is so much more to the film. Lots of women trapped in loveless marriages will identify with my character.

'Anyway, it is a great feeling to have the film rising from my shoulders,' she said. 'You know, I am much sought after. Interview after interview. The BBC just called from London. By the way, can you get a magazine called *Man's World* in London? I am on the cover. They say I have "the hottest body on the planet".'

She gave a short, nervous laugh. 'They can't think beyond this, but I guess it is their problem, not mine.'

*

Murder opened on 2 April. In his review for *Midday*, Khalid denounced the film for its 'voyeuristic flashes of semi-nudity and obscenity', mocked Mallika for her 'motor mouth and cheesy posters', and accused Mahesh of hypocrisy. But the opening box-office receipts were as good as Mallika had predicted, and within days, *Murder* had become the first successful Bollywood film of 2004.

In London I read a report about Mahesh and Mallika visiting a Delhi cinema where *Murder* was being shown. 'I come here to titillate you,' Mahesh was quoted as telling a rapturous audience. Mallika told a journalist that her father wasn't happy with the film and her mother couldn't get a ticket. She blew kisses at the audience, and said, 'I have worked like a Viagra when the market was so down.' The report said Mahesh and Mallika were planning to work together on another film.

On my last day in Bombay, I had seen Pritam standing in the small crowd outside Mahesh's office. In early April, I called Mohammed from London, and asked him to find out what if anything had happened. Mohammed reported that Pritam was still where I had last seen him. He had hoped to get his break in May, when work began on Mahesh's brother's next film, but he was less sure now. I wondered if I should ring Mahesh. And then I thought that he had been right all along: I thought that Pritam should go home.

Part II

Kashmir:
The Cost of Nationalism

1 The Killings in Chitisinghpura

ON THE EVENING OF 20 March 2000, Nanak Singh was chatting with some friends and relatives near his house in Chitisinghpura, a remote Sikh-dominated village in the Himalayan valley of Kashmir. Most of the locals were hung over, having spent the previous days celebrating Holi, the Hindu festival of colour, which the Sikhs also observe. Singh, who works for the animal husbandry department of the India-backed government in Kashmir, wasn't particularly suspicious when about seventeen armed men in combat fatigues showed up and ordered the men out of their houses, telling them to stand before the *gurudwara* (the Sikh prayer site), with their identity cards.

Singh assumed, like many other Sikhs, that the men were from the army – people in villages all across the valley were accustomed to being searched and interrogated by Indian security forces. The four million Muslims of Kashmir live precariously between the eternally warring countries of India and Pakistan. Nanak Singh is, however, along with most other residents of Chitisinghpura, a Sikh;

and thus a tiny minority of Sikhs in Kashmir, just over 2 per cent of the population, have enjoyed a tentative immunity throughout the ten years of violence; an immunity that neither the local Hindus, most of whom have migrated to India, nor the Muslims, always suspect in the eyes of Indian security forces, have had. If you were a Sikh, and worked for the government, as many of the Sikhs in Chitisinghpura did, such checking was a formality. Nevertheless, there were a few Sikhs who had premonitions and hid themselves in their houses.

It was dark and Singh couldn't really see the faces of the men, although they spoke both Punjabi and Urdu, the languages of North India and Pakistan, as they used flashlights to check the identity cards of the nineteen Sikhs standing and squatting before the walls of the *gurudwara*.

The checking done, the soldiers stepped back a few inches from the line-up. A moment passed; there was a single shot, and suddenly they raised their guns – AK-56s or AK-47s – and began to fire blindly at the Sikhs.

Singh felt the entire row of men crumple with brief cries of pain, and fell immediately to the muddy ground himself, dragged down by the weight of the dying man beside him. He assumed that he had been hit and found it strange that he felt no pain. In fact, by collapsing so early to the ground, he had missed a bullet.

Half-buried by a bloodied corpse, Singh heard the armed men move away with quick steps to the other side of the village. Minutes later, he heard more gunfire.

Soon after that the soldiers were back; they seemed to be in a hurry. Singh heard their leader instruct them to put a bullet quickly into each of the nineteen Sikhs lying there, all of whom except for him, Singh believed, were already dead.

Not daring to breathe, Singh dimly perceived a tall figure loom over him in the dark and raise his gun. He heard the shot; he felt the bullet penetrate his left thigh, felt the first warm sensation of pain, and then the man moved away.

As it turned out, Nanak Singh's luck lasted: he is the only survivor of the village massacre in which thirty-five Sikhs died.

Since 1990, thousands of Muslim guerrillas have been waging a war against the Indian presence in Kashmir: a war in which more than 50,000 people – civilians, guerrillas, Indian soldiers and policemen – have died, a war that came after four decades of Kashmiri resentment of Indian rule. The guerrillas are supported by Islamic fundamentalists in Pakistan, who wish to see Kashmir incorporated into the latter as part of a larger Islamized state. Pakistan, which was carved out of Hindu-majority India during the violent and confused Partition of 1947 as a separate homeland for Indian Muslims, has never ceased to claim the Muslim-dominated valley for itself. India has fought two wars over Kashmir with Pakistan in 1948 and 1965, and came very close to a nuclear war in both 1990 and 2002. The Indian government sees the Pakistani support of the guerrillas as a 'proxy war' and has deployed up to half a million soldiers to suppress the insurgency.

But the Sikhs have remained neutral; and over the last ten years guerrillas as well as soldiers from the Indian army camps frequently visited Chitisinghpura, their usual aggressiveness and tension defused by the isolation and serenity

of the pastoral setting – the houses with thatch and corrugated iron roofs, the vegetable gardens and the brisk
stream, and the melancholy willows and the forest of
chenar, walnut and almond, and the high mountains looming above the village – which even today make the great
turmoil of the valley seem far away. The guerrillas, some of
whom were from Pakistan and Afghanistan, used to play
cricket with the children; they often asked for wheat and
rice (Chitisinghpura is relatively prosperous, with revenues
from apple and rice farms and transport businesses). The
Indian army, which routinely patrolled the village, knew
about the guerrillas' visits from some of the concerned villagers but was strangely indifferent.

   On the evening of the massacre of the Sikhs, a patrol
party from Rashtriya Rifles (one of the Indian army's units
in Kashmir) was less than a mile away from the village; the
men heard the gunshots but, for reasons still unclear, did
not bother to investigate. Forty-five minutes after the
sound of gunfire had stopped, the first Sikh ventured out
of his house and found the corpses of his friends and
relatives. Then came a terrifying five-mile walk through
pitch-darkness to reach the closest police station – given
the circumstances, the Sikhs thought it safer to not seek
help from the army camp although it was much closer to
the village. The police arrived seven hours after the killings.

I heard the news from Abbas early next morning. He is a
Muslim, the Srinagar correspondent of an Indian newspaper. The dignity and solidity of his bearing – the tall
well-built frame, the elegantly cut Kashmiri jackets he
wears – made him reassuring to be with in the city where
everyone – the tense crowds in the streets, the jumpy sol-

diers in their bunkers, and the passionate Muslims speaking of the atrocities of Indian rule in bare dark rooms – seemed on edge. A mutual acquaintance had asked Abbas to help me out during my stay in Srinagar; and he had done so dutifully, but not without a certain wariness that I put down to some slight resentment: I wasn't the first or last of the inexperienced, and possibly biased, journalists from India he had been asked to assist.

His voice on the phone was calm. In the days I had spent in Srinagar, relatively and unsettlingly quiet days, with news of sporadic custodial killings, landmine blasts, and gun battles between Indian security forces and guerrillas coming in from other places in the valley, I had often heard him say, 'If you live here, you have to be prepared for anything. Anything can happen any time in Kashmir.' His words with their tinge of melodrama had made me wonder if he saw a certain glamour in his job, the dangerous nature of the world he worked and lived in, like the reticent taxi driver, quick to point me towards the vegetable market where seventeen Muslim civilians had been blown to bits by a bomb explosion a few days earlier in one of the random incidents of violence in the valley.

But now something even bigger had happened; and Abbas was as serene as always. He had no details yet, but he thought we should leave immediately for the village. When he arrived half an hour later at my hotel with two other Kashmiri journalists, his mood was light. The atmosphere inside the battered Ambassador was already one of good-humoured banter; and the jokes and repartee in Kashmiri, which I couldn't follow, got louder after each encounter with the frankly contemptuous Indian soldiers at roadblocks, who poked AK-56 muzzles through hastily rolled-down windows, demanded identity cards, and wanted to know where we were going and why.

In villages alongside the road, men in blue and black cloak-like *pherans* stood in worried little circles and glanced nervously out of the corner of their eyes at the cars racing past. In the rice and saffron fields, stubbly and glittering with frost, soldiers stood with their backs to the road, light machine guns slung over their shoulders. Outlined against the blue misty mountains in the distance, they were like hunters from a nineteenth-century sketch.

At the village itself, where there was nothing they could do, they looked more casual, the elite commandos almost dandyish in their black headdress and bulletproof overalls, sheepishly standing where a group of angry Sikhs had barred their way to the village. There were tiny shards of glass on the ground: some car windows had already been smashed by the Sikhs and a photographer roughed up, his camera lens broken. The soldiers had watched it all and done nothing; they now quietly watched the Sikhs rage at senior officers from the army and police who had begun to arrive, their cars disgorging more and more men in fatigues.

The Sikhs were mostly survivors from the night before; mainly middle-aged men, who had stayed in their homes when the armed men came. Others were from nearby villages who had been in Chitisinghpura since dawn. But many of the Sikhs standing before the policemen now had already assumed that the killers were Muslim guerrillas. They were shouting, beating their chests, feeding upon each other's energy. The army and police officers heard them expressionlessly. 'Give us guns and then we'll deal with these Muslims,' one man with a long grey beard kept shouting. 'They know what we did with them in 1947. We are not cowards like the Kashmiri Hindus! Do they think they can throw us out of Kashmir?! We'll show them!' And then, spittle growing at the corner of his mouth, he added, 'This is a country we have ruled.' The historical reference – to the early nineteenth century, when Sikh governors sent out by the king of Punjab had ravaged the valley, and tormented the Muslims – made the Kashmiri Muslim policeman before him flinch.

More journalists and government people arrived. The Sikhs wouldn't let anyone past, and continued to curse and lament. Behind them, a frightful clamour, like that of a thousand crows, arose from the top of the hill where the bigger *gurudwara* was situated. It was the sound of the weeping and wailing women, and it seemed to bewilder the roosters in the village, who were to go on dementedly for several hours after dawn, their exultant cries hanging discordantly above the village amid the grief and despair of the women.

Throughout the long drive to the village, I had been dreading the moment when I would encounter the dead men, but when I entered the courtyard of the *gurudwara* where the bodies had been placed on the ground, my first impression, after the early morning mistiness of the Kashmir valley, the mud-coloured villages and *pheran*-draped men, was incongruously of colour: the reds and yellows and purples of turbans and scarves and shawls and blankets. There was a crush of people inside the courtyard, Sikh men and women everywhere shouting, gesticulating, crying, wailing. I had been standing for some time, unable to move or speak, when I felt a hand on my shoulder. It was a boy, not more than ten years old, his hazel eyes under the crimson head-cloth full of curiosity. 'Are you from the media?' he asked and when I nodded, he said, 'They shot a sixteen-year-old boy.' He pointed towards one of the bodies. I hadn't wanted to look at any of the faces of the dead men; his words jolted me into doing so. The face had gone white, the flesh tight on the bones, and skull-like hollows had begun to deepen on the boy's cheeks and around his eyes. His middle-aged mother sat beside him, a jade-green shawl draped around her head; she must have been grieving all night and, in between lifting her arms and beating her chest, the tears running down her face in an unbroken stream, she forced out a tiny yawn.

Photographers and TV cameramen were already climbing the trees and the walls of the courtyard for a better view. I saw relatives gathered around a young girl in a long red skirt, talking to her in loud voices, shaking her shoulders, pointing to the dead father lying before her, but the stony expression on her face did not break, the eyes remained glassy – she hadn't cried at all, someone standing behind me said, and she needed to if she wasn't to go insane with grief.

When I walked over to the other side of the village, where another sixteen men had been similarly lined up and fired upon at close range, the bodies were still being transported to the *gurudwara* on improvised stretchers. There was a delay when a young widow sitting on the muddy ground would not let go of her dead husband. She clasped his head tightly in her lap until relatives prised her hands away and held her arms. Struggling to break free, she screamed as the men quickly carted away the corpse. Her stringy hair was loose, her pale wrists streaked with blood where the glass of her shattered bangles had bitten into her flesh, and her screams were loud. In this densely forested side of the village, the ground covered with straw and the houses roofed with thatch, the big turbanned men collecting the corpses and the overwrought widow seemed to belong to a scene of medieval cruelty.

I spoke to a few elderly Sikhs standing near a tea-shack. Some of them were away when the killers arrived, others had stayed put in their homes; and after the first few awful hours of confronting what had happened their emotions had been dulled. They didn't want to speculate about the identity of the killers. They kept saying, 'It was too dark, you couldn't see anyone.' I noticed a wariness; their response to the journalists present seemed to suggest what I had heard before from other unprotected people in India: 'You'll come and go, but we have to live here, with the consequences of what we say to you.'

But there were some Sikhs who seemed convinced that the Muslim guerrillas were the killers and they were the most aggressive and outspoken, raising slogans against Pakistan and Muslims, vowing revenge ('Blood for blood'). They surrounded the very senior bureaucrats as they arrived at the courtyard, and demanded arms to protect themselves against the Muslims. In one of the groups under attack I recognized the Inspector General of Police, a Kashmiri Hindu: just a few days earlier, I had seen him in his overheated walnut-panelled office, boasting on the telephone about the number of guerrillas killed that day. He looked anxious and lonely now, as the Sikhs confronted him.

They were especially rough with the Commissioner of Srinagar, one of the few Kashmiri Muslim officers of the

Indian Administrative Service in the valley; he was shouted down as he tried to speak. It was a senior Hindu army officer who saved him from unceremonious expulsion from the village – and a previous high-level Muslim visitor had indeed been thrown out – by joining the Sikhs in their slogan-shouting: slogans that asserted the military traditions of the Sikh faith, that came from the time of the persecution of the Sikhs and Hindus at the hands of Muslim invaders and conquerors.

The Sikhs appeared to demand a swift and brutal response. And so when the crowd of villagers, growing in numbers as the news spread across the valley (each new arrival bringing his own outrage), abused and drove out the first VIP, a senior state minister, stoned his car and shattered his windscreen; when his bodyguards let loose a few rounds into the air from their AK-47s and there was temporary panic because some people thought that the guerrillas had attacked; when men began sprinting all across the forest outside the village and the commandos threw themselves on the damp ground and prepared to shoot, the little commotion assuaged the growing need for drama and suddenly there was relief all round, and the commandos appeared less dandyish and more sheepish when they got up with muddy stains on their bulletproof overalls.

But something suspect lay in that need for drama, which, in the few hours it took to broadcast the TV images of the widows, was to be amplified all across India. There had been a small war in Kashmir in the summer of 1999 when Pakistan-backed infiltrators, many of them regular Pakistan army recruits, occupied high mountain positions past the border. Hundreds of Indian soldiers had died while trying to dislodge them; and the media, slicker but also much coarser after ten years of economic liberalization, had brought about a general intoxication with war in millions of middle-class Indian homes. Opinion polls in English-language newspapers had shown much of the middle class demanding an all-out invasion of Pakistan; letters in the popular press had even called for a nuclear bombardment of Pakistan. The media itself had joined in the frenzy: young awkwardly helmeted reporters shouting into microphones over the noise of artillery fire, 'You have got to be here to know what it is like.'

And that need for drama, for swift brutal responses to brutality, wasn't going to be appeased by Bill Clinton's condemnation of the massacre. When I left the village and returned to Srinagar later that day, the groups of worried Muslims I had passed in the morning had been broken up. They were already in roped-off enclosures, squatting on the ground while soldiers searched their houses. Buses were being stopped, their passengers lined up and interrogated by the side of the road: a multitude of localized crackdowns was taking place in the region.

Retribution was the theme of the slogans the Sikhs had shouted. It was what motivated the policemen; and the great need for some kind of retaliation would partly shape the events of the next few days.

It had begun that very morning, even as I stood there among the corpses and the wailing women. A minute's walk from the *gurudwara*, away from the Sikh-dominated part of the village, an official from the Special Operations Group (this is one of the draconian Indian security agencies set up to suppress the insurgency, and it is dominated by Sikhs) had arrived at the house of Sonaullah Wagay, one of the few Muslims living in Chitisinghpura.

Wagay is less well-off than the Sikhs; he is a peasant who makes some money on the side by selling milk from his cow, and he must have been bemused when the Hindu sub-inspector, arriving in a jeep and abruptly barging in, told him that the police were looking to recruit some local young men. Wagay told him that his youngest son is – strangely for a Kashmiri Muslim – a soldier in the Indian army, but that the eldest one is deranged and the middle one, Mohammed Yaqub Wagay, has been unemployed since finishing school, and spends his time leading the prayers at the local mosque – he was being considered as an Imam – and playing cricket with the children in the village.

It was Yaqub who had tried to prevent Wagay from rushing to the Sikh side of the village after the killings. Yaqub had returned from his evening prayers and was sitting on the timber logs outside the house, chatting with four friends, including a Sikh, when they heard the rattle of automatic guns. All five immediately ran to their homes and locked themselves in.

When they mustered the courage to emerge some time later they were warned by Sikh neighbours returning from the sites that they might be attacked by angry Sikhs, and that it might be better to stay inside their homes. And that's where Wagay and his sons spent the long tense night, until the arrival of the police in the morning.

After the first confusing lie about recruiting local youth into the police, the SOG sub-inspector didn't waste time in getting down to business. He asked for the middle son,

Yaqub Wagay. When the diminutive and very frightened Yaqub appeared, the sub-inspector gently caught hold of his arm and then ushered him towards the waiting jeep. 'Don't make a noise,' he told Yaqub's maternal uncle, a retired soldier. 'We have to talk to him.' And then he was off.

'We have to talk to him': that line has been heard in thousands of Muslim homes in the past decade. Young men suspected of being guerrillas have been taken away by Indian security men and returned, if not as corpses, then badly mutilated, the torture marks still visible in places where hot iron rods have been applied. The chances of a man returning unviolated from interrogation and third-degree torture were greater if you knew someone in the civil administration or the many Indian military organizations. But you had to get your application in very fast; and Wagay, though relatively well connected, was under no illusions about what could happen to his son. He simply ran from his house, past the rice fields, the minesweepers in the rice fields 'sanitizing' the road for the VIPs descending upon the Sikh village; past the car-loads of Sikhs and journalists and army officers hurtling down the broken dusty road, to the police station in the nearby town of Mattan.

There he pleaded that his son had nothing to do with the guerrillas, and that the Muslim families living in the region had a very good record: none of the young men had ever gone to Pakistan or Afghanistan for training in light weapons; none of them were jihadis; and indeed several of them like his son, and Yaqub's maternal uncle, had been in the Indian army. The police, some of whom were Kashmiri Muslims and sympathetic to Wagay, registered his FIR

(First Information Report), but there was little else they could do: they had no influence over the Special Operations Group, which had its own murky ways of functioning. All Wagay could do was hope for the best.

Two days later I was watching the premier Indian TV news channel at my hotel in Srinagar, the capital of India-ruled Kashmir. I had been thinking about the killings in Chitisinghpura. The question of why the guerrillas would kill Sikhs, who had never previously been targeted, and then invite international censure, kept troubling me. But the news on TV didn't seem to offer any answers. It was full of Bill Clinton's state visit to India – the first by an American president in more than two decades – which had begun hours after the killings in Chitisinghpura; his condemnation of the massacre and well-planned tributes to Indian democracy had been met with great enthusiasm and gratitude among the up-and-coming middle class, which like many Third World middle classes is fiercely nationalistic, but at the same time craves approval from the West.

The killings of the Sikhs overshadowed everything Clinton said about Kashmir and Pakistan – interestingly, the correspondents of the two major TV channels from New Delhi had arrived a day before the massacre in Kashmir in expectation of a major incident. But it was the potential shifts in the American position on Kashmir that occupied the media; the mysterious circumstances of the killings were hardly mentioned. There appeared to be little mystery at all: India's national security adviser had already blamed the massacre on Hizbul Mujahedin and Lashkar-e-Toiba, the two major Pakistan-based guerrilla outfits. L.K. Advani, the Indian home minister, and a hard-line member of the BJP government in Delhi, had spoken of a deliberate policy of 'ethnic cleansing' pursued by Muslim guerrillas, and that had more or less settled the matter. No one took any notice of the strident denials from Pakistan-based guerrilla organizations that are normally very eager to claim credit for any spectacular act of violence in the valley.

Clinton was travelling to Pakistan after his stay in India, and Indian pundits on television speculated endlessly about whether he would come down hard on Pakistan's new military ruler for his country's support of the Muslim guerrillas in Kashmir, and whether the State Department would be repulsed enough by the killings to declare Pakistan a 'terrorist state'. But the Americans themselves seemed to have some doubts: journalists from the *Washington Post* and the *New York Times*, among other major American media covering Clinton's visit, had been sceptical of the Indian version. There seemed little reason for the guerrillas to kill Sikhs just before Clinton's visit, an act that would inevitably lead to international outrage, and thus discredit their cause.

It was what intrigued me about Chitisinghpura, and so when the 'breaking news' caption appeared on the edge of the TV screen, and a senior Indian bureaucrat appeared to make a statement about the Sikh killings, I was both surprised and curious. Clinton was still in India at that time, and the home secretary had some of the breathless eagerness of the Indian reporters covering the President's visit. The Indian security forces, he announced in a jubilant tone, had made a 'major breakthrough'. They had arrested a native of Chitisinghpura village called Yaqub Wagay, who had provided valuable information about the Muslim guerrillas responsible for the killings, and 'follow-up action' was expected at any time.

It was around this time, two days after the killings, that Muslim men started to disappear from the villages around Chitisinghpura. At least three of the disappearances followed the same pattern: a red Maruti van with civilian number plates arrived in a village, and armed men suddenly emerged from it to grab an individual, usually tall and well built.

The small cramped van was used to abduct Bashir Ahmed and his friend, Mohammed Yusuf Malik, sheep and cattle traders in a village called Hallan. The same red Maruti was spotted waiting on the lonely willow-lined stretch of road outside the walled compound of Zahoor Ahmad Dalal's house in a suburb of Anantnag, the second largest town in the valley, minutes before Dalal stepped out to go to the mosque for evening prayers on 24 March.

Dalal, twenty-nine years old, slightly plump with flushed red cheeks, had done very well with the small cloth-retailing shop he suddenly inherited when his father died on a pilgrimage to Mecca in 1984. Business hadn't been easy in the last ten years of endless curfews and regular strikes; but Dalal had not only survived but actually flourished. Inside his large compound, he had built several warehouses, had planted rose bushes, dug a fish-pond, and very recently he had built a new house adjacent to the old one where his widowed mother lived. His sister's marriage – always an onerous task in subcontinental families – was happily arranged in Anantnag. He regularly made the long journey to Delhi to order fresh stock; his warm ebullient manner had earned him many friends in the valley, including the Indian paramilitary men who sat in the bunker near his house.

The visit to the mosque was part of a routine, and he dressed casually for it: nylon slippers and tracksuit bottoms under a checked shirt and maroon wool jumper. When he didn't return home that evening in time for dinner, his mother and uncle thought that he might have gone to visit one of his many friends in the area.

They began to worry later that evening, after the friends and relatives they contacted said they hadn't seen Dalal. On the morning of 25 March Dalal's uncle, Nissar, went to the local police station. The inspector there suggested that they might want to wait before registering a First Information Report. Anantnag is the stronghold of 'renegade militants' called Ikhwanis – former guerrillas who after being captured or surrendering worked for the Indian army, and who often kidnapped and killed for money. It was likely that they had seen the affluent and unprotected Dalal as a good source of easy money. The police inspector was being pragmatic: why register an FIR and endanger Dalal's life when Rs 50,000 as ransom might bring him back unharmed?

Dalal's uncle heeded the advice and immediately went to the headquarters of the Ikhwanis – a mini-fortress in the heart of the old town – and then to the headquarters of the Special Task Force, an Indian anti-insurgency organization that was known to hire the 'renegade militants'. No one at these places had either seen or heard of Dalal. At the police headquarters, the superintendent of police, a reputedly ruthless man named Khan, was not present. His superior officer told Dalal's uncle that if the Indian army had kidnapped his nephew, there was nothing anyone could do, and sent him away. At five o'clock in the evening, Nissar returned to the police headquarters and was informed that the superintendent was busy, along with units from the Special Task Force and the SOG, supervising an 'encounter' with guerrillas in a village called Panchalthan, thirty kilometres from Anantnag. There might be some news of Dalal's whereabouts when they returned, Nissar was told.

The morning of 26 March brought news of the death of five of the seventeen men allegedly responsible for the Sikh killings. I saw the news in curfew-bound Jammu where angry Sikhs had been rioting for three days. For a brief moment Chitisinghpura was back on the front pages of the Indian papers. There had been a four-hour-long 'encounter' between the guerrillas and the police and army in Panchalthan in the early morning of 25 March – a few hours after the disappearance of Dalal. The army spokesman said that all five men were 'foreign mercenaries', belonging to Pakistan-based Islamic terrorist outfits; the most important piece of evidence they presented was the army fatigues the five men were dressed in, the same uniform the killers of the Sikhs had been wearing. The police issued a separate statement in which Yaqub Wagay was mentioned as having provided the information that led the police and the army to the hideout of the mercenaries: a hut-like shelter for Gujars (shepherds) on top of a steep hill that had been shelled with mortars during the encounter. Later in the evening, the police released black-and-white photographs of three of the five dead men: the bodies were 'roasted and disfigured beyond recognition', reported the *Kashmir Times*, but the army fatigues were unmistakable, looking almost brand new.

*

Dalal's uncle met Khan and the men from Special Task Force when they returned from Panchalthan. They hadn't seen Dalal. By now Nissar was beginning to panic: on the previous day he had heard about the disappearance of Bhat and Malik, the buffalo traders from Hallan, a little before the time Dalal left his house to go to the mosque; and he had heard about the red Maruti van.

Two days later, he ran into a group of Gujars from the villages around Anantnag. Two of their friends, both called Juma Khan, had gone missing. The Gujars weren't involved in any guerrilla activity but still faced much harassment by Indian security men since their long beards, hooked noses, and tall frames made them look like Afghans. They told Nissar that they had gone in a procession to the government's local headquarters in Anantnag to lodge a complaint about the missing men they suspected had been abducted by the police or SOG.

Before the day was through, and purely by chance again, Dalal's uncle encountered another Gujar, this time from Panchalthan; he had a disturbing story to tell about the 'encounter' that had kept Khan, the notorious police officer, from his desk for so long the previous day.

Panchalthan lies at the base of the thick hilly forests that line the valley of Kashmir on its south-eastern side. Some miles south is the region of Doda where some of the most vicious battles between guerrillas and the the Indian army have been fought. Hardly a day goes by without the combatants lapsing into massacres or rape or arson or torture, and the knowledge weighs heavily on those travelling through the heavily militarized and isolated area around Panchalthan.

The road is unpaved and its perennially dug-up appearance made me worry about the possibility of landmines placed by guerrillas to ambush the military convoys that regularly make their way to the ordnance depot near Panchalthan. The day before I visited in late May 2000, the ordnance depot had been attacked by rocket grenades, and the resulting tension was palpable. Women in long black veils walked quickly, as if seized by silent panic. In bazaars along the road, sullen men lurked in dark bare shops. Tense pedestrians avoided all conversation, never forming groups, eyes always averted from the army men in the makeshift bunkers at every street crossing and bend in the road.

The closer we got to Panchalthan and the further from the nearest town – past the hostile army men at checkpoints, who pretended not to understand why we were going to Panchalthan and insisted on searching the car, one hand wrapped around the trigger of their guns – the greater my fear. And it was shared by the Kashmiri driver and journalist I was travelling with. Far too many journalists investigating strange events in remote parts of Kashmir had been killed.

But the villages along the broad valley seemed peaceful, a few hay-topped houses spread across shimmering fields where women in colourful headscarves sang traditional songs as they planted the paddy and then, when dusk fell, sat cross-legged upon little Kashmiri rugs to sip salty tea from samovars.

A hill, uncultivated for the most part, and rising almost vertically from the base of the valley, looms over the village. On the top – known to the villagers as Zountengri ('hilltop of the moon') – are two wood and mud huts used as shelters by Gujar shepherds from the village. The land slopes down steeply from here to the valley; as a military position, it is close to invincible. Nevertheless, it was here, according to both the army and the police, that the five 'foreign mercenaries' were trapped and killed and vast quantities of arms and ammunition discovered in an operation that lasted four hours – and from which soldiers and police emerged unscathed.

In a previous 'encounter', not far from Panchalthan, the army had bullied the villagers into acting as human shields as they attacked a guerrilla hideout: in remote places in the valley, you did what the men with guns instructed. But on this more recent occasion the villagers weren't asked for their help.

In the early hours of the morning of 25 March they had been woken by the noise of gunfire. It went on for some time, and then, abruptly, there were some big bangs: mortar shelling. When the firing stopped, it was light and some of the villagers ventured outside their homes. They saw four soldiers dragging large kerosene canisters up the hill. As the villagers watched, two of the soldiers stopped and partially emptied their canisters before trudging on.

A few minutes later, the villagers saw smoke rise into the misty morning air and heard the sound of crackling wood. Not long afterwards the army men summoned the elders of the village. Although scores of men from the army and the Special Operations Group stood idly by, the commanding officer asked the villagers to remove the bodies of the 'mercenaries' from the smouldering huts.

The men went in to find five charred and disfigured bodies dressed in army fatigues on the ground. All of the dead men looked as if they had been tall and well built:

quite like the guerrillas from Afghanistan and Pakistan the villagers had seen before. They noticed that one of the bodies was headless; they saw a tree trunk and two logs of wood soaked in blood. Then, as the soldiers watched impatiently, the villagers carried out the bodies and, after the briefest of religious ceremonies, buried them in separate graves around the hill.

The Gujar from Panchalthan whom Dalal's uncle met up with was one of the men who had helped bury the bodies. And after the man finished telling his story, Dalal's uncle pulled out, very tentatively, a photo of his nephew that he had been carrying everywhere with him. He asked the Gujar if any of the men he helped bury resembled the man in the picture. The Gujar stared hard at the creased photo of Dalal, and then abruptly started to weep.

After the army and policemen left in a convoy from Panchalthan that morning of the 'encounter', the villagers returned to the huts on Zountengri and found a pit full of fast-burning clothes and shoes. They quickly put out the fire, and retrieved whatever they could. It was among these scorched scraps that Dalal's relatives found the maroon jumper and checked shirt he had been wearing when he left his house for his evening *namaz* three days before.

That evening the family formally went into mourning. There was no point in investigating the identity of the killers, nor the circumstances of the killing: they were likely only to bring more trouble upon themselves. Sympathetic Kashmiri Muslim officials at Anantnag provided the family with facts – the red Maruti was one of the many 'seized vehicles' kept at Anantnag police station and had been signed out on 24 March for 'operational purposes' by a

Sikh officer of the SOG – but they didn't encourage them to follow it up. Instead, the family's efforts were now aimed at retrieving Dalal's body from the remote grave at Panchalthan and giving him a proper Islamic burial.

This wouldn't be accomplished for nearly two weeks, however, and would never have happened at all had the Gujars not initiated, in a bold pursuit of justice, unusual for Kashmir, yet another series of horrific events.

In the same pit of half-burnt belongings, a Gujar called Rafiq, the son of one of the two missing Gujars, had discovered his father's identity card, ring, shreds of clothing, and shoes. He had been looking for his father for some days; and it was purely by chance that he thought of coming to Panchalthan. His discovery had been the first sign that the five dead men had been civilians, among the seventeen who had disappeared after the killings in Chitisinghpura.

For the next few days, the Gujars, always close-knit as a community, walked fifteen miles each day to the government's district headquarters in Anantnag to appeal for the exhumation of the bodies. At first, the government officials kept stonewalling them: the relevant officer isn't present, he is very busy. But on 31 March, the Gujars managed to extract an order from the chief judicial magistrate for a public exhumation. It was a major victory: tens of thousands of Muslims had been killed by Indian security forces in Kashmir in the previous decade but there had rarely been a post-mortem or exhumation.

That wasn't the end if it, however: the army controlled the road to Panchalthan, and refused to let anyone through. The civilian administration in Anantnag, too scared to take on the army, was still waiting to know if they would be allowed to pass when the villages near Panchalthan were visited by terror: armed men from the SOG who beat up the Gujars and threatened to kill them if they went ahead with their attempts to exhume the bodies.

The Gujars, buoyed by their victory in obtaining the exhumation order, decided to protest at the harassment by the SOG. They began the long walk to Anantnag on the afternoon of 3 April. The procession included relatives of the two murdered Gujars – Rafiq walking in the front – and other sympathetic villagers. The news of the killings in Panchalthan had gone around, as had the unexpected news of the Gujars' exhumation order, and the crowd swelled and swelled at each village.

By then numbering 5,000, the procession crossed three army checkpoints without much trouble. But at a little village called Brakpora, at a little dirt-road crossing hemmed in by shacks selling groceries, men from the SOG were waiting for them.

Rafiq, the first man to establish a connection between the half-burnt personal effects at Panchalthan and the five missing men, was one of the first to be shot. In the end, nine men died in the firing – so ferocious that doctors at the local hospital removed twenty bullets from the groin of one corpse.

The unprovoked firing made the national news – in the usual vague terms: 'Eight people killed in police firing' – but the army still would not allow civilian officials to enter Panchalthan. Finally, on 6 and 7 April, the bodies were exhumed, and though badly defaced, were identified by relatives of the five men. The first grave revealed the chopped-off nose and chin of a Gujar who was found buried in a separate grave. Dalal's face had been partly gouged away; he had no bullet marks on him and may have been burnt alive. The last body was headless – the head couldn't be found – but the relatives identified him by his trousers, which he still wore under the army fatigues.

Government officials at first refused to part with the bodies, and then relented after demanding that the relatives perform the burials secretly that same night. The government made few other concessions to outraged public opinion. Khan, the police officer who had jointly led the operation with an army brigadier, was suspended from active duty, but he was reinstated very soon afterwards and then awarded a President's Medal for courage displayed in an earlier operation. Other officials were merely transferred out of Anantnag.

Accusations were formally lodged against the SOG men who had fired on the Gujar demonstrators. On 11 April, the government announced a special investigation into the Panchalthan killings. But they refused to charge anyone with murder until DNA samples taken from the dead men were matched with those of their supposed relatives.

The DNA tests seem subsequently to have been forgotten until March 2002, when the *Times of India*, India's leading newspaper, revealed their results. Apparently, the results had been officially sent to Kashmir the year before by a laboratory in Hyderabad but were suppressed by the local government, because they exposed a clumsy attempt by Indian officials to fudge the samples taken from the relatives of the five murdered men.

The turnover of atrocities in Kashmir is so high, and the

situation in general so murky, that it is hard to get to the truth. Few people in India even talk of Chitisinghpura any more. And the forgetfulness and murkiness will remain: such killings are soon supplanted by something bigger; there is the usual exchange of allegations between India and Pakistan, the usual outrage and condemnation around the world; and no more than a few people know what is really going on.

The government remained steadily indifferent to the several requests from human rights organizations and Indian political parties for an independent probe into the massacres of the Sikhs. In the Indian parliament, the union law minister asked members from opposition parties to drop their demand for an enquiry into the recent killings, since it only helped Pakistan 'point accusing fingers at India'. A spokesman for the BJP exhorted members of parliament to instead 'concentrate on exposing the evil designs of Pakistan'.

The truth about the killing of the Sikhs has yet to be discovered. There has been no official enquiry, despite many requests; and there are new facts, apart from the clumsy and brutal attempt to blame it on 'foreign mercenaries', which cast a considerable shadow on the Indian version of events.

Five years later, not a single person or group has plausibly been held responsible for the killings, and the Pakistan-based guerrilla outfits have continued to deny their involvement. Within a few days of the massacre, most of the Sikhs I had seen so vehemently blaming, without much evidence, the Muslim guerrillas – and who had then gone on to do the same on national and international TV – had left Kashmir with their families. Those Sikhs who stayed on in Chitisinghpura are even more reluctant to talk to journalists. Some complain privately about the special favours bestowed by the government upon a few chosen men: large sums of money given as 'compensation', jobs for the unemployed, special recruitment into the police.

But the appeasement hasn't prevented many Sikhs outside the village from expressing their doubts: the killings in Chitisinghpura, many of them believe, were organized by Indian intelligence agencies to influence Clinton, and the Western journalists covering his visit, into taking a tougher line towards Pakistan. No evidence has come to light to support this belief.

According to his father, Yaqub Wagay, arrested soon after the Sikh killings, was brutally interrogated by the SOG and made to sign false confessions. A senior government official admitted to me that he was innocent, and in fact he was released on bail in the Chitisinghpura case, before being rearrested, farcically, in connection with the Panchalthan case, on the basis of the evidence allegedly supplied by him about the five 'foreign mercenaries'. He is now out of prison.

For those who live in Kashmir, the expectations of justice, rarely fulfilled in the Indian subcontinent, are more than optimistic: they belong to fantasy. It makes it all the more difficult for the victims to bear their human losses. At Dalal's house, the once carefully tended plants and hedges were already running wild just a few weeks after his murder, the fish in the pond were mostly dead, and a few men sat slumped on the floor in a bare hall under the Islamic calendar of mourning. His mother, persuaded by her male relatives to emerge from the dark room she had taken to since her son's death, broke down as soon as she noticed the photos of Dalal I had been studying. The pictures showed a young man in dark glasses and trendy clothes, a happy contented man, someone who had managed to find, amid the relentless violence of the insurgency, a new style and identity for himself. When Dalal's mother – still crying, while her own mother, Dalal's grandmother, sat beside her, quietly wiping her tears with the frayed end of her head-scarf – asked what was the point of talking to the press, of speaking about her son to me – he was gone, and wouldn't come back; the people who had killed him were too powerful – it was hard not to feel pierced by the truth of what she was saying; hard not to be moved by her grief, and the pain, amid the great human waste of Kashmir, of her helplessness.

More than 50,000 people – and these are conservative figures – have been killed, maimed or have disappeared in the last ten years. The Indian army and police have lost a few thousand men, but have killed many more Muslim guerrillas and civilians. There is hardly a family among the four-million-strong Muslim population of the valley which hasn't been affected. Abbas said, when we discussed possible stories I could cover, 'You must do widows and orphans.' I had foolishly asked, 'Where can I find them?' Abbas had let the remark go; he simply said, 'Anywhere.' And it was true: widows and orphans were as ubiquitous as graveyards and ruins in the valley.

After each of my travels around the city and the valley I came back to the hotel room, relieved that the day's work was over, and that I could retreat for some hours at least from the world around me, from the stories – of torture (one hospital alone witnessed 250 cases of death by acute renal failure, caused by putting human bodies under heavy rollers in the army's interrogation centres, called Papa 1 and Papa 2), of summary executions, rapes, kidnappings, and arson – stories that emerged unprompted in the most casual of conversations with Kashmiris, and that formed the grisly background to life in the valley.

The oldest among Kashmiris often claim that there is nothing new about their condition; that they have been slaves of foreign rulers since the sixteenth century when the Mogul Emperor, Akbar, annexed Kashmir and appointed a local governor to rule the state. In the chaos of post-Mogul India, with the old empire rapidly disintegrating, Afghan and Sikh invaders plundered Kashmir at will. The peasantry was taxed and taxed into utter wretchedness; the cultural and intellectual life that had produced under indigenous rulers some of the greatest poetry, music and philosophy in the subcontinent, dried up. Barbaric rules were imposed in the early nineteenth century: a Sikh who killed a Muslim native of Kashmir was fined no more than two rupees. Victor Jacquemont, a botanist and friend of Stendhal who came to the valley in 1831, thought that 'nowhere else in India were the masses as poor and denuded as they were in Kashmir'.

But this background of constant suffering could remain invisible to the casual visitor; the physical beauty of the place – enhanced by the valley's isolation from the rest of the world, and tempting for foreign adventurers – is still, even after these last ten years of violence, overwhelming. All through my stay, memories of previous trips kept bubbling up: visits made in less troubled times, just before the insurgency began in 1990, that first visit which for me – as for anyone who had never been away from the hot dusty Indian plains – was the first exhilarating revelation of beauty.

I hadn't then really noticed the Kashmiris. They did appear very different with their pale long-nosed faces, their *pherans*, their strange language, so unlike any Indian language. They also seemed oddly self-possessed. But in the enchanting new world that had opened before me – the big deep-blue skies and the tiny boats becalmed in vast lakes, the cool trout streams and the stately forests of chenar and poplar, the red-cheeked children at roadside hamlets and in apple orchards, the cows and sheep grazing on wide meadows, and, always, the surrounding mountains – in so private an experience of beauty it was hard to acknowledge the inhabitants of the valley, hard to acknowledge the more prosaic facts of their existence: the dependence upon India, the lack of local industry, the growing number of unemployed educated youth.

Then, as the years passed, the news from Kashmir took its place with the other news – equally bad, of murders and destruction – from Punjab and the north-east: the distant struggles that were, ultimately, marginal to one's own life in a very large and deprived country where almost everyone is struggling. In any event, I found I couldn't always get the necessary information about Kashmir. There were some good books published by small imprints; but you had to search hard for them. To read what was reported in the press was to be told that Pakistan had fomented trouble in Kashmir, and the Indian army was taking care of it. It was to understand that there really wasn't a problem except one of law and order, which the relevant military and paramilitary organizations would soon deal with. The missing physical details had to be imagined; and they turned out to be much grimmer than what I once could have thought of.

Srinagar's big hotel with its vast lawns and bare trees overlooking the lake was empty; but the staff still felt obliged to work themselves up each morning, like the Indian papers, into cheerful falsehoods: 'Everything is fine today, sir, there is no problem at all, there is only as much violence here as in any Indian city.'

In their softly lit, carpet-muffled offices, with trays of tea and biscuits regularly brought in by uniformed servants, Indian officials presented statistics about the number of guerrillas killed, guns, rocket launchers, and grenades seized. In a gloomy room, the furnishings dark with grime, piles of unread newspapers in one corner, a member of the Kashmir Bar Association presented me with some counter-statistics about the number of Muslims killed (80,000 in his estimation), tortured, raped, or gone missing.

The day before I arrived, a senior guerrilla from one of the pro-Pakistan outfits had been shot dead. But weariness – there had been too many killings of that sort – and the fear of being fired upon by the Indian police or army kept public mourners in their homes; the streets remained clear of the thousands of grieving men who had once taken the corpses of 'martyrs' to the graveyards scattered everywhere in the city, often adjacent to destroyed houses; a sudden swarm of green headstones and irises in the dusty broken streets.

The festival of Eid came and went, but the shops still closed early, the tense busy-ness abruptly giving way to silence and darkness, and each evening, in little stockades beside the roads, sheep with purple paint on their backs restlessly awaited slaughter. The long boulevard along the lake, filled in my memory with holiday-makers, remained deserted and dusty, the hotels on the boulevard serving as barracks for paramilitary soldiers. The houseboats cowered under the snow-capped mountains to the north, the jaunty names on their gables – *Miss England, Manhattan Adventure* – as gaudily ironical as the 'Bright Career Institute' sighted in an alley full of spectacularly ruined houses – heaps of bricks that had already been plundered for wood. Filth lay in small mounds everywhere in the alleys and bazaars of the grey old city – the stronghold of the pro-Pakistan guerrillas – where Indian soldiers stood alert in their improvised bunkers at every bend and corner. The bunkers seemed like some kind of trap: sandbag walls roofed with corrugated iron and blue weatherbeaten tarpaulin, LMG muzzles pointing out from small squarish holes between the sandbags, behind which you occasionally saw the frightened eyes in dark faces, the helplessness of soldiers in this hostile setting, hundreds of miles away from home, somehow made more poignant by the 'Happy Eid' messages painted in Urdu on little cards stuck to the sandbags. And everywhere on the narrow broken roads you saw, and hastily stepped aside to make way for, big machine-gun-topped trucks in fast-moving convoys of three or four, often flying the defiant banners – 'India is Great' – of a besieged army.

The military controlled the roads, but the pro-Pakistan guerrillas were still at large in the countryside, the forests and hollows, the hills and flatlands of the valley. The myths once attached to them had been embellished: they now came out of nowhere – detonated a landmine, ambushed a convoy, fired and threw hand grenades at street patrols – and then vanished once more. The soldiers and the policemen emerged from the shock and blood to rage against whoever they could. The victims were often civilians, who just happened to be around when the guerrillas struck. Whole towns and villages had been laid waste in this way: shops and bazaars burned, houses razed, people shot at random.

This was how Jalaluddin's photocopying shop at Pattan, a small town a few miles north of Srinagar, came to be destroyed. The guerrillas had come early in the morning, shot a policeman on the main street and then disappeared. The police came looking for the guerrillas, and accused the Muslim shopkeepers of helping them escape. Then, before the shopkeepers could put down their shutters, more policemen arrived, this time with cans of petrol. Jalaluddin's shop was the first to be set alight, possibly because it was very new: he had only recently brought the photocopying machine and Honda generator from Delhi, in a long and difficult journey during which he'd had to bribe his way out of more than one roadblock.

The fire quickly spread to the adjacent shops, a ramshackle row of single rooms lining the highway: footwear and grocery stores, computer and typing institutes, all shaky in structure, and quick to combust, with their wooden frames. The smell of burnt wood was still in the air when I visited Pattan two days later.

'If you live in Kashmir, you have to be prepared for anything,' Abbas had said, and Jalaluddin, and other young men, had already moved beyond rage, hoping now to receive compensation from the government for the destruction of their property – large enough to enable them to rebuild their shops. The men – well-educated and articulate, and handsome, with sharp features and artlessly staring eyes in the Kashmiri manner – were matter-of-fact about the lack of options. There were no jobs to be had if you couldn't afford large bribes to government officials: Rs 50,000 to secure fourth-class employment as a *chaprasi* (servant) in a despised administration that then exposed you and your family to the fury of the guerrillas.

An old man, short and squat, with dull bloodshot eyes in a round puffy face, came and stood behind Jalaluddin as he spoke. The owner of a house that the fire had consumed, he had been lucky to get out with his wife, five daughters and two grandsons; and it was his story that the young men began to tell me – the cousin who had been killed in an 'encounter'; the son, a banana-seller in the bazaar, whom the police had kidnapped and then returned on a ransom payment of Rs 5,000.

The young men insisted on showing me the extent of the destruction. The photocopying shop had been completely gutted, the wooden beams charred and swollen into a kind of delicate filigree. The cream-coloured photocopier lay on the floor, the shiniest and most expensive thing in the shop, and it was with lingering solicitude that Jalaluddin turned it over and around to reveal the shattered glass and blackened underside.

One of the walls had collapsed, exposing the derelict shell, greater when seen from above, of the adjacent burnt house where a garish poster of a Swiss chalet remained on one of the bare walls, the broad-brushed sentiment on it still legible: 'A smile works magic like the sun and makes things bright for everyone.'

*

The Muslim middle class in the valley still largely consists of people connected to the government as elected or non-elected officials, and during the insurgency it hadn't stopped carving out private profits from public works: if anything, the violence and instability, the constant destruction and rebuilding, had offered more opportunities to raid the state exchequer. Jammu, the Hindu-majority city outside the valley, was full of newly built mansions of senior ministers and bureaucrats; in remote villages in the valley, corruption finding its own level everywhere, the massive new houses of local petty officials stood apart from the enclosing shabbiness.

Twenty miles south of Srinagar, past steep slopes and startlingly panoramic views of pear and apple orchards and rice fields and the tall mountains on the horizon, lies the hillside town of Charar-e-Sharif. It was here that the shrine of Kashmir's fifteenth-century patron saint, Sheikh Nuruddin, stood until 1995, when it was torched and destroyed during fighting between the Indian army and guerrillas. Kashmiris, both Hindu and Muslim, grieved at its loss. In Kashmir, Islam had escaped the taint it acquired elsewhere in the subcontinent from forced conversions and temple-destruction during the several centuries of invasions and conquests by Muslims from Arabia and Central Asia. It had come to the valley in the fourteenth century by way of Central Asian and Persian missionaries, and, blending well with earlier Hindu and Buddhist cultures, had taken on a uniquely Kashmiri character; it was to become known not for invaders, but for the great Sufi saints whom both Hindus and Muslims revered. Sheikh Nuruddin was one of the earliest and greatest of these saints.

It wasn't clear who started the fire: the guerrillas, some

of whom were from Pakistan and who, contemptuous of the pacifism of Sufi Islam, had turned the shrine into a bunker; or the Indian army, which had laid a siege around the shrine. But the destruction was international news and for some months various Kashmiri political and religious outfits as well as the government repeatedly promised to rebuild the shrine.

Five years later, Charar-e-Sharif and its inhabitants appeared to have been overtaken by events in the valley. The rebuilding amounted to an ungainly corrugated-iron roof over unpainted walls in the middle of a slushy field. A lot of money had been collected from shocked devotees; the government had pitched in; but little work was done, the funds disappearing, as with all delayed reconstruction projects, into many pockets.

The part of the town that had been destroyed and partly rebuilt was still a mess of rubble and open gutters and uncollected rubbish. A few new houses and shops had gone up: small bare windowless rooms, often with plastic sheets as doors, where ancient men sat embroidering wicker baskets for *kangris* (a little earthenware pot with charcoal embers that Kashmiris keep under their *pherans*), their thin legs drawn up against the wall, a hookah quietly smouldering beside them.

Word of my presence in the town had quickly spread. The car, the notebook and the camera had their own associations here, and, as I prepared to leave, about forty men appeared before the tiny stationery store where I had been talking to some schoolchildren (there are about twenty schools in the thinly populated region). The men had walked four miles from their village across the hilly countryside, after hearing that an official-seeming person was in town. The pipes in their area had burst and there had been no water for eight days. They had trudged to the assistant engineer's office but found it locked; they had gone to the local police station but hadn't been allowed a hearing; they were now melting the snow in the gullies for water, but there wasn't much snow left. Raggedly dressed, large holes gaping in their *pherans*, their thickly bearded faces white with dust, they seemed to have emerged out of a scene of eighteenth-or nineteenth-century wretchedness – the kind that made Victor Jacquemont conclude that nowhere in India were the masses as poor and denuded as in Kashmir.

The continuing backwardness of Kashmir, its failure, or inability, to join the modern world and find new identities for itself: this was what the Commissioner of Srinagar, an official of the central Indian government, had spoken to me about at his house; so too, although less directly, Abbas, who had told me on the very first day I met him that his ancestors had come to Kashmir from Samarkand in Central Asia.

Their connection to the Islamic world outside India was often exaggerated by leaders of Indian Muslims in the nineteenth and twentieth centuries; it was one way of holding onto an idea of personal and collective worth amid the general degradation of the Muslim community under colonialism. What struck me, however, was that Abbas, whose work as a correspondent for a major Indian newspaper gave him status, even prestige, in Kashmir, still needed to make the claim. But it was really an idea of dignity and selfhood that he was affirming – an idea that could take on a special urgency among such thoroughly trampled-upon people as the Kashmiris.

The troubles began, Kashmiris say, with foreign rule. After the Moguls, Afghans, and Sikhs, the valley fell in the mid nineteenth century to a petty Hindu feudal chief who had helped the British defeat the Sikhs. The British ceded the entire state – the valley together with Hindu-majority Jammu, Buddhist-dominated Ladakh and the north-western parts that later were to come under Pakistan's rule – to the chief for the meagre sum of Rs 7.5 m. The sale is still a source of rage and shame for Kashmiris.

Things didn't improve much under the new Hindu rulers. In 1877, a famine killed two-thirds of the population. Thousands of underfed, underclothed Muslims died while carrying rations on their backs for troops in remote Himalayan outposts. Muslims were rarely given jobs; the administration was staffed overwhemingly by the small minority of Hindus (about 4 per cent of the population in the valley). The Maharaja and his Hindu courtiers built up fabulous private fortunes. Even prostitutes paid Rs 100 as tax to the Maharaja; Muslims who were found slaughtering cows were banished to the remote Andaman Islands in the Indian Ocean.

The son of the last Hindu maharaja of the state, Karan Singh, records a Buddha-like epiphany in his autobiography. Born at the Hotel Martinez in Cannes, an entire floor of which had been taken over by his father, he spent his childhood in Kashmir more or less free of contact with Muslims and poverty. His father, Hari Singh, was fond of shooting and hunting and racing; also, it is said, of London prostitutes. Life in his palace was an endless search for entertainment. As Karan Singh writes, 'We spent hours working up lists for lunch and dinner parties, seating plans and menus.' Once his father asked a friend to take Singh around the city and show him the kingdom he would one day inherit. The friend drove him to the Muslim majority areas, pointed at the dilapidated buildings and shabbily dressed men on the streets, and said, 'These are your people.' Karan Singh was astonished.

The more astonishing thing about this event is its date, in the 1930s. Barely ten years later, India was free both of colonial rule and the maharajas; the Muslim elite of India were to demand and receive a separate homeland in the form of Pakistan; and the Maharaja of Kashmir, faced with a choice between joining India or Pakistan, would reluctantly accede to India, which had adopted a secular, democratic and egalitarian constitution, giving Indians a new idea of themselves, of their past and potential.

But such was the course of Indian history until then that it was mostly Hindus who took up these opportunities, who saw in modern education and the modern world the possibilities of personal and communal development. The Muslims of India, whose political power had been comprehensively destroyed by the British, and many of whose leaders remained trapped by fantasies of recapturing their old glory in India, took some time before even attempting to catch up with the Hindus.

In all this time, the Muslims of Kashmir, cut off from larger events and trends in British-ruled India, and held down by the tiny Hindu minority of rulers and administrators, were barely able to move at all. Illiteracy and poverty were widespread; political opposition to the Hindu Maharaja was met with brutality. As in India, a few educated Muslims were left to carry the burden of their country's humiliation and backwardness.

Part 2

2 The Politics of Secularism

It is no coincidence that the person who articulated best
the fears and frustrations of all Indian Muslims was a
Kashmiri, Mohammad Iqbal, one of the most important
Muslim philosophical thinkers of modern times. Iqbal was
born in 1876 in what is now Pakistan to an illiterate family
of shawl-peddlers and tailors. His parents managed to send
him to school and college, where he did very well. He was
already famous for his poetry when he went to Cambridge
in the early years of the twentieth century to study
philosophy.

Iqbal followed many other Indians in being deeply
impressed by European progress in the nineteenth century;
the idea of individual struggle and fulfilment, and the
related idea of the individual's responsibilities to society
and the nation, could not but come as a revelation to
people from listless subject communities. Iqbal came to
admire Nietzsche. The idea of the superman, of self-
creation and self-assertion, spoke to him in the powerful
way it always has to people from colonized countries. But
he was also disturbed by racism and hypercompetitiveness,
and while in Europe, struggling with the complex mix
of admiration, fear, and insecurity the place aroused, he
became even more aware of his Muslim identity. The history of Islam acquired new meaning for him; a passing
glimpse from a ship of Sicily, the setting of one of Islam's
greatest triumphs in Europe, could make him weep.

He came back to India convinced, like many Indians
before him, that the progress of his community lay not in
imitating Europe but in reforming and reviving the religion

{ 236 }

he had been born into. To this end, he began to exalt masculine vigour and the great Islamic past in his writings. He became a determined critic of Sufism, of the mystical and folk traditions within Islam that, advocating the rejection of the ego and the self, had found such a hospitable home in his ancestral Kashmir. He saw these traditions as emasculating Muslims, rendering them inadequate before the outstanding tasks demanded of the self and of the larger Islamic community.

Iqbal's ideas about Islam in India had to have political ramifications. Politics itself at that time of colonial oppression was primarily a quest for dignity, an assertion of identity first, and then only secondarily an attempt at creating new institutions. As such, it could not be separated from religion, from the larger sense of a shared culture and past which was the beginning of a political sense for all deprived and subjugated peoples. If, as Iqbal believed, Islam was weakened by incorporating the local traditions of Hinduism, then its original purity under the democracy established by the first four caliphs could never be recovered within an India dominated by Hindus. True Islam, as Iqbal conceived, could be reinstated only if Indian Muslims formed a separate nation. The idea which Iqbal put forward at an important political meeting of Muslims in 1930 was the beginning of the 'two-nation theory' which, seventeen years later, worked itself out in the partition of India and the creation of Pakistan.

For most Hindus in India, Iqbal is the misguided instigator of the movement for Pakistan. I hadn't really thought of him in connection with Kashmir until I met Dr Mohammad Ishaq Khan in Srinagar, the Kashmiri capital, in

March 2000. Dr Khan teaches medieval history at Kashmir University in Srinagar, and has done pioneering work on Islam's acculturation in the Hindu–Buddhist environment of Kashmir. He is a small, round-faced man, gentle in demeanour; he speaks slowly, as if unaccustomed to talking much of his work, but in clear qualified sentences that indicate a quietly active mind. During the past decade, the years of the insurgency, when the university ceased to function, he has produced his best work: a book on the spiritual dimensions of Islam that stressed the contemplative aspects of the faith over the ideological ones.

In one of the Kashmiri newspapers I read during a recent visit to Kashmir – papers that were full of bad news but always offering something lively in their editorial pages – I read Dr Khan's account of his visit to Pakistan. He had met many Kashmiris settled there; but he had stayed away from the awkward subject of politics altogether. When asked why he and other Muslim intellectuals in Kashmir weren't involved in the anti-India insurgency, he had thought of the Persian Sufi Rumi's words: 'The intellect is destroyed by partial reason.' Nevertheless he did visit Iqbal's tomb in Lahore; and in a striking passage he describes how overwhelmed he was with emotion as he approached the tomb: 'I couldn't control myself. Tears started pouring from my eyes.'

Dr Khan's allegiance was to the Sufi tradition of Kashmir, which Iqbal had rejected. His suspicion of Islam as ideology had grown only after the violence and suffering caused by the insurgency, which one of his own students had joined – someone whom Dr Khan remembered as denouncing, in the way Iqbal once had, Sufi Islam for turning the Kashmiris into apathetic slaves of Hindu India. The student had gone to Pakistan for training in the military camps and risen high within the leading pro-Pakistan guerrilla group, Hizbul Mujahedin, before being killed in Srinagar in 1999.

Iqbal's personal response to Europe and Islam and the melancholy beauty of his poetry had been reduced in the end to simple ideologies that had sent thousands of other young men to an early death. Nevertheless, the idea of Iqbal as the man who had brought a hope of redemption to the Muslims of the subcontinent survived, and – this is what struck me – still had the power, many decades later, of moving even someone like Dr Khan, committed to the intellectual life, to tears.

It was somewhat easier after that to imagine the impact Iqbal had on millions of Muslims across India with his poetry and philosophy – something comparable to Gandhi's influence on the Hindus; and it was somewhat easier to enter the Indian Muslim's sense of dispossession, and understand how much the charisma and persuasive power of men like Iqbal derive from the raw unformed nature of their community.

For Kashmiris, the person who came to embody their fate a generation after Iqbal was Sheikh Abdullah, once hailed as the Lion of Kashmir, who for more than half a century after the early 1930s remained the most popular leader of Kashmiri Muslims. His funeral in 1982 was attended by hundreds of thousands of mourners. But eight years later, his grave was desecrated – a moment that marks not only the beginning of the insurgency, but also the decline of the politics of personality in South Asia.

Abdullah's early mentor was Iqbal, whom he had met in 1924 in Lahore, when Iqbal was at the height of his fame. Iqbal had first visited Kashmir, the land of his ancestors, three years before, and had come away distressed by the condition of the Muslims: 'In the bitter chill of winter shivers his naked body,' he wrote, 'whose skill wraps the rich in royal shawls.' He had joined the Muslim-owned newspapers of Lahore in highlighting the fate of the Kashmiri Muslims under Hindu rule: how though they formed 96 per cent of the population the rate of literacy among them was only 0.8 per cent.

Iqbal was sympathetic to Abdullah, who, like himself, came from a family of poor shawl-sellers, and was one of the few Kashmiri Muslims who had managed to educate themselves up to the point where they found their way blocked by discrimination on grounds of religion: under the Maharaja, only Hindus, who were a mere 4 per cent of the population, were allowed to aspire to higher education and better jobs. Consequently, Abdullah had to leave Kashmir for Aligarh, near Delhi, where the first college providing Western-style education exclusively to Muslims had been set up in 1875. On his return to Kashmir in 1930, he joined a small group of graduate students from Aligarh who called themselves the Reading Room Party.

Barely a year later, Kashmir witnessed the first major disturbance in response to the autocratic rule of the Maharaja. A Muslim called Abdul Qadir who was working as a butler for a European resident was arrested for giving a seditious speech. Crowds who came to protest at the prison gates were arrested; more protests followed, and at one point the police fired on the demonstrators. Twenty-one people died. Then the procession carrying the bodies for burial became unruly, and Hindu-owned shops along the route to the graveyard were looted.

The Maharaja's Hindu army cracked down brutally on Muslim dissenters. Abdullah spent a year in prison with other members of the Reading Room Party. When he was released in 1932, he announced the formation of the Muslim Conference: it was the first organized opposition to the regime of the Maharaja in Kashmir. There was a special edge to Abdullah's relationship with the Maharaja. No two men could have been more dissimilar: the horse-racing Maharaja with a weakness for fraudulent Hindu holy men, and the devout Muslim and brilliant manipulator of the masses. In his opposition to the Maharaja, Abdullah found himself supported by leaders of the Indian nationalist movement against colonial rule, particularly Pandit Nehru, who under Gandhi's patronage had become the unchallenged leader of the Congress Party. The friendship between Abdullah and Nehru grew fast.

There was a special reason for that friendship. Nehru's Brahmin ancestors came from Kashmir, and had moved just a few decades before his birth in 1889 to Delhi and Allahabad, where they became one of the first families of modern India. There was always an air of the solitary visionary about Nehru. He was sent to Harrow and Cambridge by his Anglophile father. He was much influenced by European ideas of socialism and nationalism. His discovery of India came later and made all the more valuable for him the discovery of his roots in Kashmir, the ancestral connection deepened by the pantheistic feeling he, a man who disdained organized religion, had for the Himalayas.

Iqbal once said that though his body was confined to India, his soul existed in Kashmir. Nehru came close to making the same claim in his various scattered writings on Kashmir. He'd visited the state as a young trekker and was enraptured. In *The Continent of Circe*, Nirad Chaudhuri wrote of the Hindu sense of loss associated with the Himalayas: the cold regions the Aryan settlers of North India had come from – the longing expressed by Nehru himself when he wrote in his autobiography, 'And I dream of the day when I shall wander about the Himalayas.' In official and personal correspondence, Nehru kept coming back to what he himself described as his 'partiality for Kashmir'.

That partiality took several forms, and was to shape Indian attitudes towards Kashmir well after his death. By the time he met and befriended Abdullah in the mid-1930s, he had already begun to shape his blueprint for an independent India. In Abdullah, he saw someone who shared his conviction that the old social and economic order of India, represented by the maharajas and big landlords, had to be destroyed through land reforms and centralized economic planning. Abdullah was receptive to Nehru's advocacy of secularism: it was under the latter's persuasion that Abdullah changed the name of the Muslim Conference to the National Conference, and acquired a greater following among the small minority of Hindus in the Kashmir valley, as well as among the Hindu majority in Jammu, the southern part of the state. Though distrustful of Abdullah, they found reassuring his growing proximity to Indian nationalist leaders.

As the creation of Pakistan became a certainty, much to the heartbreak of Gandhi and others who had wanted a united India, Nehru was increasingly determined that Kashmir and its Muslim majority should be part of the India he had envisaged and so painstakingly worked towards: an India that was committed to democracy, secularism, and social-ism. He was convinced that the idea of a separate nation for the Muslims – the 'two-nation' theory first proposed by Iqbal and embraced by the feudal Muslim elite of North India – was a mistake; he didn't think it could solve the problem of the Muslim community, the problem he defined as social and economic backwardness. He thought the landlords and mullahs who had kept the Muslim masses away from the benefits of education would merely consol-idate their power in a new state.

Abdullah's own view of the demand for Pakistan was more qualified and less emotional. He felt, as he confessed in his autobiography, a subconscious sympathy for it; he saw it as a Muslim reaction against Hindu sectarianism, which he believed, despite his personal regard for Gandhi and Nehru, the Congress Party insidiously practised. Indeed, he thought he could discern strains of Hindu revivalism in Nehru's sentimental attachment to Kashmir.

He could also see that Kashmir's Muslim-majority pop-ulation and geographical location made for a natural affinity with the new state of Pakistan being carved out from the western, as well as eastern, parts of British India. At the same time, he felt himself out of sympathy with the men leading the agitation for Pakistan, particularly Mohammad Ali Jinnah, the pork-eating barrister from Bombay, who did not disguise his contempt for the Kash-miris and yet assumed that the state with its Muslim majority had no option but to join the new homeland for Indian Muslims. Abdullah also feared that the poor Mus-lims of Kashmir would get a bad deal in the feudal set-up of Pakistan. So it was that, in the years leading up to the

Partition of India, Abdullah came to think of independence and democracy as the best option for Kashmir.

The same idea, without of course the democracy bit, had struck the Maharaja, who, as the time of British withdrawal from India came nearer, was faced, as the ruler of the largest of the 562 states under British paramountcy, with a choice between India and Pakistan.

The Maharaja's autocratic ways continued as local opposition to him intensified. In 1946, he put Abdullah and other members of the National Conference in prison for running a highly popular 'Quit Kashmir' campaign against him. Nehru's support for Abdullah had already alienated the Maharaja from the Indian leadership; Gandhi's questions over the legitimacy of his rule, which had its dubious origin in a sale deed of 1846 between the Maharaja's ancestors and the British, made him more receptive to emissaries from Pakistan, who began to visit him with greater frequency. The Partition of India was three months old and he was still talking with both Indian and Pakistani representatives, hoping to buy time and preserve his regime, when a quick series of events forced him to act.

Violence and rioting during Partition had affected the southern part of the Maharaja's state, where Sikh refugees from Pakistan joined Hindu nationalists and members of the Maharaja's police in attacking Muslims. Tens of thousands of Muslims were killed. Many more Muslims fled to Pakistan, where the news of their suffering provoked the always very volatile Muslim tribesmen of the north-western provinces on the Pakistan border into declaring jihad against the Maharaja. In one of the impetuous and confused actions that inaugurated and forever marked the

Pakistani position on Kashmir, a few officers of the Pakistani army provided a ragtag group of jihad-minded tribals with arms and helped them across the border into Kashmir – at the same time as the Pakistan government was still trying to convince the Maharaja to hand over Kashmir to Pakistan.

The Maharaja's army was no match for the energetic tribal forces, who advanced swiftly through the north-west parts of Kashmir; an older generation of Kashmiris still remembers the killings and looting and rapes that they committed on their way to Srinagar. The Maharaja panicked as they came closer and closer. His son, Karan Singh, describes in his autobiography the moment when the lights went out in the palace – the invaders had destroyed the power station – and the noise of howling jackals suddenly sliced through the darkness and silence. The Maharaja appealed to the Indian government for military assistance; but the legalistic response from Delhi was that the Indian army could enter Kashmir only after the state had formally acceded to India. There was no longer any choice for the Maharaja. As the tribal army drew nearer to Srinagar, he fled the city for the Hindu-dominated city of Jammu, where he went to bed after instructing his aide-de-camp to shoot him in his sleep if the Indian government's representative didn't turn up with the instrument of accession. He never returned to Kashmir and died in far-off Bombay in 1962.

The Indian army finally arrived in Srinagar in late October 1947, and its offensive against the invaders became a fully fledged war with Pakistan that lasted more than a year. A ceasefire was eventually declared under the auspices of the UN on 1 January 1949, by which time the Indian army had driven the invaders out of the valley. However, the north-western part of the princely state, which is different, culturally and socially, from the Kashmir valley and closer to the Muslim Punjab, remained under Pakistani control, and, though named Azad (Free) Kashmir, is effectively as much a part of Pakistan as the valley is of India.

It was Sheikh Abdullah, released from prison just three weeks before the invasion, who had organized the defence of Srinagar. The National Conference came out in support of the Indian army. Abdullah not only endorsed the accession to India, but also generated popular Kashmiri support for it, which wasn't hard since the atrocities committed by the tribal army had put fear of Pakistan in the Kashmiris, and this fear took a long time to fade.

In retrospect, the tribal invasion seems to have spoiled everything. Certainly, the issue of Kashmir acquired a degree of complication from which it never recovered. Nehru took the dispute to the UN on 1 January 1948, and offered to hold a plebiscite under international auspices to confirm the accession to India. This sounds generous, given that Nehru already had physical control of the valley. But Nehru also wanted the legitimacy of popular support for Indian rule over Kashmir. He was confident that, with Sheikh Abdullah on his side, India would win a plebiscite in Kashmir.

As things turned out, the Indian offer of a plebiscite under the supervision of the UN was never redeemed. There was no withdrawal of the Indian and Pakistan armies from Kashmir, which had to be achieved before the plebiscite could take place, and the issue got bogged down in various legalities as the years passed. Pakistan remained in occupation of one-third of the state, and denounced the accession to India as fraudulent since in its view the Maharaja had surrendered all authority by fleeing Srinagar after the Muslims rebelled. The Indians kept dismissing the claim and saying that Pakistan had acted illegally by invading the state, and frequently raised the rhetorical ante – as they still do – by stating that the only unresolved issue for India concerned the return of Pakistan-occupied territories.

Positions hardened on both sides as the cold war reached the subcontinent. The US State Department under John Foster Dulles always suspected Nehru of being soft on communism, and was openly contemptuous of his non-aligned position. The US drew closer to Pakistan, which it included, in the mid 1950s, in such military treaties as CENTO and SEATO. This further stiffened Nehru's position on Kashmir; there was no more talk of a plebiscite. The Soviet Union under Khrushchev became a consistent supporter of Nehru's line, which became the official Indian line, that Kashmir was an integral part of India, and thus not subject to any international arbitration. The ceasefire line between India and Pakistan in Kashmir, called the Line of Control (LOC), became a de facto international border.

This would have been the end of the dispute: the status quo accepted by all parties as an unalterable reality. Certainly, in those early years, the populations in both Indian- and Pakistani-held Kashmir seemed resigned to being where they were. Sheikh Abdullah was now in charge, and almost the first thing he did as prime minister of Kashmir from 1948 to 1953 was to initiate a series of ambitious land reforms whereby ownership of lands in excess of twelve-and-a-half acres was abolished. In effect, this meant taking land away from the Hindu landlords and distributing it among poor Muslim tenants. It was a mini-revolution, and it assured Abdullah the gratitude and support of two generations of Kashmiri Muslims.

Less than four decades later, however, Kashmiris were to take up arms for the first time in their long history; India was to face a popular insurgency in Kashmir, and come close to nuclear war with Pakistan. The grave of Sheikh Abdullah, eight years after his crowded funeral, would require round-the-clock protection from vandals.

Jinnah's demand for Pakistan had innocuous beginnings: from the desire for a guarantee of Muslim rights in a Hindu-majority India, it developed into a demand for a confederation of India where Muslims would not have minority status but would share power with Hindus. However, the Hindu leaders of the Congress Party, so close to achieving real political power for the first time, were in no mood to share it.

The clumsily partitioned provinces toward the eastern and the western borders of India weren't what Jinnah had asked for – there were almost as many Muslims in India as in the new state of Pakistan – but they were all the Congress was prepared to part with. In the end, with the British impatient to depart and hustling everyone else, it was the Congress that was eager to settle for Partition in order to consolidate its hold on the much bigger Hindu-majority provinces and the institutions of the colonial state – the army, the bureaucracy, and the police – that were its great inheritance from the British.

Among the people who took a harder line as a result of the demand for partition was Nehru, who, over most of a lifetime spent fighting the British, had never accepted the idea of Pakistan, and held on to the idea of a united multicultural India. The bloodshed that accompanied the Partition came as a bigger blow to him; he was now more convinced than ever of the need to have, in the colonial way, a strong central government for India, with as little autonomy as possible for the diverse communities that constituted it. He regarded all regional assertiveness – and there was much of that across India in the 1950s – with suspicion. National unity, along with secularism, became his mantra, which was taken up by almost all political parties, and echoed by the colonial bureaucracy that was keen on holding on to its own power.

It was hard, nevertheless, to keep down sectarian demands in a country as diverse as India, where independence had released a new longing for self-expression, and where millions of previously disenfranchised people could find a political voice only through the community they were born to. A lesser leader would have proved disastrous here. Nehru dealt astutely with the demands for a linguistic reorganization of India, which in the South Indian state of Tamil Nadu, for example, had developed into a movement for outright secession. He used a carrot-and-stick policy – a mix of limited democracy and state repression – to pacify various regional groups and keep them within India.

But his own emotional connection with Kashmir made him wield a big stick there with Sheikh Abdullah, who, soon after becoming prime minister, had come up against the problems of running a large multi-ethnic, multi-religious state – problems not unlike those Nehru himself faced, but which Abdullah was much less equipped to deal with. He was primarily the leader of the Muslims of the Kashmir valley, who represented the majority of the state's population, 53 per cent. But there were also the influential Hindu majority in Jammu to the south, who resented Abdullah's radical politics, and the Buddhists of Ladakh, who were worried about the power of the valley's Muslims.

As usually happens, the lack of a political alternative turned Abdullah into an authoritarian ruler. Impressed by the Soviet model, he made the party inseparable from the administration; and, as the aggrieved tone of his letters to Nehru shows, he interpreted all opposition to him as an attempt to undermine his personal authority, and, by extension, the right of the Kashmiri Muslims to run the state after centuries of foreign rule.

In the early 1950s, when the Hindu nationalists in Jammu, the forebears of the BJP, organized the dispossessed landlords and followers of the sulking Maharaja into a movement for greater integration with India, Abdullah became more insecure. He had bargained hard with the Indian government to preserve the state from excessive interference by New Delhi; Kashmir, he argued, needed special guarantees for the protection of its autonomy. He now revived his idea of an independent Kashmir, bringing it up with, among other visiting diplomats, Adlai Stevenson in 1953.

This was disturbing news for Nehru. He felt Abdullah moving away from him and towards a course of action that was likely to end in the loss of Kashmir and India's secular credentials. He was quick to act: Abdullah was dismissed in 1953 and put in prison, where he stayed, initially without trial, for all but four months of the next eleven years.

This sounds rather unbecoming of Nehru, who by then was known internationally as a statesman. But national unity had become his obsession. He had praised Abdullah's land reforms; he had ensured there was no viable opposition to Abdullah; he had offered personal friendship to him. But now Abdullah was working against the 'national interest'. The support and dismissal of Abdullah was consistent with his belief that politics in Kashmir revolved around personalities. As he had told an activist who was arguing for a democratic alternative to Abdullah: there was 'no material for democracy in Kashmir'.

The other side, then, of Nehru's enchantment with Kashmir was a fear of losing control, a possessiveness that he gradually transformed into a national imperative: Kashmir, he began to argue, couldn't be separated from India without exposing the Muslims in the rest of India to retaliation from Hindu fanatics. You still hear a version of this idea in liberal circles in India today: that communal riots of the same scale and intensity as those during the Partition of India are around the corner if Kashmir is allowed to break away.

And then, in 1953, an old protégé of Abdullah's named Bakshi Ghulam Mohammed took over as prime minister of Kashmir, and did everything Nehru wanted to constitutionally integrate Kashmir into India. Promises of autonomy made earlier to Abdullah were cancelled; and fear of violence came to dictate Indian policy.

Bakshi Ghulam Mohammed was himself sidelined after serving ten years as the India-approved prime minister of Kashmir, and was imprisoned in 1965 when he sought to undermine an India-backed chief minister. Kashmir without Sheikh Abdullah reverted to what it had been for centuries under Mogul rule: a dependency, its fate controlled by a distant great power whose representatives could do what they wished as long as no one rocked the boat. Its political life, which had really only begun with Abdullah, came to be dominated by small men with small aims of personal empowerment and enrichment, by constant intrigues and betrayals.

Elections, held periodically in order to demonstrate before the world the democratic nature of the Delhi-imposed regime, were farcically rigged: the nomination papers of opposition parties would be rejected or their candidates beaten up and arrested; the National Conference won most elections unopposed. A concerned Nehru had to tell Mohammed that it might look better if he were to lose a few elections to 'bona-fide opponents'. The central government poured money into the state for development and education; and, for a handful of Kashmiris at least, the stakes for holding on to power rose higher. A new elite of politicians and bureaucrats emerged from the culture of corruption that grew around the administration.

As in the history of any dependency and its court politics, what you come to miss in accounts of Kashmir is a sense of the people, the way life went on in the villages and towns. One of the images that springs to mind is that of the corrupt government official in his large house, his sons studying in the best colleges of India. The other image is of the peasant in his rice field and mud hut, living as depressed a life as he was when, in 1831, the French botanist Victor Jacquemont visited the region.

However, the image alters as you read about the rise in literacy levels today. In all likelihood, the peasant's son of today has gone to school – one of hundreds opened by the Indian government – or even to the new university or the medical and engineering colleges; the peasant himself hasn't done badly with his apple orchards – horticulture still forms the mainstay of the economy.

In less than two decades, then, the peasant's son has become ready for a job, but he then finds that his options are very limited. Modern education has taken him away from a life in the rice fields or the apple orchards; but there is no local industry in the valley. The only jobs to be had are with the government; and here he finds himself excluded by the culture of bribery and nepotism. In India, he finds himself a foreigner, likely to be discriminated against on grounds of religion; it is not easy for a Muslim to find a job or rent a house in a Hindu-dominated region.

It was this sense of a blocked future among educated Kashmiris, along with the realization, hammered into them by repeatedly rigged elections, of their political impotence, that eventually led to the insurgency in the early 1990s.

In 1975, out of jail and once again chief minister of the state, Abdullah entered into an arrangement with the Indian government whereby he promised to give up the demand for self-determination in exchange for becoming what other men before him had been: a satrap of the Indian state in Kashmir.

The downside to the total investment of faith invited by charismatic individuals like Iqbal, Abdullah, or even Nehru, is that in the absence of institutions, the welfare of a country comes to depend on a few favoured ideas, and, more dangerously, on personal temperament. The success or failure of individuals has consequences, sometimes damaging, for many future generations. With Iqbal, the danger was always that his followers would go for the simplest and most emotional of the ideas he was trying out in his mind; and after the first flurry of land reforms, Abdullah wasn't able to offer anything more to Kashmiris than his formidable rhetoric and the glamorous myth of the prisoner of conscience.

A few months before he died, Abdullah, in the style of Third World dynasts, anointed as his successor his son, a UK-based doctor. Farooq Abdullah, inexperienced but enthusiastic, had barely begun when he clashed with Indira Gandhi, who had by then evolved her own authoritarian style. In 1975, she brought her father's anxiety about national unity to a new hysterical pitch as she arrested opposition leaders for being 'anti-national' and suspended fundamental rights.

In Kashmir, Mrs Gandhi found herself thwarted by Farooq Abdullah, who refused her offer of an election alliance between her party, the Congress, and the National Conference. Abdullah's victory in the elections of 1983, and subsequent hobnobbing with other politicians opposed to her, made Mrs Gandhi determined to get rid of him. Her tactics resembled those of the colonial state, something the British had employed to great effect: encouraging religious sectarianism in order to downplay regional disaffection with the central government. In Punjab, she had built up Bhindranwale, an illiterate Sikh preacher, as a counterweight to the province's anti-Congress government; the preacher subsequently turned into a murderous demagogue and declared war on India. Undeterred by the setback in

Punjab, she set to work on building up an atmosphere of Hindu jingoism over the issue of Kashmir.

A few stray anti-India demonstrations and violent incidents were held up as evidence of Farooq Abdullah's unreliability. The Indian press, which for decades had faithfully followed the government line on Kashmir, went along with Mrs Gandhi. Not that the Hindu middle classes needed much persuasion. By then Nehruvian nationalism had begun to degenerate into Hindu nationalism, into a search for external and internal enemies – the enemies who, when they were not the CIA or Pakistan, invariably belonged to the minority community, whether Sikh, as in the case of Punjab, or Muslim. The mass murder arranged by Congress leaders of 3,000 Sikhs in Delhi after Mrs Gandhi's assassination in 1984 came out of that frenzy of Hindu xenophobia she had herself encouraged.

Abdullah's elected government was illegally dismissed in 1984 by Jagmohan, a governor specially appointed by Mrs Gandhi after she had transferred out of Kashmir the previous governor, who had refused to act against Abdullah. The new government, made up of defectors from Farooq Abdullah's party, the National Conference, had to impose a curfew for seventy-two out of its first ninety days in office in order to keep down public agitation against it. Then, in early 1986, Jagmohan dismissed the government and took charge.

During his tenure as governor of the state of Jammu and Kashmir in the 1980s and then again in the early 1990s, Jagmohan did more than anyone else to provoke insurgency in the state. He came to be known as a pro-Hindu bureaucrat during Mrs Gandhi's Emergency when he sent bulldozers into Muslim slum colonies in Delhi as part of an attempted 'beautification' of the city. In Kashmir, an isolated state with a docile population always seeming ready to be trampled upon, he was no more subtle.

He saw the distinct cultural identity of Kashmir as something that had to be undermined before the state could join what in India is referred to, without irony, as the 'national mainstream'. With this all-subsuming idea in mind, he sought to impose a peculiarly Hindu modernity on the state, where the unrestricted sale of alcohol was permitted but Muslims were forbidden to slaughter sheep on a Hindu festival day – a pointless law since no prohibitions on meat exist for Kashmiri Hindus. The number of Muslims being recruited in government service went down. The Hindu nationalists were known to admire the resettlement policies followed by the Israeli government in the occupied territories in the 1970s, and Jagmohan may have been inspired by them in encouraging non-Muslims to work in Kashmir.

The backlash was not long in coming: what a colonized people fear most is the possibility of being swallowed up by the dominant alien culture in their midst, which is why the British had left the great religions of the subcontinent and their many subcultures more or less untouched. As in Algeria, Iran, and Egypt, anxiety about modernization, cultural influences from elsewhere, and rampant unemployment turned, because of Jagmohan, into an anxiety about religion: the notion that not only Muslims but Islam itself was in danger – the same fear that had led many Indian Muslims in the mid 1940s to suddenly embrace, after years of relative indifference towards it, the idea of Pakistan.

The popularity of Islamist parties grew throughout the

1980s, helped by the growth of madrasas, the privately owned theology schools which were often run by Muslims from Assam in eastern India, over a thousand miles away, after mass killings of Muslims in the early 1980s had forced their migration to Kashmir. These Muslims from outside Kashmir brought their own fundamentalist variety of Islam to the valley: the clerics suddenly wanted to impose new prohibitions restricting women's rights; they wished to ban Bombay films and beauty parlours.

The Islamist parties came together to fight the elections of 1987, in which Abdullah teamed up with the Congress. Just three years after being thrown out by the Congress, Farooq Abdullah decided he couldn't do anything in Kashmir without the support of the ruling party. But his power-sharing arrangement with the Congress was seen as another humiliation for Kashmir. To no one's surprise, he won the elections, and Kashmiris still talk about the active rigging that went on by Indian election officials. Opposition candidates comfortably in the lead suddenly found themselves defeated; candidates and polling agents were beaten up and tortured. Syed Salahuddin, the current leader of Hizbul Mujahedin, the leading Pakistan-based guerrilla outfit, was imprisoned after almost winning the vote in his constituency.

'There is no material there for democracy': the expressed contempt of Nehru's statement, amplified over time, began to affect a new generation of Kashmiris, the educated sons of peasants and artisans already reduced to futile resentment by corruption and unemployment. It was also around this time that the first groups of young Kashmiri men, most of them highly skilled, some even with engineering degrees, and almost all of them jobless, stole across the open border into Pakistan.

The young men were received by middle-level army officers in Pakistan, and set up with salaries and private housing. They were trained in the use of light weapons for some months; many of them were asked to return to the valley and bring back more young men. Other recruits smuggled arms and ammunition into the valley. Slowly, the traffic across the border grew: in less than three years thousands of young Kashmiri men had ventured across the border, where they formed the first guerrilla groups that declared war on India in 1990.

Pakistan was a natural ally of disaffected Kashmiris. It had twice tried to liberate Kashmir by force by sending in armed infiltrators – first in 1948 and then in 1965 – and on both occasions had failed to muster enough support among the local population, which, though not entirely happy with Indian rule, remained wary of Pakistan. But the fast-growing disillusionment with Indian rule through the 1980s made many Kashmiris look towards Pakistan for assistance: it was the only country in the world that consistently affirmed, at least rhetorically, the Kashmiri 'right to self-determination.'

For the Pakistani army officers who received the Kashmiris, the creation and support of the guerrilla groups required no expertise; they had done similar things, on a much larger scale, for the Mujahedin fighting the Soviet army in Afghanistan. Most of the officers worked for the Inter-Services Intelligence. Set up to coordinate the war effort in Afghanistan, the ISI had close links with the CIA and had come to play a considerable extra-constitutional role in Pakistan.

The army's control of Pakistan had not weakened since the last months of 1947, when the war with India over Kashmir transformed the new country, lacking the administrative centre or the infrastructure of the former colonial government, into a national security state, with over 70 per cent of the national budget being spent on defence. Islam turned out to be a weak nation-building glue in Pakistan. The feudal and professional Muslim elite's fear of being overwhelmed by Hindu India mutated into an anxiety about the assertion of ethnic identities in Sind, Baluchistan, and East Pakistan. The need to pacify ethnic minorities while affirming the power of the central government – a tricky manoeuvre that in the stronger and more democratic state of India had ended up promoting political life – only further expanded the role of the army and the bureaucracy in Pakistan.

In 1979, when the Soviet Union invaded Afghanistan, Pakistan was thirty-two years old, and still without a coherent political life. Just eight years before, it had suffered the traumatic secession of East Pakistan with its large Bengali Muslim population, which became, with India's assistance, Bangladesh. What remained was ruled despotically by an army general, Zia-ul-Haq, who had just hanged his former prime minister, Zulfikar Ali Bhutto, and the primitive economy with a tiny manufacturing base was propped up by the export of cheap labour to the Middle East.

The CIA found Pakistan a ready host for its proxy war against the Soviet Union. Billions of dollars' worth of arms and ammunition arrived in Pakistan over the next ten years, transforming the social and political landscape of the entire region while creating a strong Islamic fundamentalist movement all around the world.

The arms went to the mujahedin fighting the Soviet army, and their sale in the black market was also used to finance an illegal drugs trade – a disastrous link that eventually resulted in, apart from cheap heroin on the streets of New York, an estimated five million heroin addicts in Pakistan. The army was brought into the civil administration, and organizations like the ISI acquired their currently limitless and sinister power during this time.

Most damagingly, Zia-ul-Haq revived the idea of an Islamic society in order to postpone the transition to civilian rule he had promised soon after his coup against Bhutto. The state funds available to Islamic organizations went into raising armed outfits that attacked Muslim minorities such as the Shi'ites and the Ahmediyas; and violent conflict within rival Islamic groups broke out in many parts of the country.

Of the three million Afghans who came as refugees to Pakistan, many went to the province of Sind, where local opposition to their presence developed into a particularly savage civil war in Karachi, the largest city. Hundreds of thousands of Afghan refugees were given food, shelter, and elementary Islamic instruction at madrasas run by an Islamic organization close to the Pakistani army and sponsored by Saudi Arabia. It was the students at these madrasas that, assisted by Pakistan, went on to form the extremist Taliban.

The Soviet retreat from Afghanistan in 1989 was claimed as a victory by the fundamentalists. The fantasy of a new extensive jihad, such as the one in the seventh and eighth centuries that had established Islam as a world religion, attracted thousands of Muslims to Pakistan, from countries including Egypt, Algeria, Yemen, and Sudan. This globalized jihad, which began as a CIA-initiated move to unite all Muslims against godless communism, found new promoters after 1989, such as Osama Bin Laden, whose network of Muslim militants now spans the world. Many of the Muslims initially trained in Afghanistan became leading activists within Islamic fundamentalist movements in Egypt, Algeria, and the Central Asian republics.

About 100,000 unemployed men from Pakistan fought the jihad in Afghanistan; a few thousand among them would go on to fight in Kashmir. The Pakistani army itself was infiltrated by Islamic fundamentalists; and the possibility of these fundamentalists seizing political power in a nuclear-armed Pakistan is ever-present. Among other equally ruinous after-effects of the American–Pakistani adventure in Afghanistan, the generous American and Saudi Arabian support for the mujahedin in Afghanistan created and enriched a powerful lobby composed of army officers, smugglers, and drug barons, whose particular, often conflicting, needs have shaped Pakistan's domestic and foreign policies, and usually work against Pakistan's own larger interests.

Jihad alone brought about a degree of consensus among Pakistan's corrupt ruling elite; holy war having been the very profitable *raison d'être* of many of them. When American interest in Afghanistan dwindled in the early 1990s the ISI turned its attention to the long-standing dispute over Kashmir, which had always aroused much patriotic sentiment within Pakistan. Throughout the 1990s, the uprising against Indian rule in Kashmir, and the hectic mobilization by the ISI for a fresh jihad against India, proved especially handy as distractions from the widespread social and economic breakdowns within Pakistan.

India was always the significant enemy. The war with India over Bangladesh in 1971 had ended in utter humiliation for the Pakistani army, with 90,000 of its soldiers taken prisoner; and revenge motivated many ISI officers as much as the need to keep invoking jihad. One reason why American arms and money for the mujahedin in Afghanistan were so eagerly accepted by Zia-ul-Haq was that they seemed to give Pakistan 'strategic depth' in any potential conflict with India over Kashmir. In the mid 1990s, the government of Pakistan risked international isolation in supporting the Taliban, partly because the latter provided facilities in Afghanistan for the training of Muslims committed to the jihad in Kashmir.

The war in Afghanistan thus brought Pakistan to an unexpected fulfilment of its original mission: instead of becoming the pure homeland of Muslims, it became the capital of a global movement for jihad, a holy war against infidels, who seemed to be everywhere. It wasn't what Iqbal, insecure after his time in the West, thrown back to regretting the dead glory of Islam in Europe, could have imagined when he first proposed a democratic society of believers. And it wasn't what the Kashmiris, accustomed to a more benign version of Islam, could have imagined when they turned spontaneously to Pakistan for assistance in their struggle against India.

The first murders, kidnappings, and bombings by Pakistan-backed guerrillas began in Kashmir in 1989, while Farooq Abdullah was still heading a civilian government. Later that year the daughter of the home minister in the federal government in Delhi, a native of Kashmir, was taken hostage, and then released in exchange for five guerrillas. Large crowds welcomed the released men on the streets of Srinagar. They were fired upon by Indian police; five men died. There were more protests, bigger and bigger demonstrations: hundreds of thousands of men and women filled the streets of Srinagar, shouting '*Azadi, Azadi*' ('Freedom, Freedom'). People still speak of the strange energy in the air at the time: everyone shared the heady expectation that freedom was just around the corner, and news of the Soviet withdrawal from Afghanistan and television images of the fall of the Berlin Wall and the great demonstrations of Eastern Europe only deepened the delusion.

It was then, early in 1990, that the Indian government again appointed Jagmohan as governor; he arrived with a sense of mission whose fanaticism approached that of the Islamic guerrillas. Farooq Abdullah resigned, leaving Kashmir without an elected leader. A series of ruthless actions quickly followed. Hundreds of young men suspected of being guerrillas were taken away from their homes, tortured, and sometimes killed. Unprovoked attacks on demonstrators alone cost hundreds of lives – thanks to jumpy soldiers far from home, given a simple idea of the enemy, and licensed to kill. Thousands of Indian soldiers were brought into the valley – their current number is between 300,000 and 400,000 – while foreign journalists were expelled and local journalists found themselves confined to their houses.

A range of severe laws was introduced – not that many were needed, since all safeguards for civil liberties had

completely collapsed by then. You could be picked up anywhere and interrogated, or killed; and no one would ever
come to know what happened. The Kashmiri-American
poet Agha Shahid Ali quotes a doctor who attended to a
sixteen-year-old boy released from one of the interrogation
centres: '"Did anything in his lines of Fate reveal that the
webs of his hands would be cut with a knife?"'

By the time Jagmohan was replaced, after six months as
governor, the entire Muslim population of the valley had
revolted against Indian rule. The local police had mutinied;
the legal system staffed by Kashmiris was close to collapse;
more than 100,000 Hindus had fled; while the hospitals
were flooded with tortured and maimed young men,
and thousands more were missing, presumed dead, or in
Pakistan.

3 The Unending War

The unprovoked firings on unarmed demonstrators by the
Indian police and army – a recurring, if little-reported,
event in Kashmir over the next few years – alienated even
pro-India Kashmiris. Coming after the corruption and
arbitrariness of Indian rule in the previous four decades,
they created a vast number of humiliated men in Kashmir
– people likely to be attracted to the upsurge of nihilistic
energy in Afghanistan and Pakistan. So intent were the
Kashmiris upon fighting for independence that their cultural and political differences with the Pakistanis became
relatively unimportant. The first men who went over to
Pakistan were still thinking of an independent and secular
Kashmir. But as the movement grew and the ISI found

increasing numbers of Kashmiris willing to fight for integration into Pakistan, the country stopped bankrolling those secular Kashmiri guerrillas who were seeking independence. They were betrayed to Indian intelligence agencies, and many of them were also killed by the more militant pro-Pakistan guerrillas. These new insurgents were seen as hard-line Islamic terrorists, especially after they kidnapped and killed Hindus and, later, European and American tourists in Kashmir. Among Kashmiri Muslims, who belong to the peaceable Sufi tradition of Islam, they came to be feared for their fanaticism, which often erupted into violence against women and other unprotected civilians.

Kashmiris, who had expected as much international support as had been given to the East Germans and the Czechs when they filled the streets in late 1989, were surprised by the cautious pro-India policies followed by the EU and America. But diplomats and policymakers in the West had their reasons to be worried. In 1994, as the Taliban achieved major victories in Afghanistan, the network of radical Islamists began to spread. Islamic fundamentalist outfits in Pakistan became stronger; so did the ISI, which played a large role in shaping Pakistan's domestic and foreign policies. As the Taliban began to consolidate its position in Afghanistan, the ISI and the fundamentalists began to export jihad to Kashmir, where guerrilla groups were brought together by the ISI in an umbrella organization called the United Jihad Council. The guerrillas, once raw young Kashmiris, were trained in the use of light weapons in Afghanistan and Pakistan, and then sent back to wage war on India. The traffic across the border grew very busy. Even now, almost every Kashmiri Muslim you meet has friends or acquaintances who went to Pakistan. However, the Pakistani involvement in Kashmir reached a new pitch when, in the summer of 1999, Kashmiri guerrillas along with Pakistani soldiers were discovered to have occupied strategic Himalayan heights in India-held Kargil.

There were other, larger reasons behind the insurgency in Kashmir, which lay in changes in India. In addition to the shift in Indian politics throughout the 1970s, there was a later cultural shift in the early 1990s, when India's nominally socialist, protectionist economy was opened up to foreign investment, giving rise to a new middle class of people in business and the professions. As with most new middle classes, its members were eager to hold on to what they had recently acquired; and their politics were on the whole conservative. Many of them felt that India's stability should be ensured by brute force, if necessary, in places like Kashmir and the north-eastern states, since stability was essential for business, both locally and internationally. This was an attitude most strongly articulated by the Hindu nationalist party, the BJP, which the middle class helped elect to power in 1998.

Under the Hindu nationalists, India's economy was further globalized, creating a small elite of business tycoons and reanimating the cultural and emotional links many affluent Indian-Americans had with their home country. The BJP attempted to give India, and this global Hindu middle class, a greater international presence by conducting nuclear tests and lobbying for a permanent seat in the Security Council of the United Nations. The government's obsession with India's unity, and its deep suspicion of internal and external enemies, moved beyond the nationalism of the Congress Party. As the party in power, the BJP had more opportunity to enforce its nineteenth-century idea of nationhood – one people, one culture, one language.

The BJP had kept up a steady rhetoric on Kashmir throughout most of the 1990s, before they came to power, even as a harsh crackdown in the state went on: India, they said, had become a 'soft' state, easily bullied by its neighbours and by secessionists; they spoke of a 'proactive' policy and 'hot pursuit' of terrorists across the border into Pakistan. In 1999, the battles with Pakistan-backed infiltrators in Kashmir broke out, the first in India to be fought before TV cameras, and suddenly many in the middle class adopted the BJP's extreme rhetoric about the 'Kashmir problem'.

During the long years of rule from Delhi, most middle-class Indians had been generally indifferent to local politics in Kashmir; for the more affluent, the valley itself was a holiday destination, cherished for sentimental reasons. However, with Pakistan seen increasingly as an ever more implacable enemy, renewed patriotic sentiment and the televised demands for an end to Pakistani support for the guerrillas affected the Indian army: a friend back from the front told me of a Pakistani soldier in Kargil whose arms had been cut off and who, as he bled to death, kept pleading in vain with indifferent Indian soldiers to take his money out of his pocket and send it to his children and ageing mother in Pakistan.

As the Indian army announced one improbable victory after another, TV reporters and newspaper journalists emerged as cheerleaders, and then in July 1999 when, under American pressure on Pakistan, the infiltrators withdrew from the strategic heights, the media led the country in celebrating what the Hindu nationalist government described as Pakistan's military and diplomatic defeat.

If the battles in Kashmir hardened public opinion in India, the well-reported arrests of Muslims, allegedly terrorist agents of the ISI, in various parts of India further fed Hindu suspicions about Muslims in general, and Kashmiri Muslims in particular.

According to popular Hindu sentiment about the Kashmir problem, human rights violations by the military could be a means of reasserting Indian authority over the state. In the southern, Hindu-majority city of Jammu in the plains, I met a leader of the BJP, Mr Khajuria, one of the up-and-coming men within his party. Supplicants – job-seekers, men with big shiny boxes of sweets to offer Khajuria – thronged outside his flat, often spilling into the living room furnished with the regulation green carpet of government offices and sofas upholstered in dark blue velvet, with model aeroplanes on display in the glass cabinet, below large framed pictures of stern-looking BJP ideologues. Khajuria, a small round man with a big wart on the bridge of his nose, would gently scold the waiting group as he pushed his way through: 'Can't you see I am doing an interview?'

He had been a leader of the student wing of the BJP at Jammu University, and still had the sweetly ingratiating manner of the ineffectual student politician. I could have predicted before the meeting most of what he said: India was facing 'total war' with Pakistan which could only be ended by invading and conquering Pakistan; the ISI was encouraging Indian Muslims to increase their population in India through hectic breeding; and Muslims were at best unreliable.

But I was still taken aback when – eager to make an impression, and bolder now in his remarks – he said that Kashmiri Muslims only understood the language of the *danda*, the policeman's baton. That was the lesson of the maharaja's rule. 'Give the security forces a free hand,' he said, 'and the Kashmir problem would be solved in two weeks.'

The Kashmiri Muslim politician Mirwaiz Omar Farooq told me that the Hindu nationalists were determined to hold on to the valley but had little interest in the Kashmiris, and knew very little about their long history and culture. Still in his early thirties, Farooq is the youngest of the leading separatist politicians in the Muslim-dominated valley. Most of his colleagues were in prison in the western Indian state of Rajasthan when I saw him in June 2000; he himself was under house arrest, and while we talked policemen outside were asserting their presence by checking all incoming cars for bombs. On the clean-cut lawns where the trimmed tall hedges looked, distractingly, like giant hand grenades, a small group of men waited for an audience. Though much older, they were reverential toward Farooq, who was also the religious head of old Srinagar, a position occupied by his father, an opponent of the pro-India chief minister Sheikh Abdullah, until his assassination in 1990.

At the age of eighteen, Farooq had become the leader of the coalition of parties fighting for liberation from Indian rule: the news, I remember, was greeted with derision in India, as a sign of Kashmir's political immaturity. But people grow up fast in adverse times, and Farooq spoke with the subtlety and skill of an older, more experienced politician.

He was among the majority of Kashmiris, he said, who thought the insurgency had failed, and not only that: it had also undermined an ancient and gentle culture by introducing it to the dangerous cult of the gun. The only hope lay in a dialogue between India and Pakistan that would also involve representatives of Kashmir. Although he opposed Indian rule in Kashmir, and worried about the hardening of attitudes in India, he was also concerned about the rise of fundamentalist Islam in Kashmir. There was no alternative to a secular democratic state and rapid economic progress. It was Nehru's vision for India all over again, although, ironically, in Kashmir, that vision had been dissolved by the same Indian state that was entrusted with the great power to realize it.

Still, the Kashmiris themselves are quick to embrace the modern world whenever the opportunity comes their way. Movement and growth are visible even after more than a decade of damage. Education suffered most in ten years of endless curfews and strikes, and yet even so, one of the most popular small businesses in the valley remains the primary 'English-medium' school or 'coaching institute'. A small room and a graduate are all that is initially needed. You are assured of customers: parents who can't afford anything better but are anxious for their children to make their way into the larger world of jobs and professional careers, their anxiety so great and widespread that even the madrasas – the schools run by the fundamentalist Jamaat-I-Islami – where moderate Muslims often send their children, have had to secularize their syllabus.

At the time when political activity was restricted by the insurgency, Omar Farooq accumulated degrees in computer science and political science. When I first met him in

2000, he was studying for an M.Phil. degree in Islamic studies. In the market in Pattan, a few miles north of Srinagar, regularly destroyed and rebuilt after each battle between the police and guerrillas, I found two 'computer institutes': tiny rooms really, with a computer in each, full of restless young men – restless because there was no power and they paid by the hour to become familiar with Windows software. At Kashmir University in Srinagar – its vast green campus bordering a lake and monitored by snow-capped mountains – the lines of students for enrolment in the new semester are very long. Students with guns ruled the campus not so long ago. The university, set up in 1948 and already in 1988 known as one of the best universities in India, effectively ceased to function in the 1990s. Most of the Kashmiri Hindus on the faculty left. The anomie and corruption elsewhere had infected the university: there was mass cheating in exams and as a result the percentages of students passing their exams was an unusually high 90.5 per cent. The lowest point was reached in 1992, when the university awarded degrees without holding examinations.

But the India-backed drive to restore peace to the state after the elections in 1996 benefited those in education. During the brief respite, the faculty was restaffed with more Kashmiri Muslims occupying senior teaching positions. Seminars and conferences were held again. The percentage of students passing their exams returned to normal. Some of the Muslim students who had been attending colleges and universities in India also returned, after being continually harassed by the police; the university set up new departments of biotechnology and geology for them.

*

For more than a century after 1846, when the British left, the Kashmiri Hindus had dominated the Muslim-majority population of the valley. Then the land reforms of Sheikh Abdullah, introduced during his time as the India-backed leader of Kashmir from 1948 to 1953, and the spread of free primary education, created a new class of ambitious Kashmiri Muslims. However, no new institutions were provided to accommodate them; and existing facilities were monopolized by the minority of Hindus who ran the schools and colleges and had a disproportionate presence in the state's administration.

At first, the abrupt departure of the Hindus after the insurgency began in 1990 was felt as a blow. Over time the space vacated by them has been filled. Alongside the insurgency and the bloodletting, a new generation of Kashmiri Muslims has emerged to take their positions in the bureaucracy, the universities, and the media; and it is hard not to be impressed by this new middle-class intelligentsia, by the journalists, academics, and politicians in the valley – people like Abbas, my Muslim guide in Kashmir, Dr Khan, the thoughtful scholar whom I had met in Srinagar, and Omar Farooq himself. They make it possible to believe that, along with immeasurable suffering and pain, Kashmir has acquired a new political and intellectual life; that as had taken place once in India, the struggle for greater liberty has turned out to be a rite of passage, an awakening that owes as much to modern education as to the still-strong Sufi Islamic traditions of tolerance and civility.

Pakistan – busy exporting jihad everywhere even as it slowly imploded – couldn't have been expected to be responsive to that awakening; the section in north-west Kashmir which it continues to hold is the most underdeveloped part of Pakistan, and it has done little for it. India is the bigger, economically stronger, more democratic country that can accommodate Kashmir, make it part of its overall growth. But the gap between India and Kashmir has grown even wider in the last decade.

The government keeps inviting the separatists to renounce violence and engage in dialogue; army and police officers speak routinely of 'winning back the hearts and minds of the Kashmiris'. But this isn't going to be achieved simply by sending Kashmiri schoolchildren on tours of India – one of the Indian government's populist measures, which, as one army officer told me, would not only appease the new generation of Kashmiris but would make them realize what a big and powerful country India is. That is a message that has already been conveyed by hundreds of thousands of Indian troops in Kashmir – the various army and paramilitary groups, some of whose more protected members, more than ten years after the insurgency began, have done well for themselves.

In Srinagar in March 2000, I met Mehbooba Mufti, the daughter of a senior pro-India Kashmiri politician, who was then one of the brave people who travelled around the valley investigating the excesses of both the security forces and the guerrillas. When I saw her she had just returned from visiting the border with Pakistan near the distant north of the valley. The area was known for timber smuggling; and three timber smugglers, caught while murdering some villagers, had fingered the commanding officer of the local army unit as their protector. That wasn't all. The fabled beauty of the women in the area invited trouble from the Indian soldiers stationed there. There had been accounts of prostitution and rape in the past, and, just a few months ago, an incident with a commanding officer who wanted to marry one of the seven daughters of a peasant. The woman was already married; and so was the army officer. The peasant father, who refused to sanction the relationship, was taken away; pieces of his body were later returned in a sack to the village. The army claimed that the man knew of a guerrilla hideout and was leading an army patrol to it when he stepped on a mine.

There were similar stories everywhere – stories either left unreported in the Indian press or deemed too dangerous to investigate, since the 'national interest' was at stake – it was the excuse the India-backed chief minister of Kashmir, Farooq Abdullah, had himself used in 1999 when asked by Yusuf Tarigami, the lone communist in the state legislature, to reveal the killers of fifteen Muslim villagers in Jammu. It was also, Mr Tarigami told me, why there was going to be no independent investigation into the killing of the Sikhs at Chitisinghpura, despite repeated requests by human rights organizations.

One of these organizations, Amnesty International, identified Indian intelligence agents and 'renegade militants' whose patrons are the Indian army, alongside armed opposition groups on its list of those likely to be responsible for the killings. These 'renegade militants,' were so called after the army began to recruit captured or 're-formed' guerrillas for operations where the costs in human lives and the army's reputation were likely to be too great for the army to use its own men. They are the most dreaded group in the valley, more feared than the jihadi guerrillas, more than the army and police officials in remote areas or the jumpy soldiers in their bunkers.

In the early years of the conflict, 1994 to 1996, these renegades had proved very handy: they helped the army rebuild its intelligence network in the valley and also assisted in tracking down and killing hundreds of guerrillas trained in Pakistan and Afghanistan. They proved less effective against the Fedayeen, the new 'suicidal' guerrillas, often Pakistani citizens, who had started to arrive in the valley in larger numbers after the battles of 1999; in fact many renegades had been murdered by the Fedayeen. Nevertheless, they still threatened, and sometimes killed, the families of guerrillas living in the valley or those journalists and human rights activists who were seen as too eager to report the excesses committed by the army. In return, the army and the civil administration looked the other way when the renegades kidnapped and killed for money. A senior government official spoke of them to me as Frankenstein's monsters; the renegades were, he said, the most visible and hated symbol of Indian rule over the valley, and it wasn't going to be easy to tame them.

At Anantnag, a town thirty-five miles south of Srinagar, I tried to see the local 'commander' of the renegades. But he was away in Delhi – an unexpected sign of his status with the Indian government; the renegades had recently helped set up the BJP office in Anantnag. A polite policeman directed me to the home of another commander in the same protected compound. Parts of the house looked relatively old, and the rest was under construction, the money for it coming, it seemed, in instalments. When finished it was going to be a huge house, its size and the high walls topped with glass shards making it look like something from an affluent Delhi suburb.

A young, good-looking man in kurta pyjamas came out

after much apprehensive peeking through the holes in the heavy iron gate. It transpired he was the brother of the commander, Rashid; Rashid himself was at his headquarters a couple of miles away, and the brother drove me there.

The headquarters was a large building that had been vacated by a Kashmiri Hindu family. It had been transformed into a mini-fortress, with boarded-up windows and a tall corrugated-iron gate, behind which, in the courtyard, young men stood dramatically poised with light machine guns to repulse any attack. There were good reasons for their defensiveness: one of the commanders of the renegades had been shot dead a week before in a crowded bazaar, and some months ago an improvised explosive device hidden in an auto-rickshaw and intended for the renegades had turned a house ten metres away into a huge mound of rubble.

Rashid was waiting outside the gate, and to see his bodyguards – teenage boys with oversized guns – was to feel the fear and uncertainty their presence brought to the neighbourhood, to the tense men in the little meat shops and bakeries lining the alley. As for Rashid himself, his lean, wiry frame, sharp features and thick moustache, his thick gold ring and blue jeans gave him a Bombay movie-star glamour and an impression of brute power until the moment he spoke. Then the quivering jaw and broken syllables betrayed his jitteriness: the jitteriness, I thought, of the doomed man; it made him an attentive host and a keen talker. He saw me as taking back an important message to the Indian government conveying his anger at what he perceived as India's disregard for the renegades, the poverty and isolation to which they had been reduced, the temptation they felt to go back to Pakistan; and he shouted at the bodyguards when they showed up with lukewarm tea.

It was hard to get him to talk about the things I was interested in, which he mentioned indifferently when pressed: the bachelor's degree in science from the local college, the lack of work, the journey to Pakistan with no clear motivation along with twenty-eight other men, the training in light weapons in Pakistan and Afghanistan for eleven months, then the return to the valley as a guerrilla, the sudden disillusionment with the armed movement for independence, and the recruitment by the army. He was frankly puzzled when I asked him to expand on little details in his narrative – about the camp commander in Pakistan named after Aurangzeb, the last great Mogul emperor and persecutor of Hindus; the deception in Pakistan where he'd had to present himself as a fundamentalist pro-Pakistan Muslim in order to receive his training and small salary. But he elaborated at some length about his local patron, a senior army officer in the Indian army.

The senior army officer had asked him to lead an anti-guerrilla operation very recently, and he had obliged by killing two guerrillas who had infiltrated an army camp. Here Rashid pointed at the thin, unshaven, middle-aged man in grimy kurta pyjamas I had assumed to be a supplicant awaiting his turn: he was the one who had covered Rashid as he stormed, guns blazing, the little room where the guerrillas were holed up; the one who shot a dying man to prevent him from reaching for a hand grenade. This thin, unshaven man, Rashid said, had been rewarded by having a police report lodged against him for 'asking' a rich merchant in the town for some money. But what, after all, could he do with the little money he was given by the government?

It was at this moment that something hit the high corrugated-iron roof sloping into the courtyard: at the deep, heavy sound, everyone – Rashid, I, the three boys with guns – froze for an agonizing second. It was several minutes after the scruffy cork cricket ball had pattered off the roof into the open drain around the courtyard that I heard my heart pounding wildly.

Rashid's face had gone white; and the shame of that inadvertent confession of fear was, I think, what made him grow wild when I asked him about the Fedayeen, the suicidal guerrillas. He and his men were the true Fedayeen, he shouted – people who were being martyred for being faithful to India. Then he added that he was ready to take on the Fedayeen any time. All he needed was a 'free hand'.

A 'free hand': I heard those words very often in the valley, and they spoke, as nothing else did, of the breakdown of communications, the end of dialogue, and the unthinking preference for violence and terror. Rashid was bemused when I asked him to explain what he meant by a 'free hand', because he had already done so, at least indirectly: he had made it clear, without saying so explicitly, that the government, and busybodies from the press and human rights groups, should look the other way while the families of the guerrillas were harassed, and suspected informers were tortured, and civilians mistreated.

Rashid's idea of a 'free hand' wasn't very different from that of the government. The words were part of the accepted vocabulary, more potent than the previous talk of 'pro-active policy', which really meant pursuing guerrillas

across the border into the training camps – easy to fanta-
size about in Delhi but impossible to achieve without
starting, as almost happened in 1990, a war with Pakistan.
The borrowed phrase 'ethnic cleansing' was even less effective. After each killing of Hindus, it was said that the
guerrillas were engaged in 'ethnic cleansing'; but, ethni-
cally, the Sikhs and Hindus were no different from the
Muslims of the valley. In the end, the few attempts at subtle
rhetoric always collapsed into crudely aggressive demands
for a 'free hand'.

The 'free hand' means that the cycle of retribution will
continue for a much longer time. In Pattan, outside Srinagar, just a few days after I left, the local police station was
attacked with grenades and rockets. In response, the frustrated policemen looted and burned down the entire
market. I didn't go back; I didn't feel I could face the helpless shopkeepers I had met on my previous visit. I went
instead to Jammu, the city of the plains, where, far away
from the new mansions of the politicians and bureaucrats,
thousands of Hindu refugees from Kashmir now live.

It was in early 1990, during Jagmohan's few months as
India's appointed governor in Kashmir – and, some say,
with his active encouragement – that most of the 140,000-
strong community of Kashmiri Hindus left the valley.
Jagmohan had originally been made governor in 1984,
appointed by Mrs Gandhi in order to dismiss Kashmir's
elected government; he had served for five turbulent years
during which his aggressively pro-Hindu policies further
alienated Muslims in the state from India. His limited
comprehension of the insurgency – as simply a limited
law-and-order problem which could be contained fast – is

apparent in his memoir about his time as governor of Kashmir. Many Kashmiris believe that he wanted the Hindus safely out of the way while he dealt with the Muslim guerrillas.

The Hindus had formed a kind of elite in the valley; and made their presence felt in the bureaucracy, both there and in Delhi, where government policy on Kashmir often came to be dictated by the fears and concerns of this tiny minority. Their connections with India, and their relative affluence, made them highly visible targets during the first few months of the insurgency in 1990; several government officials were assassinated by pro-Pakistan Muslim guerrillas who also committed random atrocities against Hindu civilians: rapes, murders, kidnappings.

Approximately 130,000 Kashmiri Hindus left the valley within two months of the insurgency beginning; few have been able to return. The ordeal of displacement was less difficult for the professional elite of doctors, engineers, and academics, who, on leaving the valley, renewed their links with the outside world: they now form a distinct diaspora within India and in the UK and America, where large numbers have settled.

It has been the less well-off Hindus in the countryside who have suffered the most. A few miles out of Jammu, on a stony, treeless plain, you suddenly come across hundreds of one-room tenements where thousands of Kashmiri Hindus have been living for the last ten years, waiting, without much hope, for things to improve. It was early spring in the valley and still cold when I visited the camps, but around Jammu the temperatures had begun to rise, and the sun felt more severe on the rocky, exposed ground. The tar that held together the thermocoal roof of the igloo-shaped tenements had already begun to melt, and more tar was hard to find: you had to bribe the roadworks labourers.

This wasn't the only thing that worried Gautam, the Hindu I met in one of the camps. In 1990, he had left his apple orchards near Baramulla in the north of the valley with just Rs 65 in his pocket. There had been no water for eight days and the plastic buckets used for storage had begun to run dry.

Gautam sat behind a window with iron bars, half-slumped on the single wooden cot in his half-sleeved vest and pyjamas. The smell of burned onion drifted from the tiny room where all five members of his family slept. The walls were bare except for a calendar with pictures of Rama and Sita; there were a few steel utensils on the shelf over a rusty gas cylinder; a small television sat on a rickety stool. Outside, in the cramped little courtyard edged with an open drain, a mangy dog slumbered in the shade of the overburdened clothes-line, and the tin doors of the public latrines were cut so low that you could see the blank face of the person squatting over the hole in the floor.

I wasn't invited in. Gautam, when he relaxed more with me, said bitterly, 'We are like a zoo, people come to watch and then go away.' He felt betrayed by Jagmohan and the other politicians, especially the Hindu nationalists, who had held up the community as victims of Muslim guerrillas in order to secure Hindu votes, but had then done very little to resettle them, find jobs for the adults or schools for the young. Gautam had been back to the valley just once: he had been persuaded to do so by his Muslim neighbour who personally came to the refugee camp to escort him back to his village. The warmth between the Hindu and

Muslim communities of the valley – so alike in many ways
for the outsider, so hard to tell apart – had remained intact,
and had acquired a kind of poignancy after such a long
separation.

But when Gautam returned, he found his house had
been plundered; children were playing cricket in his apple
orchard where the trees had been cut down for firewood.
Then he was kept awake by fear on his first night at the
sound of gunfire, a sound his Muslim neighbours had
become used to. In the morning he had heard news of the
deaths of five Indian soldiers in the gun battle with guerrillas. Enraged soldiers were expected at any minute to
launch a 'crackdown'. Gautam followed the young men of
the village and took the first bus out.

He hadn't been back again; he didn't know if he could.
His son, fourteen years old now, had very few memories of
Kashmir, had grown up in a different world, with a sense
of injustice and the rage of the young. Gautam often had
to stop him from denouncing Muslims and Islam.

I didn't see the boy: he was at school. There was a picture of him in a small plastic frame; with large serious eyes
in his pale Kashmiri face, he reminded me of the Muslim
boy I had met some days earlier at a graveyard in Srinagar.

It was my first day in Srinagar. A famous guerrilla had
been killed by the army the day before but there had been
no public mourning. At the Idgah cemetery for 'martyrs' –
placed at the edge of a vast, bald field scarred with muddy
puddles, and full of signboards with exhortations: 'Lest
you forget that they gave their today for our tomorrow' –
there was one fresh grave but, again, no mourners. The
grave was that of a young man who had been taken by the
police from his home for interrogation. A very old man sat

nearby with a teenage boy in large thick-framed glasses, both hunched over a *kangri* – the little pot with charcoal embers they carried under their cloak-like *pherans*. The boy, Jamal, took me around, stepping agilely across the graves, his dark eyes sombre behind his glasses.

The earliest graves in that Srinagar cemetery had claimed the most reverence and space: they were set in large plots, adorned with bead necklaces and plastic garlands. But as the numbers had begun to rise, and the graves had been set closer together, the headstone engravings acquired a uniformity of message and style: the green-painted word 'martyr' occurred in all of them.

The boy pointed out the new grave: the earth still moist under the wrinkled plastic sheet; it had no headstone yet, but a narrow, freshly dug bed of yellow irises ran around the perimeter. Irises were, Jamal said, the flowers used to honour the Muslim dead in Kashmir.

He couldn't have been more than five years old when the insurgency began but he knew the names of all the 'martyrs'. There were some in his own family: his elder brother, who had been killed two years ago, soon after he returned from Pakistan; his father, who had died of his injuries after being tortured with hot iron rods. Jamal had dropped out of school, and now came to sit in the graveyard each evening. I asked him why, and he said, his large eyes earnest, that he wanted to be close to the martyrs; they had died a holy death in the cause of jihad, and were now in paradise. Later, he said that his mother was worried about his visits to the cemetery; she had been going to various shrines and making him wear amulets to prevent him from becoming a 'militant' like his brother.

He wanted to know what Indians in India thought of

their army killing the Kashmiris, and it was the guilt brought on by this question that made me stay longer with Jamal. Windows opened in the rain-dampened houses overlooking the graveyard, and curious faces appeared in them, watching me talk to him. The day, already grey, began to die quickly. The taxi driver grew nervous: the area was the stronghold of the pro-Pakistan guerrillas.

When I left, the image I carried with me was of the young boy and the old man sitting against the dirty overcast sky, the mist-hazy mountains and the flat, puddle-stained field; it added to the desolation of those first few days in Srinagar, which – although the terrible scenes of the massacre were yet to come – had already begun to contaminate my early memories of Kashmir, of the landscape that had once been a revelation of beauty.

On one of my last days in Srinagar – one of the many days of protest strikes, enforced by the guerrillas, the city surreally deserted in the middle of the long, sunny afternoon – I went back to the graveyard. There were more graves; and, with spring finally resurgent in the valley after many cold days, the irises were in full bloom. But Jamal was gone. The old man sat all alone in the middle of the graveyard, and didn't know where Jamal was. He hadn't been to the graveyard in several days, but his mother had come looking for him.

It was some weeks after I left Kashmir that I read a newspaper account of a teenage boy who had driven a car full of explosives into the army cantonment in Srinagar: it was the first suicide bombing in the valley. The boy went to a local school, and neither of his parents had known about his connections with the jihadi outfits. It couldn't have been Jamal, who had only one parent, but it was while reading about this boy that I thought of Jamal again; I remembered the wide serious eyes; I remembered his talk of martyrdom and paradise and death.

The cycle of violence and destruction has been swift and severe in Kashmir; the insurgency has poisoned and destroyed many lives. Yet the insurgents' political cause remains as lonely and hopeless as before. Independence, which a majority of Kashmiris seem to want, or integration with Pakistan, which for many Kashmiris is the second-best option after independence, are not possibilities that any Indian government can ever consider without immediately losing the support of the Hindu middle classes. The European Union and the US are unlikely to risk antagonizing India, with its lucrative markets and resources and the trappings of a democracy, by taking up the Kashmiri cause.

It seems unfair: that all Kashmiris can hope for at present is a change in Indian attitudes, a bit more breathing space, a bit less heavy-handedness; that the tens of thousands of victims of the decade-long violence will have to wait much longer for even some partial justice.

But then you can't hope for much justice in the subcontinent, where fulfilment comes to very few among the needy and restless millions, and where aspiration itself can feel like a luxury. In Kashmir, isolated and oppressed, and then dragged into the larger world of competing men and nations and murderous ideologies, more people have been confronted with this awareness in the last ten years than in all of its tormented modern history.

There will always be young men like Jamal who attempt to dissolve the pain of that awareness in the nihilism of jihadi martyrdom. At the same time, there are many more Kashmiris who wish to make their peace with that pain, who are wearied by the bloodletting and resigned to their lack of options. They now want the relative stability of the time before the insurgency to return, even if it involves living with the humiliation of continued Indian rule over the valley: the same private, uneasy accommodations with the world that keep the deprived millions elsewhere in the subcontinent from exploding into rage and destruction.

Pakistan:
Jihad Globalized

PESHAWAR IS A MESS. And during my stay there in January 2001 – when the smog above the city trapped the acrid smoke from the burning tyres that the Afghan refugees huddled around for warmth, and Pakistani traffic policemen wearing new-looking gas masks flailed helplessly in the slow swirl of donkey carts, trucks, auto-rickshaws and cars – I began to wonder, somewhat resentfully, if the romance of Peshawar had been an invention of jaded adventurers from the West: of the eager-faced white men and women you could still see walking in the narrow alleys of the old quarters – visitors in the first flush of their enchantment with the Orient, for whom all those aggressively encroaching shanty colonies and the precariously defended middle-class suburbs, all the Afghan beggar children with startlingly green eyes, and the heroin addicts slumped on broken pavements, could easily fade into the general quaintness of the East.

Fifteen years ago, Peshawar had glamour. The Soviet army was in Afghanistan, just forty miles away, propping up a communist government; and Peshawar was the

front-line city for the jihad against Soviet communism that
the United States and its allies were sponsoring. Spies from
the CIA, KGB, Mossad, and ISI worked the streets and
refugee camps where more than one million Afghans lived.
The local papers were full of cryptic paragraphs about
assassinations and bomb explosions. Margaret Thatcher,
George Bush, Kirk Douglas, and Princess Anne, among
other celebrities, showed up to raise the spirits of the anti-
communist Afghan mujahedin. European and American
journalists crowded into Dean's Hotel, waiting to be smuggled onto the battlefield by their favourite 'Muj'. At Lala's
Grill, local fixers cadged kebabs from backpackers looking
for the frisson of holy war, and gossiped about the number
of heroin laboratories near the Khyber Pass. You might
even have come across rich Saudis like Osama Bin Laden,
busy enlisting Arab mercenaries into the jihad.

By early 2001, these excitements had died away, except
among nostalgic middle-aged local journalists, whom the
proxy war had temporarily rescued from ill-paid obscurity.
Dean's Hotel had closed down a few months before my
visit. Lala's Grill had acquired the dark-windowed facade
of an Indian–Pakistani dive with pretensions; and although
a sign asking visitors not to bring in their guns still stood
by the main entrance to the Pearl Continental Hotel, the
bright cloth banner outside advertised cooking classes for
'ladies'.

I felt oppressed by the city; its shapeless squalor as well
as its new aspirations to respectability reminded me too
much of the small-town India I had grown up in. Relief,
along with proportion and order, seemed to lie only in the
British-created cantonment: in the low red-tiled bungalows, whitewashed trees and brick-lined flower beds, and

the lone guard standing stiff before long smoothly gravelled driveways. It was where I often found myself in the
long evenings – somehow longer in an unknown city –
browsing through the boldly pirated American and British
paperbacks at Saeed Book Bank and visiting newspaper
offices in Saddar Bazaar.

I was never less than nervous while visiting the cantonment. My visa for Pakistan said, 'Not Valid for Cantt
Areas'. I wasn't sure what this meant since cantonment
areas in the cities of the subcontinent are impossible to
avoid. I was expected to stay away from 'sensitive military
installations'; but since I didn't know what these were I
had to play it safe. I never turned my head sideways when
my rickshaw passed the grander-looking buildings, never
made it apparent that I was curious about anything except
the dreary progression of the well-paved road, and the
proud replicas of new Pakistani missiles mounted on
traffic islands – the missiles named provocatively after the
Muslim conquerors of India.

This timidity was partly created by the three men in a
beat-up Toyota Corolla who followed me every time I left
my hotel. I presumed them to be representatives of one or
all of the three major intelligence agencies in Pakistan, but
their interest in me seemed exaggerated: a reflex from the
days of the spy-infested jihad. It would have mortified
the very amiable Pakistani diplomats in New Delhi who
arranged my visa and gave me, an Indian writer, what I
later learnt was an unprecedented liberty of travel within
Pakistan. But then to be an Indian in Pakistan – or, for that
matter, a Pakistani in India – is to be trapped by the prickly

nationalisms of the two neighbouring countries; it is to be automatically suspect.

Not that the spies did anything – or even looked – particularly ominous: the most visible amongst them, a plump, rosy-cheeked man in a pink salwar kurta, could easily have been one of the shopkeepers standing idle behind open sackfuls of dry fruits in the narrow, dark rooms of the old bazaar.

Still, if you are not used to being followed and watched, it can get stifling: the world seems full of a vague menace; the friendly, rather camp bellboy with slicked-down hair that you think you have tipped generously turns into an ungrateful informer (so does, at one point, everyone else); and the liveliest street scene begins to look like an elaborate preparation for an arrest.

Paranoia was what the spies embodied, and then, by their very presence, instilled in me. But there was a deeper unease I felt throughout the first three weeks I spent in Pakistan, waiting to go to Afghanistan: an unease about Islam and Muslims I had so far seen in others: something I sensed, while living in London, in the reports and outraged editorials in the British and American press, about the Taliban and Osama bin Laden and other Islamic extremists and to which I thought I would be immune after my experience of Kashmir.

Tens of thousands of people – militants, soldiers, civilians – have been killed since the uprising began in 1990. The Indian press prefers to describe the situation in the valley as a spillover from the jihad in Afghanistan, the timid Kashmiris having been overwhelmed by Pakistani and Afghan terrorists looking to wage fresh holy wars.

This broad picture, which depicted Pakistan and Islamic fundamentalists as the major villains, had blurred and then dissolved altogether during the several weeks I spent in Kashmir the previous year: most Kashmiris still followed an unorthodox Sufi version of Islam, and the brutalities of the 400,000 Indian soldiers in the valley was what had pushed a small number of young Kashmiri Muslims into jihadi extremism.

My articles on Kashmir appeared in an American magazine. Soon after they came out, officials from the Indian IB (Intelligence Bureau) visited my retired parents in India and interrogated them at some length about my 'pro-Pakistan' proclivities (which would have been confirmed for them when the Pakistani High Commissioner in New Delhi praised my articles in print and then, not long afterwards, arranged my exceptionally generous visa for Pakistan). Senior Indian columnists denounced me as unpatriotic and while wondering what would lead an apparently well-to-do upper-caste Hindu to betray his country in an American magazine, concluded that I was pandering to white pro-Muslim audiences in the West.

This was optimistic. In the days before 9/11, you wouldn't have known that such audiences existed, judging from the little attention paid to Kashmir, or Chechnya – another place where Muslims led a popular but hopeless uprising against a powerful pro-West nation-state – in the British or American press. Bereft of any recognizable context, the international news pages often seemed to offer a kind of brisk atrocity-mongering; part of their purpose seemed to be to verify the free world's privileges – as with the luxuries on display in the more expansive sections on shopping, food, sex, and celebrities; and Islam with all its diversity appeared primarily as the West's 'other', in the way communism once had been: the aggressive ideology of an underprivileged and dangerously deluded people.

It wasn't a conclusion I ever expected myself to reach about Islam and Muslims, particularly when, soon after returning from Kashmir, I thought of travelling to Pakistan and Afghanistan. I wanted to find out more about the CIA-led jihad in the 1980s and the rise of the Taliban, although there were related, less specific things I was curious about. One evening in Srinagar, an old Muslim politician, routinely described as 'fundamentalist' in the Indian papers, had spoken to me of how the West feared Islam even more since the demise of communism because it alone offered an alternative to the modern civilization of the West. It was hard for me then to work through such large generalizations. Later, when I began to read more in Islamic history, it became clearer to me how quickly, after the centuries of cultural and technological backwardness, the West had caught up with, and then begun to politically subjugate, the Islamic world in the nineteenth and twentieth centuries.

As it turned out, it wasn't very difficult to understand how people in demoralized societies could grow inflexible while trying to protect their older lifestyles. But this understanding came from the books I read in London, before I spent any time in a Muslim-majority country; and when, not long after I arrived in Peshawar from London, Jamal said, 'They are all such fanatics here,' I immediately warmed towards him, for I had found myself silently nurturing this commonplace prejudice, although I wouldn't have wanted to articulate it myself.

Jamal worked as a sub-editor for the *Frontier Post*, one of Peshawar's English-language dailies, at whose offices

I spent many hours on those bleak winter evenings. As I drove up to the box-like narrow building, the three spies parked their car a few metres behind, on an empty lot where scrawny dogs loitered around mounds of assorted rubbish. The men had already ordered tea and barely looked at me as I walked past the pale mist-blurred lights of the tea-shacks. Inside, at reception, an old Pathan in a coarse-textured military coat hunched over a rickety table, a Kalashnikov leaning against the seat of his wicker chair; on the floor beside his feet squatted a bar heater, and occasionally he would bend towards its weak orange glow, palms stretched and facing outwards, to gather some warmth. Upstairs, low doors led in and out of one cramped smoke-filled room after another; and in the room where I usually sat, a windowless cube really, the cigarette smoke stayed suspended in the air, the delicately curled plumes outlined against green walls and brown paper files and ageing computers with grimy screens.

It was a difficult time for the newspaper. Its owner, a local Pathan businessman called Rahmat Shah Afridi, had been arrested in 1999 on a charge of drugs trading. His son, a young easily distracted man who ran the paper now, told me that the small amount of cannabis found in his father's Mercedes had been planted there by agents of Mian Nawaz Sharif, then prime minister of Pakistan. It seemed like a typical Pakistani story: big men pursuing small private feuds and vendettas – and perhaps not entirely inaccurate: a few weeks after I left Pakistan, a special anti-narcotics court in Lahore sentenced Afridi to death. In any case, the smaller people were suffering: the staff had been working without salaries for three months.

But the shared austerity had made people jollier; the

door to the room opened every two minutes to reveal a newcomer, announcing his presence with a joke, an anecdote, a filched cigarette, and a curious friendly glance at the visitor from India. A teenage boy, his oversized brown salwar flapping around his ankles, kept bringing trays full of chipped cups steaming with thick milky tea; the rim of the cup's bottom would be already wet by the time you took your cup, and there were so many visitors that at the end of three hours the broad dusty table glistened all over with small overlapping circles.

Jamal was as much of a cigarette-cadger and tea-drinker as anyone there. But he looked restless amidst the bonhomie of his colleagues, among whose ruddy handsome Pashtun, or Pathan, faces his swarthy blunt features, so much like that of a South or East Indian, looked alien. I often felt his dull yellow eyes fixed upon my face; there was, I sensed, something he wished to tell me in private; and when the moment came early one evening, it was this difference that he was so keen to establish.

I hadn't been misled by his appearance. He was a Bengali, from Bangladesh. In 1975, when the country was just four years old, he had, as a young captain in the Bangladeshi army, taken part in the military coup against the government. He had been present on the morning when the prime minister, Sheikh Mujibur Rahman and his family were gunned down at their official residence. 'An accident,' he said, 'we didn't mean to kill him.' Whether accidental or not, the moment was firmly in the past, part of Bangladesh's history. But Jamal had spent the quarter-century since then dealing with the consequences.

After the 1975 coup, he spent four more years in Bangladesh, waging a futile insurgency against the government, before finally escaping to Pakistan. There was no other choice: Pakistan, still bitter about its lost province, was the only country that wouldn't deport him straight back to Bangladesh where he was sure to be executed for Rahman's murder.

Jamal hadn't liked his new country one bit, however. He had arrived in Pakistan just as General Zia-ul-Haq was beginning his programme of Islamization; there was enough of the liberal Bengali, the reader of Tagore and Nazrul Islam, in Jamal to be repelled by the brutal imposition of religion on everyday life. But he couldn't object too loudly; as a political refugee, he had to be grateful that he wasn't being hanged or shot. He had to manage as best he could; and so he had done, moving from job to job, city to city, from one kind of meanness to another.

Jamal's story was refined and embellished over several evenings. I wasn't always sure how to respond to it, especially when he added that he had a wonderful book inside him. After all, he had been eyewitness to the murder of Rahman, and the world was still waiting to hear the truth behind those events in Bangladesh in 1975.

The heaviness in his yellow eyes disappeared briefly when he said this. I didn't feel like telling him that all he had was a story; that a book was something else; and that the world wasn't much interested in what had happened that morning in Dacca all those years ago.

I didn't want to discourage or alienate him. He had known such a damaged life, and then only a kind of survival in Pakistan. Besides, he was on my side: a fellow stranger in Pakistan, adrift among the fanatics with whom Pakistan appeared to be, during my first days there, alarmingly replete: there were the black-turbanned heavy-bearded leaders of the Taliban, arriving at their embassy in Islamabad in gleaming new Pajero cars; the retired general in Rawalpindi declaiming on the nobility of jihad; the crudely painted donation boxes for the jihad in Kashmir in the bazaars; the fundamentalist demagogues in small towns threatening to march upon Islamabad if the sharia (Islamic law) and interest-free banking weren't immediately introduced; the tribals in the so-called self-administering areas near the Afghan border cutting off a few arms in their attempts at proper Islamic justice. Almost every day, Sunnis murdered Shias and vice versa; a few young mujahedin achieved *shahadat*, or martyrdom, in Indian Kashmir – and the newspapers alone, while reporting on all-consuming religious obsessions, could take you to the point where you began to sense something hard and fierce in even the simple devotion of the skull-capped men half-prostrate, on chilly evenings, on the streets of Peshawar.

But here I had to look out for my own prejudices. There had been many Muslims in the railway towns of North and Central India where I had grown up. I couldn't distinguish them from the low-caste Hindus among the railway labour gangs my father supervised. My father certainly had Muslim colleagues. But I cannot remember identifying any among the exhausted men in sweat-drenched white shirts and grey pants who returned home with my father for a cup of tea after a long day out on the tracks, although the tea must have been served to them not in cups but the special glasses kept aside in our kitchen for Muslims and low-caste Hindus.

Most Muslims in the towns of my childhood were, in fact, very poor – much more so than us – and this was the reason I noticed them. They lived in ghettos inside the older parts of the town, where, after the expansiveness of the British-built cantonment and Civil Lines and Railway Colony, the streets and houses suddenly shrank and were edged with open drains, the women disappeared behind sinister black burkas, flimsy rags curtained off the hanging carcasses at the butchers' shops, and the gaunt-faced men with pointed beards standing outside dark houses looked quite capable of the brutality that our prejudices ascribed to them.

The prejudices were bred partly by our own lower-middle-class deprivations: the anxieties about money, status, and security that came to be related, in the usual unreflective way, to the alien-looking community in our midst. We weren't the kind of people who incited or ever took part in Hindu–Muslim riots. But we did believe the stereotype that fuelled these brief explosions of rage and despair; we had no trouble imagining the bearded Muslim as a fundamentally violent aggressor, who could murder a Hindu with as much avidity and relish as he slaughtered the cow whose chopped-up flesh, thrown inside temple courtyards, usually inaugurated the savagery.

Another quite common, and somewhat subtler, cliché presented Muslims as backward-looking, as a drag on modernizing India, if not fifth columnists for Pakistan. Of course, the blunter dismissal was: Why don't these Muslims simply go to Pakistan? After all India had been partitioned in 1947 in order to create a new homeland for Indian Muslims. Pakistan was what most of them had asked for, so what were they doing in India?

It seems a crude question now; but it wasn't easy to answer, although politicians and other privileged men tried. However, their assertion that India was a secular country which was open to people from all religions didn't convince those of us – upper-caste Hindus – who lived in straitened circumstances and practised as well as suffered discrimination. And so, feeling frustrated and demoralized ourselves, we redirected most of the pity and scorn with which if we could, we would have seen our own lives. Most Hindu women probably deserved as much sympathy as was expended, in any cursory discussions of the minorities, on Muslim women, who were imagined to be leading terribly oppressed lives, forced to breed like rabbits and wrap themselves in heavy burkas.

The clichés bubbled up only when we noticed the Muslims. For the most part this depressed minority was invisible – and remained so for me even after I left home and went to university in Allahabad, where Hindu caste politics in the 1980s managed to overshadow Hindu–Muslim discord.

In the late 1980s, when I moved to a university in Delhi, the Hindu nationalist agitation to demolish the Babri mosque in Ayodhya had just picked up all over North India. There was much opposition to this inside my university campus; in fact, it was there, in the isolated and artificial world of university politics, that I became slightly more aware of the peculiar status of Indian Muslims. The student politicians organized almost daily protests inside the campus, which many of the Muslim students – most of whom came from the nearby riot-prone town of Aligarh – joined, and where one speaker after another denounced the Hindu nationalists for attempting to destroy the great Indian traditions of tolerance and accommodation.

The student leaders were eager to make themselves

known; they worked hard to make their protests as noisy and disruptive as they could, and the library, where I spent most of my time, was often closed early in the evenings.

The fuss over a disused tottering mosque in the middle of nowhere seemed excessive. Then came the day, in December 1992, when the mosque was demolished by a frenzied Hindu mob.

The student politicians in the campus raged for some weeks afterwards; but the Muslim students stayed away from their rallies. They appeared bitter and haunted. I began to look differently at them as they huddled around the dining table and spoke in low voices, eating swiftly all the while with their fingers.

I still couldn't feel involved. I had my own anxieties to deal with; the university degree I was working towards was only the first stage in what then seemed a long slow climb out of the relative poverty my family had lived in for much of my childhood. Occasionally, I would attend the after-dinner lectures by visiting left-wing journalists and academics – articulate, suave men who discussed the historical bonds between Hindus and Muslims and the uniquely syncretic civilization of India. These ideas about India's past and present didn't always match my experience – the sense I had of the distrust and hostility between Hindus and Muslims, and the keener sense I'd had, in the course of my travels through small-town India, of the stagnant resentments of the Muslim ghettos. But I didn't have the courage to contradict them then, and even now feel insecure before such powerful liberal pieties.

Pakistan has its own marginalized but vigorous liberals: indeed its small English-language press is intellectually more adventurous and engaging than its Indian counterpart. This is probably because the country seems to have few pieties left over from its fifty years of existence. The bookstores are full of such titles as *The Years of Disillusionment*, and *Whither Pakistan?*; the newspapers carry long letters by retired army men expressing concern over the number of educated Pakistanis wanting to emigrate.

Very early in Pakistan's history, its foundational myth had been broken: a shared religion, it turned out, couldn't solve the problem of how people with different ethnic and linguistic backgrounds were to live together. Urdu-speaking Muslims from India, arriving in large numbers in Sindh, found themselves resented by the poor Sindhis, who in turn felt oppressed by the rich and dominant majority of Punjabi-speakers in the north. The Bengalis revolted and broke away in the early 1970s; the Baluchi attempt to secede was put down with a lot of difficulty; and the disastrous Pakistani imperative to control events in Afghanistan grew out of the urgent need to pacify the Pashtun separatists of the North-West Frontier. The country, which many Hindus in India still imagined to be the natural home of Indian Muslims, had created its own ghettos, where resentments were anything but stagnant.

India has had its share of restless minorities: the Tamils, the Sikhs, and the Nagas. But it has also had a consistent political life; the semi-democratic institutions it inherited from the British. Since Partition, elected politicians themselves have wrecked Pakistan's frail democratic structures when given half a chance by the army officers and the bureaucrats, who have otherwise been the real rulers: the major newspaper story in Pakistan when I was there in early 2005 offered details about how a few army officers working for the ISI cobbled together a coalition of quasi-Islamic political parties under Nawaz Sharif in order to overthrow the government of Benazir Bhutto in 1990.

The rulers of course lived separately, in well-fortified enclaves, indifferent to all the associations of Third World sleaze they gave off: there wasn't much subtlety in the town houses with their carpets and chandeliers and servants and guards with automatic rifles, or the large farmhouses outside cities, whose brick-walled boundaries meandered far and invisibly into the countryside, and where cheap French wine bootlegged by African diplomats flowed by the glimmering pool, and people discussed the latest article on Kosovo in the *New York Review of Books*, and grew very worried about the 'bearded fundos' and the imminent – or, depending on who you talked to, ongoing – Talibanization of Pakistan.

The phrase 'Talibanization of Pakistan' was one I heard often. It was a new way of referring to troubles that had begun much earlier, in 1979 in fact, when Soviet troops entered Afghanistan and the United States responded by arming anti-communist Afghans with the help of the military dictator of Pakistan, General Zia-ul-Haq.

Although something of a tyrant, Zia was not without his Pakistani supporters. His Islamic zeal was admired by those religious parties who received government patronage for their largely unsuccessful attempt to Islamize Pakistan. He was popular, too, among senior officers in the military. As he himself described it, Lt. General Hamid Gul was one of the early jihadis in the military, and much loved by Zia, who first made him director of military intelligence and then director-general of the ISI. While holding these positions in the 1980s, Gul was one of the three or four most powerful men in Pakistan – who, under Zia's patronage, could get away with just about anything.

But then in 1988 Zia and other senior army men died in a still-mysterious air crash. Benazir Bhutto, the daughter of the man Zia had hanged, became prime minister of Pakistan; and got rid of Gul at the first available opportunity in 1989. Gul turned into an intriguer: he led the frustrated power-hungry officers of the ISI in a successful conspiracy to bring down Bhutto in 1990.

Retirement from the army diminished Gul. He attempted to reinvent himself as a full-time jihadi, writing columns in the Urdu papers and sending long faxes, as an exasperated editor told me, to the offices of the English-language press, usually denouncing the new military government for surrendering before India and America.

Gul's awareness of his lost authority seemed present in his swift response on the telephone when I told him that the men shadowing me might stop me from travelling to his home in the Chaklala air base near Rawalpindi. 'I'll see', he said, in a controlled voice, 'who dares stops you from visiting my home.'

Palladian columns – the mansions of military officers in Pakistan are always grand – guarded the front of Gul's house which was otherwise remarkably un-Roman. On the walls of the living room, framed photos of the Kaaba in Mecca seemed to look away from the suffocating excess in the middle: the huge crystal decorations on the centre table, the shiny life-size brass deer, the green satin upholstery, the animal-skin rugs, and the glittering trophies.

Beardless, and sporting a trimmed moustache, western-style tweed jacket and vigorously polished brown moccasins, Gul seemed closer in style to his background as a cavalry officer than to the austere world of jihad. His English was mostly Urdu-accented and only occasionally, when he ceased his loud declamations, lapsed into the Sandhurst inflections and phrases of an older generation of army men. He dealt awkwardly with my more personal questions, revealing only, with obvious irritation, that his family was originally from the hilly district of Swat, and that he had gone to a village school before attending a government college in Lahore.

These were humble origins when compared to the 'brown sahibs' Gul was known for attacking at every available opportunity – the men Anglicized and groomed to assume power at influential establishments like Aitchison College, Lahore, and St Patrick's College, Karachi. His background partly accounted for Gul's immodest ambitions and claims. In February 1989, when the Soviet army withdrew from Afghanistan, he was, as director general of the ISI, leading the jihad. As he described it, his role in the jihad had begun even while he was a lowly brigadier. Three weeks after the Soviet intervention in Afghanistan in 1979, he wrote and circulated a policy paper, in which he advocated Pakistani support for a low-intensity guerrilla war against the Soviet Union and their Afghan allies, gradually extending it right into the Muslim-majority Central Asian provinces of the Soviet Union.

The paper reached Zia, who was impressed by Gul's energy and ambition. A meeting with the general followed. 'I told General Zia', Gul said, 'that if we defeated the Russians, and I was very optimistic that we would, then there was no reason that the borders of our great Islamic world should stop at the Amu dariya.' (Amu is the Oxus river, which formed the boundary between Afghanistan and the former Soviet Union.)

The paper, Gul claimed, was read carefully by high-placed officials of the CIA, and formed the basis of later incursions into what William Casey, the director of the CIA under Ronald Reagan, described as the 'soft underbelly of the Soviet Union'.

Much of this seemed like boasting, however. The cold warriors of the Carter administration had long been waiting for the Soviets to slip up in Afghanistan. Zbigniew Brzezinski, national security adviser to President Carter, who wanted to 'sow shit in the Soviet backyard', had arranged for clandestine aid to the radical Islamists in Pakistan a few months before Soviet troops arrived in Afghanistan. The Soviet intervention gave them the pretext they needed to raise the ante. In the letter Brzezinski wrote to Carter on the day the Soviet army entered Afghanistan, he was exultant: 'Now, we can give the Soviet Union its Vietnam War.' It was this trap for the Soviets that the CIA, under Casey, deepened through the early and mid 1980s by providing billions of dollars' worth of arms and aid.

In fact, Casey, a veteran of the OSS, and a fanatical cold warrior, wanted the ISI to involve the Muslims of the Soviet Union in the jihad; and he wasn't satisfied with the ISI-arranged smuggling of thousands of Korans into what is now Uzbekistan and Tajikistan, or with the distribution of heroin among Soviet troops. One officer of the ISI, and a critic of Gul, told me that the ISI received plenty of unofficial encouragement from Casey himself to attempt operations more damaging to the Soviet Union – but nothing that could be traced back to the CIA or the government of the United States. The senior officers of the ISI, flush with unaudited funds, were running their own little battles by the mid 1980s; and one of them arranged for the mining and bombing of military installations a few kilometres deep inside Soviet territory. The Soviet Ambassador in Islamabad immediately left some ominous messages at the Pakistan foreign office; and Gul, confronted with the possibility of a Third World War, hastily had to withdraw the saboteurs from Soviet territory.

When I met him, Gul had nothing but abuse for his former bankrollers in the CIA: 'A self-serving people. All they wanted was to turn Afghanistan into a Vietnam for the Soviet Union. They used us for this purpose, and then they lost interest after the Soviets withdrew.'

This was a commonplace sentiment in Pakistan: you heard it from liberal journalists who had from the very beginning highlighted the folly and risk of fighting other people's wars; you heard it from the jihadis hoping to fight another day. American involvement in Afghanistan and Pakistan had become the story of the cynical arrogance of cold warriors like Brzezinski and Casey.

The jihad that Gul imagined himself to be leading turned out to be under neither his nor the ISI's control. Many different realpolitik interests had brought it to Pakistan, and would, in time, take it away. The Americans wanted to rouse the Muslims of the world against the Soviet Union; the Saudi royal family, which matched the American assistance dollar for dollar, wanted its own version of Sunni Islam, Wahhabism, to triumph over the then-resurgent Shi'ism of Ayatollah Khomeini of Iran. For these larger battles, Pakistan was merely a base, where CIA operatives could, for a while at least, mingle happily with such rich Arab jihadis as Osama bin Laden.

After the Soviet withdrawal was agreed in Geneva in 1987, American interest in both the jihad and Afghanistan dwindled. The CIA promptly scaled back and soon ended its aid to Pakistan and the mujahedin.

Left pretty much to their own devices, the ISI and Gul began to flounder. In 1988 came the still-mysterious fire in Ojhri, halfway between Islamabad and Rawalpindi, in which the 10,000 tons of arms and ammunition supplied by the CIA to the ISI for the Afghan mujahedin exploded in a spectacularly violent firework display visible in a twelve-mile radius. Many people took it to be the beginning of war between India and Pakistan; the rain of rockets and missiles lasted a whole day, killing 100 people and injuring thousands more.

Then, in 1989, Gul abandoned the usual mode of guerrilla warfare in Afghanistan, and conceived and supervised what turned out to be a disastrous frontal assault by the mujahedin on the communist-held city of Jalalabad in Afghanistan. Four months later, the mujahedin had lost 3,000 men and were further away than ever from taking Jalalabad. The Afghan communist government in Kabul lasted another three years, during which the mujahedin turned to declaring jihad against each other.

The divisions between the seven mujahedin parties recognized by the ISI had been deepening since 1979, due less to ethnic and linguistic differences than to the inequitable way in which the ISI parcelled out the largesse from America and Saudi Arabia. The ISI under Gul was most generous to a particularly brutal mujahedin leader called Gulbuddin Hekmatyar, whose aggressive Islamism remained apart from the production and smuggling of heroin that created his wealth and power. The ISI expected Hekmatyar to install a pro-Pakistan government in Kabul after the fall of the communists. But Hekmatyar turned out to be unacceptable to most other mujahedin leaders, especially those who had fought the Soviets without much American or Pakistani assistance.

When the Tajik mujahedin commander, Ahmad Shah Massoud, finally drove out the communist government of Kabul in 1992, a full-scale civil war broke out in Afghanistan. Hekmatyar, backed by the ISI, rocket-bombed Kabul for months – more people died in the city during the fighting in the early 1990s than during the decade-long jihad against the Russians. International powers stepped in once again to bankroll various factions: the Saudis supported the Sunni fundamentalists, Iran backed the Shia Hazaras, Tajikistan and Uzbekistan had their own favourites among the Tajik and Uzbek mujahedin; and the ISI hadn't lost faith in Hekmatyar when in 1994 the student militia of the Taliban suddenly emerged out of nowhere and conquered most of Afghanistan.

Gul, still trying to prop up Hekmatyar, initially denounced the Taliban as CIA agents. These actions were more than personal or professional misjudgements and failures; they undermined whole societies. Reckless but high-placed adventurers like Gul, pursuing absurd fantasies of a pan-Islamic empire, had taken a largely poor and illiterate country to the edge.

Gul himself had done well out of it all. There was the Palladian-fronted house in Rawalpindi; there was a farmhouse and, rumours said, more properties elsewhere; there was the lucrative transport business that his daughter apparently ran in Islamabad.

And there were new jihads and jihadis to root for. 'These Americans now accuse Osama bin Laden of terrorism. Once upon a time they used to call upon him in Peshawar and ask him to recruit more Arabs for the jihad,' said Gul, anxious, like all jihadis I was to meet in Pakistan, to claim a special intimacy with bin Laden. 'I met him in Sudan in 1993. Such a wise and intelligent man. So much spirituality on his face. But this is the effect of jihad. It is a very noble state to be in. That's why I look so young, although I am sixty-four years old. Jihad keeps me young, gives me a great purpose in life.'

Gul's enemies in Pakistan – and there were many – scoffed at his Islamic fervour: it was, for them, another kind of opportunism: a private pipeline to power and to at least some of the money flowing in from rich Muslim countries for organizations devoted to Islamic causes. And listening to them you could easily begin to think of jihad as another racket in a poor backward country. Certainly, renewed faith alone doesn't account for the many sectarian groups that sprang up over previous years, whose exploits – shootouts, bomb explosions, arson – dominated the national news.

Many sects and ideologies of the Islamic world have travelled to Pakistan: the Muslim Brotherhood in Egypt influenced the leaders of the Jamiat-i-Islami, the biggest of the religious parties, several of whom had studied at Cairo; the Saudis arrived late, but their open-fisted generosity has ensured a speedy embrace of Wahhabism among the poorer members of the clergy: a wall of Sunni madrasas partly funded with Saudi money lie alongside the borders that Pakistan and Afghanistan share with Shia-majority Iran.

Among these imported Islamic schools, the Deobandis are the most powerful, and closest to the Wahhabis. The name comes from the original madrasa set up in 1866 in a small town near Delhi called Deoband. The madrasa was part of the insular Muslim response to British rule in the nineteenth century: the work of men who felt that Western-style education of the kind proposed by the British, and embraced by the Hindus, would fracture the Muslim community; men who were convinced that a training in the fundamentals of the Koran and the Sharia would shield Indian Muslims from the corruptions of the modern world.

A couple of years ago, I read an American academic's book about Deoband; then one hot summer day, while I was on my way to the hill station of Mussoorie, I saw a sign for the town itself alongside the rutted road. The building – a wide low quadrangle overlooked by minarets – seemed shrunken in the vast dusty land. I wasn't welcome inside; the thin timid-looking young men in skullcaps didn't want to talk to me; wouldn't even let me in. I later discovered that Muslims had recently been massacred in a town not far from the madrasa.

My image of Deoband after that was of the fearful Muslims marooned among the Hindus of the Indo-Gangetic plain. In Pakistan, however, this image dissolved fast. The large courtyard of the Binori Town madrasa in Karachi, one of the largest and oldest of Deobandi institutions in Pakistan, has marble floors. Students from Africa, Central Asia, the Philippines, and Malaysia swarmed confidently through the large complex, its several hostels and kitchens, although in the classrooms a Koran-oriented syllabus first created in India in the nineteenth century was still being used. The noticeboard displayed beautifully typed appeals for volunteers in various jihads in Kashmir, Chechnya, the Philippines, and Afghanistan. The Taliban seemed a big draw, and quite appropriately: most of the Taliban's leadership as well as many of the foot soldiers of the Taliban have emerged from the Deobandi madrasas in Pakistan and southern Afghanistan.

It was Jamal who said, 'You must go to the Deobandi madrasas. That's where a lot of the Taliban were trained, and a lot of Pakistani young men there also go to Afghanistan to fight for the Taliban. You'll find lots of fanatics there.'

I did want to find a few fanatics; I also wanted to travel to Afghanistan. On both fronts, however, my attempts were being thwarted. At the Taliban's chaotic embassy in Islamabad, where gruffly inefficient former soldiers in black turbans ran or limped in and out of rooms furnished with peeling paint and dusty rugs, my visa application, deposited and redeposited several times, seemed as much of an illusion as the existence of an Afghan state or government. It wasn't easy to find the jihadis. The names Jamal sold me – at quite a high rate: he said he hadn't been paid his salary, he needed the money, and I didn't argue – turned out to be those of men long retired, and living now in isolation. All the leads offered to me by the other English-language journalists I knew came to nothing. A Pakistani acquaintance in London had warned me that this might happen, that the jihadis knew too well how the English-language press in Pakistan felt towards them and were suspicious of anyone carrying their references. I began hanging out at the offices of the Urdu publications, many of which were sympathetic to the jihadis; and it was at the office of a plump young editor in Islamabad, one of the professional cheerleaders of the jihad, and another self-proclaimed friend of Osama bin Laden, that I ran into Shafiq.

Shafiq looked old, although he was only in his mid forties. When the editor introduced him as a veteran of the jihad in Afghanistan, he raised the sleeves of his kurta and displayed a bullet wound in his left arm. He didn't speak much; his Urdu was a low growl – the furtive tone, it turned out, of a fixer. His demands for money were more extravagant than Jamal's; and we were forced to meet early in the morning or late at night – the only time when my spies were off duty. It was difficult to arrange these meetings, for Shafiq's mobile phone, he claimed, was tapped by the ISI. But he usually had the information I required.

It took him some time to come up with someone to meet in Karachi: it wasn't his 'area', he said. And then he added, with the glint in his eyes that always appeared in expectation of more money, that he had found someone special for me: an activist from the Sipah-e-Sahaba, one of the most dreaded anti-Shia groups in Pakistan, whose acronym, SSP, featured often in the daily papers, usually with regard to attacks on or by Shias. He would, Shafiq promised, using the English words, provide me with 'good material'. All I had to do was shake off the spies and show up at the madrasa.

One early morning, when the spies were still asleep, I took a flight from Peshawar to Karachi, relieved to find no strange men in beaten-up cars awaiting me at the other end. Everywhere on the wide swift boulevard leading to the city centre there were signs of Karachi's financial eminence: the billboards, the glass-fronted boutiques, and the fancy patisseries. I had expected a meaner place, acting out its reputation as the setting for violent battles between militant groups of Muslim migrants from India and the police; and instead, with the spies gone, in this port city – its warm sea-scrubbed air and clear light and colonial buildings so much like Bombay, and so unlike the ingrown seediness of Peshawar or the diseased grandeur of Lahore and the wide suburban vacancies of Islamabad – suddenly I felt freer than I had ever before in Pakistan.

I felt, I think, as a Pakistani visitor to the city might; and it was as a Pakistani journalist from London that I introduced myself to Rahmat. The deception was necessary, Shafiq had told me: the connection to India would throw Rahmat; he would not want to talk. In any case, it gave me a new assurance the evening I went to the Binori Town madrasa: in my salwar kurta that I had bought earlier in the day, I could have been one of the hundreds of young men heading in and out of the evening *namaz*.

Rahmat was waiting for me, as Shafiq had said he would be, at the small shop selling Afghan caps and Korans just inside the tall gateway to the madrasa. He was younger than I had expected; and the grimy white kurta, the worn plastic slippers, and the dense beard that framed his face, only highlighted his exceptional good looks, wide delicate cheekbones and shyly quizzical eyes.

We sat and talked in one of the garishly lit shops and cafes that hemmed in the madrasa. Shafiq had exaggerated:

Rahmat wasn't a student but an odd-job man at the madrasa; and he had never been a member of the Sipah-e-Sahaba. He wasn't even sure whether the madrasa he had gone to near the city of Faisalabad was Deobandi – he only remembered that the teachers emphasized jihad as the primary duty of Muslims. As for the SSP, some members of the group had helped him and his family after his brother had been charged with murdering a Shia landlord.

The murder had happened near Rahmat's ancestral village in the Punjab, where his father had an auto-repair shop. Rahmat had been languishing there after his stint at the madrasa, along with his parents, four brothers and two sisters, waiting for a job to come his way. Things hadn't been bad in the 1980s, in the days of Zia-ul-Haq's Islamization, when you could still get a job after a madrasa education. But Rahmat had gone to the madrasa at the wrong time; and had come out of it to join the hundreds of thousands of unemployable young men in Pakistan. Some of his friends had mustered enough money to travel to the Gulf, and he was hoping to follow them when one day his brother murdered the landlord.

The landlord was a much-hated figure among his tenants, despised for the mistresses he kept in semi-servitude as well as for his financial crookedness. When he had falsified the records of Rahmat's family's ownership of a piece of fertile land, Rahmat's father and brothers had been too powerless to argue. But then he had tried to manipulate the mortgage on Rahmat's father's auto-repair shop. This had enraged Rahmat's brother.

Rahmat said, '*Zamindar bada powerful banda tha*' ('The landlord was a powerful man'). The many relatives of the dead man arrived in a Pajero and flogged Rahmat's father in front of his family, before destroying the auto-repair shop. The police ransacked his house a few times; even locked Rahmat up for a few days, although he himself had been in the fields with a friend at the time of the murder.

The revolving disco-like lights on the ceiling glistened on Rahmat's perspiring face as he spoke. The shop was busy. It seemed, rather incongruously, to be part of the celebration of wealth and leisure I had seen elsewhere in the city: the solemn-faced skull-capped visitors to the mosque inside the madrasa were easily outnumbered by the paunchy men in tight jeans and T-shirts who staggered out from badly parked Mercedes cars, strode fast to the shops and then returned holding mini-mountains of shiny cello-phane-wrapped sweetboxes.

Shoe-polish urchins, their thin arms slinging wooden boxes, lapped at their knees. It was them Rahmat watched, turning his head away from me. His heavy-lidded eyes were even more unreadable when he turned back, and then, as if out of habit, he wiped his mouth and then his forehead with the sleeves of his kurta, already damp from his pre-*namaz* ablutions.

Only the men at the mosque in the nearby town, Rahmat said, had been able to help his family. They had employed his teenage younger brother at their own madrasa; they had worked through their contacts in the police to ease the pressure on Rahmat's family. Rahmat knew vaguely that they were members of the SSP, and opposed to the Shias; but he hadn't given it much thought. Then one warm evening in 1995 one of the SSP men, someone not much older than Rahmat, who often led the *namaz* on Fridays, called for him.

When Rahmat got to the mosque on his bicycle, he found a small crowd of young men already there, including a couple of men from his village, people who had been tormented by the now-dead landlord. None of them knew why they had been summoned. Then the man who had called them arrived, accompanied by an Afghan wearing a black turban, and addressed them briefly.

He said that the guest with him had come all the way from Afghanistan where a new jihad had commenced. There were many corrupt men like the landlords of Punjab in Afghanistan: they called themselves mujahedin, the man said, as though they were engaged in jihad, but they were no worse than bandits and rapists, and now a new force had arisen to vanquish them and establish the law of the Prophet. The soldiers fighting the jihad were young Talibs, students, but Allah was with them.

It was the first time Rahmat had heard about the students, or the Taliban. There had been several Afghans at his madrasa, but he had kept away from them. The Afghan refugees had had a bad reputation in his part of Pakistan; they were seen as liars and thieves. His father dealt with them all the time in his auto-repair shop: their heavy trucks that they had brought from Afghanistan damaged the roads, and the drivers were often high on opium.

And so when the Afghan man began to speak, Rahmat was sceptical. He spoke Urdu with a heavy Pashto accent that, Rahmat remembered, made some of the men smile. But the Afghan remained serious, and he didn't waste much time: he said he had come to ask for volunteers for the jihad in Afghanistan. He couldn't promise much in return, except food and shelter; the way of Jihad was not strewn with roses; it was a holy duty for Muslims, and *sha-hadat*, martyrdom, was all they could expect from it.

Most of the young men weren't interested. But Rahmat, with a brother in jail and the auto-repair shop – the sole source of his family's income – now gone, couldn't so easily disregard what the Afghan had offered. His father and brothers wondered what he was getting into but didn't try to stop him. Rahmat remembered riding with other young men in a chartered bus to Quetta in Baluchistan, and then crossing the border illegally one night. On the other side there were, along with Pashtun Afghans, many more Pakistanis. There were even Pakistani army officers at the training camp where Rahmat learnt to fire an automatic rifle, and also men from Chechnya, Kashmir and Uzbekistan. It was in this training camp, in a rocky valley near the border, that he had grown his beard, not under any pressure – although men in Afghanistan were required to wear four-inch-long beards – but because of his desire to be a good Muslim.

Rahmat and other people in his group had been at the camp for less than two weeks when they were summoned to the western provinces where the Taliban were fighting to capture the city of Herat. By the time Rahmat reached Herat, it was already under the control of the Taliban. He and his fellow mujahedin were like conquerors in the city. But it was a strange place. It was very cold; the locals spoke Persian, not Urdu or Pashto; they even looked like Iranians. Even more alien were the young Pashtun men of the Taliban who went around shutting down schools, smashing TVs and VCRs, and tearing up photos. One of them discovered a semi-nude photo of an Indian film actress in the tent Rahmat shared with eleven or twelve other Pakistanis, and there was some awkwardness between the Afghans and the Pakistani volunteers for a while after that.

Rahmat hadn't liked the rough ways of the Taliban: they were backward people, he thought. They were cruel to their women and religious minorities and military opponents; someone in his village had been forced to participate in the massacre of civilians belonging to the Shia Hazara community in central Afghanistan. Rahmat was a bit frightened of them. But he couldn't deny that they had brought peace to Afghanistan, and when the Pakistanis he was with spoke of imposing a similar peace in Pakistan, where there was so much injustice and banditry, it seemed like an attractive idea.

Rahmat hadn't stayed long in Afghanistan as he was wanted as a witness at the trial of his brother. He hadn't returned to Afghanistan after that, although other young men he knew in his village had gone and were still going to fight with the Taliban.

Back in his village Rahmat met up again with the men at the mosque. It was with one of them that he had come to the Binori Town madrasa three years ago and then stayed on. There was some money to be made doing small menial jobs for the students and teachers; Rahmat could eat cheaply and he could always find a place to sleep. Things were better here than in the Punjab where his brother was still in jail and his father close to death.

Rahmat had shaken his head when I first asked him if he wanted to eat anything. But when I ordered another plate of halwa, he was quick to reach out and place his hand on the arm of the waiter, startling him slightly. After the food came – an oily plateful of what looked to my furtive eyes like mutton – Rahmat became more expansive; his Urdu, replete so far with Punjabi slang, became more formal, full of difficult Arabic and Persian words. He began to speak with his mouth full, of the greatness and necessity of jihad, of how Muslims were being oppressed everywhere, in Kashmir, Afghanistan, Chechnya, Egypt, Palestine, how the Jews in Israel could get away with anything because they were supported by Western powers.

I had heard, and was to hear, a lot of this talk from both the leaders and the foot soldiers of the jihad. It wasn't without its quota of truth, and you had to be careful neither to dismiss it nor to swallow it whole. It was easier to see through the self-aggrandizement and deceptions of people like Hamid Gul. But the idea of oppression and injustice that Rahmat spoke of was more than just rhetoric he had picked up from the teachers at his madrasa and the ISI officers at the training camp in Afghanistan; it had a basis in his own experience of the world.

Rahmat was like the young men of my own class in the Indian small towns of the 1980s and early 1990s – people for whom the world didn't seem to have much place. The idea of religion as redemption, the unquestioning submission to one creed or philosophy – this was what my background had required of me, and it had taken some effort, and much luck, to be able to move away from it, to redefine myself as an individual, and to enter new, more complicated affiliations with the larger world.

Others weren't as lucky: these were people whose frustration and rage over their many deprivations could easily be appropriated into ideological crusades and for whom hallucinations of great power allayed their crushing sense

of a very real powerlessness. The Hindu nationalist movement – also funded primarily, like the jihad, from abroad,
from rich Hindus in the US and UK – had found its foot
soldiers among the young unemployed men in small towns.
These were the men who formed the faceless mobs, who
were in charge of the dirty stuff, of the necessary lynchings
and destruction.

The Hindu disaffection, however, was of a different
order: the young Hindus I knew were frustrated by their
exclusion from the middle class; they did not, despite their
rhetoric of an Indian golden age, seek radically to change
the ways of the world, or hold up alternative visions, as
Mahatma Gandhi once had, of what a good and true life
was, and could be. Even the most extreme Hindu ideologues did not, in the end, wish, like the jihadis, to
challenge or reject the knowledge and power of the West.
They were content to take the world as they found it, dominated by the West, and then find a niche for themselves in
it: they were, above all, sly materialists. This pragmatic collaboration with the West is what has produced the new
Hindu renaissance of the last 150 years – a regeneration of
which the software tycoons of Silicon Valley and the Indian
writers in English are related aspects. Gandhi's ambition –
to form a society as different as possible from that of the
West – has few takers left in India. Ironically, his distrust
and fear of Western modernity is now amplified best by the
radical Islamists of Pakistan, where a westernized postcolonial elite – those men from the posh colleges that
Hamid Gul despised, who now spoke helplessly in their
farmhouses of the Talibanization of Pakistan – had dis-
credited itself.

It is why, while India daily moves closer to the West,

Pakistan seems much further away. It is also why Rahmat, although he imagined me to be a Muslim, saw me essentially as an alien, someone very removed from him: a resident of London, the city of Sodom and Gomorrah; and why I was startled when, looking up from his hectically ravaged plate of mutton and rice, Rahmat asked me if the women in London went around with their legs exposed.

This was a question that came from my own past: the kind of thing I would turn around in my mind when I was still a boy in isolated towns, with no TV or cinema around to inhibit my imagination. It was strange and unsettling to think how quickly that past, along with all its peculiar material and sensory privations, had vanished; how dramatically my circumstances had changed. No one before me in my family had ever left India, while I spent much of the year in London, and travelled to many different parts of the world. I published in American and British newspapers and journals; depended upon them, in fact, for a living.

Globalization had also opened up the West; there was more space there for people like me – people who would have had to struggle harder for a similar space in their native countries. I still felt myself on the margins, writing about subjects that appeared remote from the preoccupations around me, the obsessions with food, sex, money, movies, celebrities that I saw reflected in the weekend papers in Britain. But the first cultural shock had worn off. As a colonial, I was a child, however distinctly, of the West. Britain was, after all, the place where I as an adult had chosen to be; and I had, in time, come to see something brittle and selfrighteous in my exasperation over the articles about boyfriends and hemlines.

In any case, I spent most of my time in London at my desk, and had only a shallow relationship with the world around me. In the beginning I was unsettled by the devout Muslims I would often see on Brick Lane, quite near my flat. However, as often happens, the more money you have the more liberal you become, the more in tune with the cosmopolitan city and its bland middle-class tolerance. In London, where I knew security and stability for the first time in my life, I became someone without a past; and as the months passed the Muslims faded into the promiscuous bustle of the gay discos, leather retailers, balti restaurants, music halls, coffee and bagel shops.

But this kind of Westernization can also be superficial: you can quickly lapse into an older cultural conservatism. Your political loyalties can be more mixed-up than you and other people assume. It explains my unease at the American embassy in Islamabad a few days after meeting Rahmat, where stern experts on the Taliban and Islamic fundamentalists kept using the words 'us' and 'them', impressing upon me the urgency of forcing 'those guys', the Taliban, to give up their special guest, Osama bin Laden. Although I, with my beard and Afghan cap, looked like one of 'them' – the desperate men just outside the embassy's fort-like walls – the Americans had no doubt where I belonged: I was one of 'us': part of a powerful imperial civilization that, in this remote vulnerable outpost, was denoted by bowling alleys, cocktail bars, and the framed photos of suburban barbecues on office walls.

*

No ambiguities existed for the diplomats: they defended the government they worked for with as much passion and vigour as the jihadis – the 'them' of their vocabulary – spoke of jihad; and they could make you feel that the war they were fighting was also your war, and the side we were all on had both truth and power behind it.

It was hard to demur when you considered the opposition. Far from offering a blueprint for a new civilization or society, the Taliban seemed perversely intent on annihilating the few bits and pieces of Afghanistan's cultural heritage that had survived the long war. I was in India when I heard the news about the Taliban's intention to destroy all Buddhist statues in Afghanistan. At that point I'd still not visited the country and I wasn't sure what was going on. I rang a Pakistani journalist in Peshawar. He confirmed some of the theories I had seen in the Pakistani papers on the internet: the Taliban were frustrated by the sanctions imposed on them by the UN, and wanted to draw international attention to the plight of Afghans facing drought and starvation; there was a struggle between the hardliners and moderates within the Taliban, and the former had won this time.

The journalist wasn't sure about the statues, however. The tall exposed Buddhas in Bamiyan had been around for centuries; they could not be removed. And the museum in Kabul, which held the best examples of Indo-Greek sculpture, had been looted long ago, first by the mujahedin who took over the city after the fall of the communist regime in 1992, and then by the Taliban in 1996. There was not much left; foreign journalists who toured the museum were shown only some rubble, although that could have come from anywhere. For years now, statues had been smuggled out of Afghanistan and transported as far as New York and Tokyo; you could still find a few with the antique dealers in the bazaars of Peshawar.

I had already seen some of these statues, almost by chance, in the somewhat banal setting of a house in an upper-middle-class suburb of Peshawar, where they stood in glass cases before a large fake fireplace. They belonged to General Naseerullah Babur, another of Pakistan's powerful military men, and Benazir Bhutto's 'favourite uncle'. He wouldn't say how he had got hold of the statues, most of which I recognized from photos I had seen, and only mumbled something about finding them during excavations. It wasn't hard to guess, however; and subsequently I discovered that the manner in which he had acquired the statues was as much of an open secret as his original sponsorship of the Taliban.

He was also responsible for suppressing a particularly savage civil war in Karachi between local Sindhis and Muslim migrants from India. In fact, Babur told me many such stories himself, his broad face often cracking into childlike smiles: he appeared every bit the retired man, who had made his little pile, albeit rather dubiously, and was eager to establish his role in great events: the brave Pashtun of legend, as an admiring taxi driver described him to me, who would patrol Karachi during the worst violence in an open, unescorted jeep.

Babur's connection with Afghanistan had begun when he was the governor of the North-West Frontier Province in the 1970s. It was then he first met the Afghan Islamists, who became famous names in the jihad, and introduced them to American diplomats in Islamabad.

Part 2

In 1993, Benazir Bhutto returned to power, three years after being overthrown by the ISI and Hamid Gul, and Babur became interior minister. By then, Afghanistan was in chaos. The roads, bridges, schools, orchards, and irrigation systems lay in ruins. But even more disastrous was the moral breakdown that occurred in the years after the Soviet withdrawal in 1989. The modern state with its law-enforcement policies had barely existed outside the cities, while civil war and the consequent displacement of millions of people further undermined the tribal and religious codes that had previously governed the lives of ordinary Afghans. Warlords and gangsters flourished in the vacuum. Gulbuddin Hekmatyar, the mujahedin favoured by the ISI, had already branched off into heroin manufacturing and smuggling; many other mujahedin commanders took to smuggling and highway robbery. Men with guns stood at improvised checkpoints on all major roads. The situation was particularly bad in the Pashtun-majority provinces of southern Afghanistan, where several commanders raped young boys and women and plundered at will.

One day in 1994, in a village near the city of Kandahar, a Pashtun man in his thirties called Mohammed Omar heard about two women who had been abducted and raped by some local commanders. Like many young Pashtuns from his village, Omar, the son of landless peasants, had participated in the jihad against local and foreign communists. He had been wounded several times, and lost his right eye. After the Soviet withdrawal he had recommenced teaching at his village madrasa. He was deeply aggrieved by the anarchy around him, and often spoke with his friends in the village about ways to end it and establish the law of the Koran. The news of the raped women finally incited him into action. He went out to the local madrasas and raised a band of thirty students for a rescue mission. The students mustered about sixteen rifles between themselves. They then went and freed the girls and hanged the commanders from the barrel of a tank. A few months later, there was another incident in which two commanders fought a gun battle in the streets of Kandahar over a boy both wished to rape. Once again, Omar showed up with his students, releasing the boy and executing the commanders.

These were the stories Rahmat had heard in his mosque in the Punjab; they were also the stories Babur heard in Islamabad. The fame of the Taliban had grown very fast. Afghans everywhere began to appeal to them for protection from the warlords. Very soon, requests for help, along with large cash donations, came to the Taliban from the traders and smugglers who needed peace and open roads in southern Afghanistan to ensure the transport of goods to Iran and the Central Asian republics.

Babur himself had long been looking into roads and oil and gas pipelines through Afghanistan to the Central Asian republics. There had also been much interest from multinational oil companies. But Kabul was still being fought over. The ISI, which both Babur and Bhutto distrusted, insisted on supporting Hekmatyar, who was far away from imposing the stability needed to conduct business in Afghanistan. The only other route to Central Asia ran through southern Afghanistan, but anyone taking it risked an infinite number of toll booths and other forms of banditry.

Babur produced a plan to rebuild the road from Pakistan to Herat with funding from international agencies; in

October 1994, he took a group of Western and Chinese diplomats on an exploratory trip to Herat. Later that month, he attempted something riskier: he arranged for thirty Pakistani trucks to drive through Afghanistan to the capital of Turkmenistan, Ashkhabad.

Babur told me that he was advised against this. The commanders who controlled the roads in southern Afghanistan were reportedly very angry with him. They hadn't been told about the visit with the diplomats; and thought it meant Babur was supporting the Taliban, who just a few days previously had captured a massive arsenal built up during the days when the CIA sent arms to the mujahedin.

Babur said, 'I went ahead. It was an experiment. I thought, let's see what happens.'

A few miles outside Kandahar, the convoy was stopped by local commanders. They ordered the Pakistani drivers, including some army officers, to park in a nearby village. The men were outnumbered and so did not resist, merely passing on to their superiors in Islamabad the demands from the commanders: money, share of the goods on the convoy, and a promise to stop supporting the Taliban.

For three days, Pakistani officials in Islamabad wondered what to do: a commando operation to rescue the convoy was discussed and finally dropped. Then, Babur asked the Taliban to help.

The students assaulted the village where the convoy was parked, and chased out the commanders and their men. That same evening they attacked Kandahar and after two days of fighting conquered the city and expelled the remaining warlords from the area.

This was the absurdly successful beginning of the military campaign that brought the Taliban almost the whole of Afghanistan in just two years. Early in 1995, they took Herat; a year later, they were in Kabul. They didn't do it all by themselves: thousands of Pakistanis like Rahmat volunteered to fight with them, while cash bribes fund-raised by transporters and smugglers neutralized most of the warlords; and Babur put considerable Pakistani expertise at their disposal.

He sent Pakistani engineers to replace the phone system, to repair Kandahar airport, and to improve the roads; and although Babur wouldn't deny or confirm it to me, and only broke into his impish smile again, Pakistani army regulars allegedly fought alongside the Taliban and high-ranking officers planned their campaigns. Babur himself closely monitored the capture of Kabul in 1996, from where he was to carry away, like the invaders of the past, his own booty: the statues of the Buddha and Bodhisattva that now adorned his living room.

Five years later, the 'boys', as Babur called the Taliban, had grown more ambitious. They weren't content, as in the old days, to expel the warlords and institute a kind of rough and ready justice. They wanted to create the purest Islamic society in the world. Their leaders called themselves mullahs, although few had had the necessary educational qualifications – Mohammed Omar had gone a step further and anointed himself Amir-ul-Momineem ('Commander of the Faithful'). They had designed a new flag for Afghanistan. Men from the Department of Prevention of Vice and Promotion of Virtue were responsible for checking the length of beards and beating up women without male escorts.

Babur disapproved of the Taliban's restrictions on women. But they no longer turned to men like Babur for advice. They had their own boosters: the mullahs of rural Afghanistan, and the jihadis, Islamist politicians and ISI officers of Pakistan.

And they had their sympathizers: Ishrat was one of them, although he hadn't lived in Afghanistan since 1981, when as a sixteen-year-old refugee he had made the long journey from the southern province of Helmand to Pakistan. He had gone to a school in Peshawar during the anti-Soviet jihad and picked up enough English to be able to act as a guide and interpreter to foreign journalists. Ishrat was, Shafiq said, the best person to take to Afghanistan; his English was excellent, he knew his way around not only the police and customs men, but also the potentially troublesome tribals in the border areas.

'You must write the truth', he kept saying, 'and see things in context. Don't be influenced by what you read in the Western media.' There was, he said, nothing unprecedented about the Taliban's restrictions on women, their harshness towards petty criminals, their religious strictures: the tribal system that had ruled the lives of the majority of Afghans had always been severe.

Ishrat was a short man; the beard hanging from his small face seemed very long; the salwar kurtas he wore were always too big for his thin body. I thought his admiration for the Taliban contained something of the fascination that the physically unprepossessing have for demonstrations of brute power and strength.

It made me uneasy; but I was stuck with him. And there was that discomfiting kernel of truth in his wildest assertions. In the two months that had lapsed since my first trip to Pakistan, the Taliban had destroyed the giant Buddha statues in Bamiyan; and Ishrat was obsessed with the attention given to the event in the West. 'Why do Western people care so much about old Buddhist statues no one worships? Why are they not writing front-page articles about millions of starving and dying people in Afghanistan? They want to give money for the statues and take them to their museums but what about human beings?'

It was hard to respond to Ishrat, partly because I wasn't sure of my own feelings. I had visited the refugee camps near Peshawar where whole families huddled under tiny plastic tents erected between narrow lanes muddied with soapy water and urine. I had read the alarming NGO reports about famine and mass starvation in Afghanistan. I knew about the UN's failure to fund-raise even $221m. as humanitarian aid for Afghanistan.

I had also just started writing a book about the Buddha, and had been reading about the way merchant caravans had travelled with his ideas from North India to Central Asia. In Pakistan, I had travelled to some of the sites where the merchants had built great monasteries. I hadn't been much interested in Bamiyan: the giant statues looked ugly in the photographs, and there was Robert Byron's testimony, offered in the early 1930s, about them lacking 'even the dignity of labour'. Nevertheless, their antiquity gave them a kind of poise – for fifteen centuries, standing quietly in a broad mountain valley, they had weathered the change of seasons and religions around them; and the news of their defacement appalled me.

But then, as the days passed, I grew somewhat weary of the outrage and scorn; there seemed something too easy and glib about the demonizing of the Taliban. In India, the loudest protests had come from those Hindu nationalists who had demolished the Babri mosque in Ayodhya in 1992. In the angry editorials in London, the Taliban once again appeared as particularly vicious barbarians from the Middle Ages instead of the bastard children they increasingly seemed to me of the West's arrogant meddling in Afghanistan in very recent times. Much history was either forgotten or ignored in even the more ambitious denunciations: the earlier Muslim attempts to destroy the Buddha statues; British vandalism in Herat, and the relative newness of the West's reverence for monuments from the past. And when Ishrat said, 'It is all hypocrisy, the Western people are afraid of Islam, they want to protect the statues; but they had never heard of these statues, they don't know anything about Afghanistan, they are not interested in whether people live or die there,' I kept quiet.

In Afghanistan, I had an argument with Ishrat. He wanted me to go to Jalalabad and talk to Hindus and Sikhs who would confirm his account of the great peace and stability brought to the country by the Taliban. But it wasn't what I wanted to do: the story had been done by twenty journalists. I wanted to go to the villages.

'What will you do in the villages?' Ishrat asked. 'There is nothing there.' I thought he resisted me only because his contacts were all in the cities. But in the end, he backed down. He said he knew someone I could talk to. He kept up the propaganda inside the taxi. 'During the jihad against Russia', he said, 'the whole place was full with drugs smugglers. You have heard of the Afridis? Pashtun tribe people. They control the drug business. Poppy grown in Afghanistan, turned into heroin in Pakistan and then smuggled out to Europe and America through Iran and

Karachi. No one was writing about that. America's favourite mujahedin, Hekmatyar, was running dozens of heroin laboratories. Now Taliban has banned poppy, the smugglers are angry at them, but they say heroin is against Islam. They lose money because of their faith. But still no one is writing. They all talk about Osama bin Laden. But who is bin Laden? He is America's man, America made him who he is.'

Ishrat pointed to the ancient-looking cassette of Indian film music on the dashboard, and said, 'See, Afghans can listen to music. All you Western journalists are saying Taliban banned music.' But then a checkpoint appeared in the distance and the driver reached for the cassette and stuffed it quickly into the pocket of his frayed jacket before the boys with black turbans and Kalashnikovs could strut over to the car, poke their tender-skinned faces through the open window and ask severe questions.

Ishrat was quiet after that. The sun rose higher; the light steadily grew harsh, draining colour even out of the roadside tents of the nomads; a pall of white dissolved the sky, veiled the high distant mountains, and then hung over the barren fields overrun with bush and the low mud houses set against stone-littered hillsides. There was little traffic: big trucks that small straggly families by the road would try to wave down – Ishrat identified them as Pakistan-bound refugees from the Tajik-majority northern provinces – and more frequently, Toyota pick-ups, fast and dangerous on the broken road, black-turbanned men with Kalashnikovs and blank stares crammed uncomfortably in the back.

The Toyotas – famously the vehicles with which the Taliban had achieved their military victory in Herat – kicked up vast swaying clouds of dust that were then quietly absorbed into the stubborn white haze. There was more dust once we turned off the road to Jalalabad, and the car began to rock and shudder through a rutted dirt path: the dust blew in through the rolled-up windows and settled in a film on the battered brown leather of the car seats; powdered the beards of Ishrat and the taxi driver; blotted out the occasional groups of children and chador-draped women carrying dung cakes on their head; and scared off the scrawny goats sitting in the narrow shade of the mud wall before which we suddenly stopped.

Yellowed grass sagged from the web-like cracks in the wall. But then the low wooden door opened; a tall man with a long white beard came out and embraced Ishrat; and his quick quizzical glance at me modulated into a smile as Ishrat explained my presence, suddenly speaking fast and unintelligibly in Pashto.

He took us – not saying much, either to Ishrat or to me – through the empty hay-littered courtyard to what seemed like a special room for visitors. He then brought me water in a shallow trough; he indicated the place in the courtyard – before a furrowed drain that ran around the compound – where I was to wash my face and hands. He came back with green tea shortly afterwards. The tea tasted slightly of dust, and made the bone china cup – an unexpected touch of luxury in the bare room – seem as if it had been sitting unused in one of the dark low-roofed rooms around the courtyard, in one of the little niches in the wall, for a long time.

I felt expectant; also slightly exhausted by the drive, by the nervousness that the Taliban men in the Toyotas caused in me. Ishrat hadn't promised much in the car. He had given me the name of our host – Faiz. He had told me about his involvement in the anti-Soviet jihad, and the injuries – always glamorous items in these accounts of the muja-hedin – he had sustained from a mortar attack by the communists.

And it was of that life Faiz spoke to me intermittently that afternoon and evening in that cool bare room – Ishrat translating, the driver looking on blankly – and he spoke not as a man who thought himself successful would, with pride or nostalgia. He spoke – leaning against the wall, his knees drawn up, narrow eyes wandering restlessly across the room – with the neutral air of a man who had simply lived his life, in the only way he could.

He could barely remember his childhood, when his father owned a few cows and goats. But he spoke vividly of the time in the 1970s when the desert-like area around him was irrigated with Soviet assistance, and orange and olive orchards sprang up on previously infertile land. Faiz's family was one of the beneficiaries. There had been a brief moment of relative prosperity: the house we were sitting in had been built then; Faiz's elder brother had been sent to Kabul for higher education.

Very soon afterwards, there was trouble. Faiz couldn't remember the date, but his brother was probably killed in 1978, during the purges that followed the communist coup. He was suspected of being an Islamist, although he was only a student and kept away from politics altogether.

The communists had even come to the province; had rounded up and killed a few mullahs; and arrested anyone they suspected of being counter-revolutionary. And then the Russians had arrived.

Ishrat, translating and embellishing at the same time, told me of the Afghan rage and contempt for foreign invaders, and how every Afghan spontaneously joined the uprising against the Russians. But this didn't match what he translated immediately afterwards: how Faiz had stayed away from the young men in the province who came together to fight the Russians. He was married by then; he had a young son; there were the orchards to look after.

But then the bombing began, from the Russian helicopters, in response to guerrilla attacks on communist convoys. Many of the cultivated fields near the highway to Kabul were mined; and once the canals were destroyed it became harder and harder to keep the orchards going.

Faiz's parents, on their way to Jalalabad for a wedding, died when the bus they were travelling on was hit by a stray mortar. There were other tragedies. Faiz's son turned out to be 'insane' – Ishrat used the Urdu word, '*paagal*', and I didn't feel I could ask him to clarify. Faiz took him to a number of shrines and pirs, including one near Jalalabad famous for curing insanity, and made him wear various amulets. But none of these attempts worked.

Faiz's two brothers were already with the mujahedin when he began fighting alongside them. It wasn't a full-time job. There were specific expeditions he joined: mostly ambushes of government convoys. He was home the rest of the time, taking care of his diminishing farmland.

It was Ishrat who volunteered the information in Urdu – while Faiz looked on uncomprehendingly – that Faiz had earned a reputation as a brave man very early in the war. It was why he was smuggled across the border and into a hospital in Peshawar when he suffered serious injuries in the abdomen during a mortar attack on his position in the mountains around Jalalabad.

Pakistan, where he met Ishrat, was a revelation for Faiz. It was where he first saw how the jihad against the communists had become big business. Some of the so-called leaders of the Afghan mujahedin, living in grand villas in Hayatabad, were not even known to him by name. But there they were, handling the disbursement of arms and aid to the refugees and the mujahedin. They made him think with pity and rage of the poor young men he was fighting with – men who started out with just a few .303 rifles amongst them until they managed to ambush an arms convoy and equip themselves with the latest Soviet weaponry.

By the time Faiz returned to Afghanistan, the jihad against the Russians was almost over. A local mujahedin commander was already ruling over his home province, and so peace came quickly, and lasted longer in his part of Afghanistan. White men from UN agencies came to repair the canals; many of the destroyed orchards and fields were got going again.

Faiz wasn't one of the lucky farmers. None of the canals close to him was repaired. He had to go back to where his father had started out, making a living by selling the milk of the few cows and goats he had left over from the days of the jihad; he also made a bit of money by working as a labourer.

This was at a time when great wealth was being created all around him. Most of the restored fields grew poppy, under orders from the mujahedin commander, who lived in a mansion, and maintained a private army. He wasn't as bad as the warlords in Helmand province; he wasn't a bandit or rapist. In fact, he was quite helpful to people who had fought in the jihad. But everyone knew he was involved in smuggling and drugs: the big business Faiz had seen in Pakistan had come to Afghanistan. Planes arrived in Jalalabad from Dubai loaded with colour TV sets that were then smuggled into Pakistan on big trucks. The opium went out to labs in southern Afghanistan and then, as heroin, to Iran.

This was why Faiz had first thought well of the Taliban, when they came from the south and chased out the commander. He didn't mind their severity: only people in the cities chafed at their restrictions on women. But they hadn't altered the essential things. The smuggling had gone on; the poppy cultivation was stopped only recently, and he knew of people who were still at it. A few well-connected merchants and traders in Jalalabad had grown rich. Most other people became poorer: his own two brothers had left with their families for Pakistan, where they worked as truck drivers. And there was the harassment: some young men had showed up at his own house in order to draft his son into the war against the Tajiks in the north, and had to be persuaded that he was unfit to be a soldier. Faiz also didn't like the Taliban's dependence on Arab and Pakistani jihadis, many of whom he saw in the province. Foreigners had done enough damage in Afghanistan; it was time for them to leave the country and its people alone.

Dismay appeared on Ishrat's face as he translated this; and a brief argument now broke out between him and Faiz. I couldn't follow most of it; and I didn't trust the account I heard from Ishrat, who claimed to be arguing that the Arabs and Pakistanis helping the Taliban were fellow Muslims, and not infidels like the Russians and Americans.

*

I had wondered all afternoon about the emptiness of that large house, the absence of Faiz's wife and his son. I now saw two emaciated cows stumbling into the courtyard, followed by a thin stubble-faced man with a stick: this was, Ishrat said, Faiz's 'insane' son. He tethered the cows to an iron pigot and then walked out of sight. A little later, I heard the shuffling of pots and pans in an adjacent room and then I saw a chador-clad figure move briskly across the courtyard to throw some hay before the cows, and then swiftly retreat. She had been there all through the afternoon, possibly sleeping or lying down silently on the ground.

When Faiz left the room briefly, I asked Ishrat if it was possible to talk to her for a few minutes. He was quick to catch the hesitation in my voice. 'Why do you want to talk to her?' he asked, slightly aggressively.

I didn't have time to respond. Faiz, who had gone out, came back to the room at that very moment: the lantern he held filled the room with the smell of kerosene. Ishrat explained my request to him in Pashto while I looked on with some apprehension.

I saw Faiz's face go tense; I felt his narrow shrewd eyes on me before they turned towards Ishrat.

The answer was no. Ishrat, speaking once again on his own, said that local custom did not permit strange men to talk to women.

Faiz suddenly interrupted him; he said that he could convey my question to his wife and bring me her reply.

It was better than nothing, so I asked the obvious question about life for women under the Taliban. It took a while for Ishrat to translate this, and I wasn't sure if he had done so accurately until the answer came back with a slightly more relaxed Faiz.

Faiz laughed as he spoke, revealing childlike teeth; and Ishrat himself smiled as he translated. The thing she disliked most about the rule of the Taliban was the travelling in buses to nearby towns. The roads were broken; the buses were few; and the journeys were roughest for women who were forced to sit squashed at the back, separate from the men in the front of the bus.

The light outside the room grew softer; and it was in the grey-blue dusk that Faiz and Ishrat went out to offer *namaz*. I watched them from the room: two silently vigorous figures on the scruffy floor of the courtyard, bending and straightening almost in unison, expressing a common faith, but so apart in their experiences: the fixer for foreign journalists in Peshawar, in touch with and amplifying ever-new ideologies and passions, and Faiz the retired fighter, all his previous disappointments and griefs bleached by his present struggles for survival, by the bare house and courtyard, and the greater blankness outside.

Later, I went outside myself and climbed up to the flat roof. Night had descended swiftly and it was very quiet. The air carried a mysterious soft tinkling, and then a couple of goats became clear in the distance. A bright half-moon outlined the mountains in the south and north, bestowing calm upon the stony treeless plain between them.

In the morning, when the convoys of the Taliban had raced across it in great trails of dust, the plain had seemed a staging post for countless conquerors and marauders. Alexander the Great himself had crossed it on his way to

India: I had picked up this fact from the books and it had given the flat futile land a kind of aura.

I saw it differently now. Faiz's story had animated it with many different human achievements and disasters: the irrigation systems, the olive orchards, the helicopter bombings, the mines, the poppy cultivators, and the drugs smugglers.

And you could, if you wanted, connect them to larger histories and geopolitics, to the Cold War strategists in comfortable suburban retirement in America and the generals in their mansions in Pakistan still fantasizing about pan-Islamic empires, trade routes, and oil pipelines. But when you saw it from Faiz's point of view, the events still lacked a redeeming pattern. They spoke – in the house with the emaciated cows and the mad son and the unseeable woman with her silent sufferings – only of the dwindling of human possibilities, and the steady grinding-down of individual lives.

In Peshawar later in 2001 I heard about Jamal from one of the other men I had met at the offices of the *Frontier Post*. Terrible things had happened to both Jamal and the newspaper. Just a few days after my previous visit, a letter had come by email. It started innocuously enough but then insulted the Prophet Muhammad in the grossest terms. Jamal approved it for publication without reading through to the end. No one else noticed it, before it was pounced upon by one of the fundamentalist organizations, always waiting to undermine the English-language press. A mob of bearded men emerged from nowhere and burnt down the press. The police sealed the offices and arrested several journalists; the editor I had met managed to escape the

police and was hiding with his fellow tribesmen somewhere near the Khyber Pass. Most of the journalists had
now been released but Jamal was in prison, awaiting trial
for blasphemy.

The punishment for blasphemy in Pakistan is death. But
Jamal was already close to dying; the journalist was surprised to discover that I didn't know, or hadn't guessed
from his dull yellow eyes, about his heroin addiction. It had
begun soon after Jamal arrived in Peshawar and got to
know some drugs dealers; he had been in and out of several hospitals.

No one could do anything for him now, the journalist
said. I was shocked at first at the callousness, and then I
felt slightly guilty myself. In London I had received a
couple of emails from Jamal about the book he wanted to
write. I hadn't responded: the book had seemed to me a
doomed idea.

The journalist, who himself had barely escaped the fury
of the fundamentalists, was only being truthful in a brutal
unarguable kind of way. I didn't feel that I could even offer
to help. My own situation in Pakistan, as a Hindu and
Indian, was already complicated. It would have been too
risky to get involved with an assassin, a heroin addict, and
a blasphemer.

'They are all such fanatics here!' Jamal had said at our first
meeting and I had been grateful for the sentiment, even
though I knew it to be a commonplace exaggeration,
because the words stoked something I felt during my early
days in Pakistan – that deeper anxiety about Muslims I
began to acknowledge to myself only after I left Pakistan
and felt safe again in India.

The unease had never entirely gone. But I had felt myself change during the weeks in Pakistan; and there had been an unexpected moment towards the end of my stay. I had gone to see a Mogul mosque in Peshawar. The spies hadn't followed me into the courtyard, where a few men sat in the late afternoon sun, and I felt I was alone until I saw an old man sleeping in one dark corner. He was obviously an Afghan refugee. His long white beard and sharp features made me think he was from Herat, or the western provinces close to Iran. His head, resting on a silk-wrapped bundle, displayed the fine profile of monks and wayfarers in Persian and Mogul miniatures; and watching him in the decaying old building – where the inlaid tiles were all faded or chipped, the broad-blade fans swayed dangerously as they spun, and birds invisibly chattered somewhere above in the dark domes – I suddenly felt myself pulled centuries back. I had a sense, fleeting but vivid and exhilarating, of the greatness of the old global civilization of Islam, the glory and splendour of once-famous and now devastated cities – Herat, Balkh, Baghdad – of the whole life and world the religion had once created.

That world was now in turmoil; it had been broken into by the invincible modern civilization of the West. From the outside it seemed capable only of producing fanaticisms of the kind that had crushed Jamal, and it was hard not to be repelled by it.

'The foreigners should leave us alone,' Faiz had said. 'We will find our own way.' But countless men had tried and failed, many societies had been exposed to new kinds of pain, and it still wasn't clear what that way could be, whether the new versions of Islam could bring justice and peace and prosperity to the faithful, whether they even stood a chance against globalization.

In any case, I could always feel myself distant from these debates and struggles. None of them had touched my own life before I went to Pakistan and Afghanistan. I belonged to another, more fortunate world. The American diplomats in Islamabad had guessed correctly: I already had my side chosen for me.

But I was confused. I had thought Jamal an ally. His fate, however, was tied to the faceless people on the other side – people who were persecutors as much as victims. I couldn't see how things, given the way they were now, could work out for them. But the thought of their failure was painful. I wanted these people to flourish. I wanted them to have as much dignity and freedom as I had been allowed in recent years, even though I couldn't but feel the absurdity of my wish, and increasingly doubted whether the kind of life I lived was what these apparently deprived people longed for, or could be content with.

Afghanistan: Communists, Mullahs, and Warlords

MUCH OF KABUL IS built of mud. And when it rained before the Christmas of 2004 – relieving a long and severe drought – the whole city seemed to melt. The piles of slush on its unpaved lanes rose, as though in a slow-moving tide, until they spattered everything: the big white Land Cruisers of aid agencies and Afghan ministers, the beat-up yellow taxis, the bombed-out palaces of western Kabul and the bullet-pocked huts on steep hills, the fortified foreign embassies and UN offices, and even the high billboards exhorting Afghans, in idiosyncratic English, to 'national reconciliation and peace'.

Despite the rain and the cold, the bazaars were crowded. Shopkeepers representing almost all of Afghanistan's ethnic groups – Pashtuns, Tajiks, Hazaras, Uzbeks, and Turkmens – hawked oranges, carpets, Chinese-made windbreakers and electronic goods, while beggars – mostly disabled children and widows in burkas – squatted beside the sewers and tugged at the wide trousers of passing men. Thousands of refugee families huddled around small bonfires at the abandoned Soviet embassy, amid bomb-shattered slabs of concrete and open manholes.

It was strange to see no white faces in these crowds. Even in the modern part of Kabul, where thousands of Europeans and Americans live – mostly soldiers, diplomats, aid workers, and businessmen – the streets were empty. Afghan guards with Kalashnikovs stood in front of iron gates set in high concrete walls topped with barbed wire. The gates occasionally opened to reveal a new or renovated mansion, and to release or admit a Land Cruiser with tinted windows.

To be a foreigner in Afghanistan, it seemed, is to move from one protected enclave to another. An Indian journalist I met soon after arriving in Kabul that December told me that security had deteriorated soon after the presidential election in October, which the Taliban had failed to disrupt, and which Hamid Karzai had won convincingly. That same month, a suicide bomber, apparently from the Taliban, had killed an American woman and injured three European soldiers at a shopping district a few metres away from my hotel.

The Indian journalist seemed lonely, frustrated by the restrictions on both his travel and social life. For some months now he had wished to set up an FCC (Foreign Correspondents' Club) in Kabul, on the lines of one in Hong Kong. One cold rainy evening I travelled to his home with one of the foreign journalists he had invited to join the club. When we arrived we found several other potential members already there.

As usual, there was no power. A diesel generator spluttered outside the journalist's fortress-like home, one of the thousands running simultaneously in Kabul, giving to the city its characteristic low rumble. Inside, Afghan servants, chauffeurs, and bodyguards – part of the new service economy of Kabul – bustled around, replenishing bowls of dried fruits. The journalist opened a case full of alcohol – smuggled bottles gleamed wickedly in the dim, flickering light. Sipping Scotch whisky and German beer, the journalists loudly exchanged local gossip I would hear repeatedly in the next few days from Afghans: about kickbacks from an Afghan mobile phone operator to a cabinet minister, and about $1m. allegedly missing from the coffers of Ariana, the Afghan national airline. They speculated about whether Karzai would be confident enough to exclude the most corrupt and powerful warlords – defence minister Mohammed Fahim and his deputy, Abdul Rashid Dostum – from his new cabinet. There were complaints about extravagant UN agencies and NGOs pushing up rents in Kabul (up to $3,000 for a dingy two-bedroom apartment); about the arrogant employees of the American company DynCorp who worked as Karzai's bodyguards.

The Indian journalist abruptly called for silence, and read out what he said was a draft constitution, adopted from the FCC in Hong Kong. He then asked for suggestions. As it turned out, almost every idea proposed that evening ran into an obstacle. The club needed a permanent home. But this seemed possible only when rents in Kabul were less extortionate. High-paying corporate members? Perhaps, when there were many more multinational corporations in Afghanistan. Honorary memberships for such visiting foreign dignitaries as Dick Cheney, or the powerful US Ambassador to Afghanistan, Zalmay Khalilzad? Possibly, once the American embassy had become more accessible. Even a bar – indispensable to foreign correspondent clubs – seemed unobtainable. Seeking official permission for the consumption of alcohol in Kabul could only cause offence in what was still a deeply religious and conservative country.

Returning to my hotel late that night, past the sandbagged, barbed-wire-topped compounds of foreign embassies and UN offices, I felt sorry for the journalist. He had seemed right to argue, as his cherished project foundered, that Kabul had advanced greatly since the collapse of the Taliban, and that with its new, one-million-strong population of repatriated refugees – many of them rich people who had spent decades in liberal societies – it was poised for a social revolution.

Earlier that evening, I had seen two Afghan girls at a pizza parlour. They wore tight blue jeans; their faces were uncovered, and they sipped Pepsi-Cola as they watched American women playing softball on ESPN. They would have been an unthinkable sight in the Taliban-ruled Afghanistan I had visited in early 2001. Almost four years later, Kabul was full of such surprises: new walled-off villas with mock-Palladian facades, well-stocked supermarkets, internet cafes, beauty parlours, restaurants, and stores selling DVDs of Bollywood as well as pornographic films. Sitting in one of Kabul's great traffic jams caused by the Land Cruisers, surrounded by the vivacious banter of Afghanistan's new radio stations and children hawking newspapers, I felt as if I was in a small Indian city, among people prospering under the globalized economy.

In brightly lit and heated offices, diplomats, NGO workers, and government officials radiated optimism as they offered facts and figures attesting to progress in Afghanistan. The first-ever presidential elections in the country had been successfully conducted without any major disruptions. Three million Afghan refugees in Pakistan and Iran had expressed their confidence in their homeland by returning to it. More than three million children had been enrolled in schools, as compared with 900,000 under the Taliban. The 8,000-strong International Security Assistance Force (ISAF) under NATO command was beginning to cover regions beyond Kabul. A human rights commission had been established. The $4.4bn. pledged by international donors in Tokyo in 2002 for Afghanistan was coming in – albeit slowly.

There was finally a tarmac road, stretching from Kabul to Kandahar, 300 miles away to the south. More roads linking major Afghan cities were being constructed and renovated. Small civil–military provincial reconstruction teams (PRTs), which repaired schools and roads, and were run by the United Kingdom, Germany, and the Netherlands, existed in the northern provinces and were expected to cover the entire country by 2007. Japan was at the forefront of the DDR (demobilization, disarmament, and reintegration) programme, targeting warlord armies, and had disarmed about 25,000 of the more than 150,000 fighters in private militias. The US was creating the Afghan national army, with 10,000 soldiers already trained. The US and Germany had trained 18,000 police officers. The UK was leading anti-narcotics efforts. The Italians were reforming the judiciary.

To hear this litany of efforts was to feel the words 'international community', which Afghans commonly used, acquire a moral dimension in Afghanistan. With one of the lowest life expectancies and the highest infant mortality rates in the world, Afghanistan seemed to need all the help it could get. But three years after the US brought together several nations to rebuild Afghanistan, many Afghans tended to blame rather than praise that international community.

Where was much of the money for reconstruction going? they asked, pointing to the Land Cruisers and the high-rent houses and offices of the expatriate community. Disarmament was a failure, and would remain so until there was better security and rule of law in the country: most militia fighters had simply concealed their best weapons and turned in those that were old and ineffective. The new Afghan army was already afflicted with desertions. There was no comprehensive plan to house and feed the millions of repatriated refugees. And, though Afghans had turned out enthusiastically for their first-ever direct elections, they were disappointed to see US-backed warlords still ruling much of the country.

One evening, early in my time in Afghanistan, I went to see Dr Massouda Jalal. In October 2004, she'd been in the news as the lone female candidate in the presidential elections. She had got only 1.2 per cent of the votes cast, as compared to 55.4 per cent for Karzai. But the very fact that a woman could stand for high office hinted at the immensity of the changes occurring in Afghanistan.

So it was disconcerting when Dr Jalal, sitting in a very cold, dark room and speaking in slow, precise English, denounced the elections, and the registration process preceding it, as a fraud perpetrated upon Afghans – largely a show put on by the US government to impress American voters in the year of the presidential elections.

The international community, Dr Jalal kept saying, believed in 'quantity' – statistics about elections and registration processes – but was indifferent to 'quality'. The elections had not been free and fair. Many people had registered more than once, she claimed, and voted several times. Often, men with guns had forced people to vote for Karzai; they had also tried to intimidate Dr Jalal herself during her election campaign.

Western nations, she said, had not given her a single dollar while pouring millions into Karzai's campaign. Worse, they had forgotten about women's rights, which Laura Bush and Cherie Blair had so ardently embraced in late 2001, and which were trampled upon daily across Afghanistan by men hired by the United States in its war on terror. Educated women like herself were not allowed to participate in political decision-making. Karzai's cabinet was dominated by corrupt warlords and had hardly any 'qualified people' – people with the training and experience, she explained, to translate Western concepts of democracy into Afghan terms.

As with other Afghans I had met, I felt unable to assess much of what she said. Given that there were only 250 international monitors for the elections in Afghanistan, caution does seem necessary when considering claims that 10.5 million people registered to vote, and that 70 per cent of them actually voted in October 2004. However, the scale of Karzai's victory suggests that a better organized election would have had the same overall result. It seemed to me that the election, though flawed, had been a positive step.

As it turned out, within a few weeks Dr Jalal was appointed as minister in charge of 'women's affairs'. It again occurred to me that in places like Afghanistan outsiders like myself bring their own assumptions of what constitutes progress, and risk being limited by them.

But to know, as the days passed and I travelled around Afghanistan, that the new mansions with the architectural adventurousness of Los Angeles belonged to corrupt government officials, often built upon lands stolen from poor Afghans; to learn that the provincial governor, who spoke fluently of 'peace', 'reconstruction', 'international community', and 'poppy eradication', was a drug lord; to find out that the Revolutionary Association of the Women of Afghanistan (RAWA), which was briefly famous in the West for highlighting the Taliban's harsh treatment of women, was too fearful of radical Islamists to announce its presence in Kabul – to know all this was to begin to have a different sense of the change that had come to Afghanistan in the last three years. It was also to realize that like the millions suffering from contaminated water, power and housing shortages, warlords, and disease, a club for foreign journalists would have to wait for better days.

Few countries in modern times have had to wait for better days as long as Afghanistan. A bright future seemed imminent in late 2001, when the United States overthrew the Taliban regime. But the past seems hard to shake off in Afghanistan, and no events more so than the Soviet invasion of the country in 1979, and the American decision to help radical Islamists wage a jihad against Soviet communism.

In the decades before the Soviet invasion, Afghanistan had been slowly making its own way into the modern world. It is hard to imagine now, but for students at Kabul University, 1968 was no less hectic a year than it was for students at Columbia, Berkeley, Oxford, and the Sorbonne. A king, Mohammad Zahir Shah, had been presiding over the many ethnic and tribal enclaves of Afghanistan since 1933. But he knew enough of the world elsewhere to attempt, cautiously, a few liberal reforms in his capital city, Kabul. The university was set up in 1946; a liberal constitution was introduced in 1964; the press was technically free; women ran for public office in 1965. By the 1960s, many students and teachers had travelled abroad; and new ideas about how to organize the state and society had come to the sons of peasants and nomads and artisans from their foreign or foreign-educated teachers.

In the somewhat rarefied world of modernizing Kabul, where women were allowed to appear without the veil in 1959, communism and radical Islam attracted almost an equal number of believers: to these impatient men, the great Afghan countryside with its antique ways appeared ready for revolution. It was from this fledgling intelligentsia in Kabul that almost all of the crucial political figures of the next three decades emerged.

Less than five years after 1968, King Zahir Shah was deposed in a military coup by his cousin, the ambitious former prime minister Mohammad Daoud. Daoud initially sought help from the communists, whose influence in the army and bureaucracy had grown rapidly since the 1960s: together, they went after the radical Islamists, many of whom were imprisoned or murdered for ideological reasons. But when Daoud, wary of the increasing power of the communists, tried to get rid of them, he was in turn overthrown and killed. In April 1978, the communists – themselves divided, confusingly, into two factions, Khalq and Parcham, that roughly corresponded to the rural–urban divide in

Afghanistan – assumed full control of the government in Kabul, and in their hurry to eliminate all potential opposition to their programme of land redistribution and indoctrination – an attempt, really, to create a communist society virtually overnight – they effectively inaugurated the brutalization and destruction of Afghanistan.

Within just a few months, 12,000 people considered to be anti-communist, many of them members of the country's educated elite, were killed in Kabul alone; thousands more were murdered in the countryside. Thousands of families began to leave the country for Pakistan and Iran. A significant number of radical Islamists of Kabul University were already in exile in Pakistan by 1978; some of them had even started a low-intensity guerrilla war against the communist government. Several army garrisons across the country mutinied, and people in the villages, culturally very remote from Kabul, began many separate jihads against the communist regime.

In 2001, in Peshawar, I met Anwar, whose father and uncle were among the earliest Afghans to take up arms against the communists. Neither were Islamists. Anwar's father, a farmer, lived in a village north of Kabul, near the border with what is now Tajikistan: although a devout Muslim, he knew little about the modern ideologies of Islam that had travelled to Kabul University from Egypt, Pakistan, and Iran. It was Anwar's uncle, an officer in Zahir Shah's finance ministry in Kabul, who was a bit more in touch with them. He was friendly with Gulbuddin Hekmatyar, then one of the prominent radical Islamists at Kabul University.

Initially, the Russians were busy consolidating the communist hold over Kabul and securing the country's main highways, and seemed very far from rural Afghanistan, which in any case had had relative autonomy from the government in the capital city for years. But later, with the aggressive campaigns of land reforms and Marxist indoctrination emanating from Kabul, resistance built up swiftly throughout the country. Anwar's father and uncle joined one of the mujahedin groups that, though equipped only with .303 Lee Enfield rifles, managed to keep their region free of communist influence. Then, in December 1979, the Soviet army entered Afghanistan in order to protect the communist revolution, which was being threatened by factional fighting among Afghan communists and rebellions by the army; and the position of Anwar's family became more precarious.

In 1983, Russian planes bombed the villages where Anwar and his relatives lived, in retaliation for attacks on Afghan army convoys by the mujahedin. Although Anwar's father and uncle stayed to fight and to look after the animals and fields, there was no choice for many of the women and children but to leave.

Anwar, seven years old at the time, couldn't recall too many details of the long walk that took him and his mother and young brother to Pakistan. He did remember that it was very cold. There was snow on the ground and on the hills, and Anwar and his family walked all day, resting at night in roadside mosques. The 350-mile-long road to Pakistan was busy with thousands of refugees, but they had to avoid moving in large groups, which would attract fire from the Russian helicopters buzzing ominously overhead. They also had to stay as close as possible to the main road, for there were mines in the fields and on the dirt tracks –

tiny 'butterfly mines' that floated down from the helicopters and then lay in wait for unmindful children and animals.

I still heard about the mines when I travelled in the spring of 2001 on the road that links Kabul to Pakistan, through Nangrahar province. The land seemed vacant, and the stubborn bareness of rock and desert was relieved only occasionally by a green field and a black-tented encampment of nomads. This was the land that was reclaimed for cultivation, with Soviet assistance, in the days of Zahir Shah; and orchards and fields, watered by broad canals, sprang up. In a half-abandoned village, rusty padlocks hanging from the doors set into long mud walls, an old Afghan was startled when I mentioned that time. Rasool had been in his late teens then; had known some of the prosperity that came to the region; could even, with some prompting by me, remember the white men – Russian experts – travelling through the fields.

Unlike Anwar's father and uncle, Rasool wasn't a mujahedin: he hadn't revolted against the Russians or the communists; he had been content to tend his land. The jihad had almost bypassed him; and he had known hard times only when, sometime in the mid 1980s, Russian planes bombed the canals that brought water to his land. There had been another recovery after the Russian army withdrew in 1989, when white men, this time from the UN, came and supervised the repair of the canals. By then, the local mujahedin commanders were in charge. They taxed all the traffic on the roads, and took over the land that had once belonged to the Afghan state, forcing the farmers to grow high-yield poppy.

There was no point in Rasool defying the commanders;

he wouldn't have got cash credit from the traders in the town for anything other than opium. Not that poppy-growing had improved his circumstances. It was the muja-hedin commanders who had grown very rich from converting the poppy into heroin and then smuggling it across the border into Iran and Pakistan.

And then, suddenly, before Rasool had even heard of the Taliban, its young soldiers arrived from the south-ern provinces, banished the mujahedin commanders, and claimed the checkpoints. They supervised, and profited from, the drug business until 1999, when they abruptly banned the cultivation of poppy, leaving most farmers with no sources of livelihood, and the option only of migrating to Pakistan.

Rasool still lived in the vast, now arid, land, enduring, in just three decades, a whole fruitless cycle of Afghan his-tory. The long reign of Zahir Shah was no more than a faint memory. All the slow, steady work of previous generations was cancelled out; Afghanistan was even further away from its tryst with the modern world.

But then, like many Muslim countries suddenly confronted in the nineteenth century with the rising power of the West, Afghanistan's route to modern development could only have been tortuous. The Afghan empire of the eighteenth century had reached as far as Kashmir in the east and up to the Iranian city of Mashhad in the west. Like present-day Afghanistan, it contained many different ethnic groups: the dominant Pashtun tribes in the east and south, Tajiks and Uzbeks in the north and west, and the Shia Hazaras in the central provinces. Almost all of them were Sunni or Shia Muslims. Fiercely autonomous and proud, they had successfully resisted the British attempt to extend their Indian empire up to Kabul; but after two Anglo-Afghan wars, in 1838–42 and 1878–80, the Afghans had been sufficiently subdued to serve as a buffer state between the expanding empires of Britain and Russia.

The British were content to exercise influence from afar without troubling themselves with direct rule. It was under their supervision that the present-day boundaries of Afghanistan were drawn, leaving a lot of Pashtun tribes in what is now Pakistan. The British also subsidized the Afghan army. Until 1919, when the Afghans won complete independence from the British, the ruler in Kabul reported to Delhi in matters of foreign policy, which essentially involved keeping the Russians out of Afghanistan.

The British-backed rulers of Afghanistan in the nineteenth and early twentieth centuries were insecure and ruthless, obsessed with protecting their regime from any local challenges as well: Afghanistan's continued isolation was in their best interests. During the twenty-one-year rule of Amir Abdur Rahman (1880–1901), one of Afghanistan's more pro-British rulers, only one school was built in Kabul, and that was a madrasa. Condemned to playing a passive part in an imperial Great Game, Afghanistan missed out on the indirect benefits of colonial rule: the creation of an educated class such as would supply the basic infrastructure of the postcolonial states of India, Pakistan, and Egypt.

Afghanistan's resolute backwardness in the nineteenth and early twentieth centuries was appealing to Western romantics: Kipling, who was repelled by the educated Bengali, commended the Pashtun tribesmen – the traditional rulers of Afghanistan, and also a majority among Afghans – for their courage, love of freedom, and sense of honour.

These clichés about the Afghans – which would be amplified in our own time by American journalists and politicians – also had some effect on Muslims themselves.

One such man was Jamal al-Din al-Afghani, a polemicist of the nineteenth century, who sought to alert the Muslim peoples to their growing subjugation to the imperial powers of the West. The radical Islamists I spoke to didn't remember that in 1968 – while student groups at Kabul University were organizing large demonstrations, distributing fiery pamphlets, and fighting one another on the streets – a huge mausoleum for al-Afghani went up inside the campus, to honour someone who, although born in Iran and educated in India, adopted the pen name 'al-Afghani' and even began to tell people that he was from Afghanistan.

The increasing influence of the West, and the related undermining of Muslim power, was the inescapable reality of al-Afghani's lifetime; he witnessed it more closely than most Muslims during long stints in India, Iran, Egypt, France, England, and Turkey. But Afghanistan had hardly been affected by the lifestyles and new knowledge of Europe, by the passion and energy of white men from the West that were transforming old worlds elsewhere in the nineteenth century. This resistance to Western-style modernization would have impressed al-Afghani, who, while stressing the need to modernize Muslim societies, disapproved of the wholesale adoption of European ways of the kind Kemal Atatürk would impose upon Turkey just two decades after al-Afghani's death in 1897.

Nevertheless, al-Afghani failed to see how even small but strategically placed countries such as Afghanistan were being drawn into the great imperial games of nineteenth-century Europe, and then sentenced to isolation and backwardness as buffer states. Behind his romantic attachment to Afghanistan lay fear and defensiveness – his painful awareness, shared by many other educated people in once-great Asian societies, that they had fallen behind the West, and that they not only had to catch up, but also to keep in check its increasing power to alter their lives, mostly for the worse.

For many educated people in pre-modern societies, communism offered a way of both catching up with and resisting the West; and the ideology had a powerful, and often generous, sponsor in the Soviet Union. But the hasty, ill-adapted borrowings from Soviet communism – the simplistic notion, for instance, of Afghans as feudal people who had to be turned into proletarians – more often than not imposed new kinds of pain and trauma on such a traditional society as Afghanistan; and helped to push the country even further away from the modern world.

The Soviet Union had supported the communist coup of 1978 in Kabul, and had subsequently grown concerned about the clumsy and brutal way in which the Khalq faction of the Afghan Communist Party, led by the fanatical ideologue Hafizullah Amin, a one-time student at Columbia University, had hijacked the coup, and then had tried violently – and, as spontaneous revolts across the country proved, disastrously – to weld the incoherent ethnic–tribal worlds of Afghanistan into a communist society.

As records of Politburo conversations reveal, the ageing leaders of the Soviet Union at first resisted military intervention in Afghanistan. However, they feared that the United States, unsettled by the fall of the Shah of Iran, was hoping to find, with the help of the wily Amin, an alternative anti-Soviet base in Afghanistan. They suspected Amin of being 'an ambitious, cruel, treacherous person' who might 'change the political orientation of the regime'.

This sounds like cold war paranoia. It wasn't softened by the mutinies against the communist regime by Afghan military garrisons, one of which, in the city of Herat, ended in the deaths of several Soviet and East European advisers. In the last days of 1979, when the communist regime looked close to collapse, a contingent of Soviet soldiers flew into Kabul, stormed Amin's palace, and killed him. A more moderate leader, Babrak Karmal, who belonged to the urban-based Parcham faction, took his place and attempted to avert the collapse of the Afghan state and bring an end to the brutalities.

Karmal was only partly successful in restoring order, however. In 1986, the Soviets replaced Karmal with Mohammad Najibullah, the head of KHAD, the communist intelligence agency. Najibullah, known for his role in the execution and torture of anti-communists, tried even harder to win Afghan support. He toned down the Communist rhetoric, emphasized his faith in Islam, and began reaching out to the refugees and mujahedin, speaking all the time of compromise and national reconciliation. But his government couldn't possibly acquire legitimacy among Afghans while being beholden to a foreign power. And in any case, things were out of his control: Afghanistan had already begun fighting in a new proxy war that would kill a million or more Afghans over the next decade.

In the derelict Pashtun village I visited east of Kabul in the spring of 2001, five months before the attacks on the

World Trade Centre and the Pentagon, in an area heavily bombed and mined by the Soviet military, people talked, as they did elsewhere, of the irrelevance – indeed the non-existence – of the Taliban government. They spoke, too, of the good deeds of the white men from the foreign NGOs and the UN, who were active throughout the previous two decades of war, supplying seeds, food, and health care, despite the constant danger of being kidnapped and beaten up by the Taliban.

There were three Afghans sitting on the floor of the bare, low-roofed room, all of them in their late forties, variously disabled during the anti-communist jihad, and prematurely aged, even the dim light from the lantern seeming harsh on their sunburned wrinkled faces and wiry grey beards. Only men like these remained in the village. The soldiers in black turbans came regularly to look for fit young men. Those young men who had escaped the draft had fled to Pakistan, where many of their relatives already lived in the much worse conditions of the refugee camps.

The conversation inside the room was of the quality of seeds, the lack of fodder and drinking water for livestock, and the refugees from the war in the north, who, turned away at the border with Pakistan, were now draining away the already meagre supply of food and water in the province. The three-year-long drought and ongoing civil war had created more than half a million internal refugees. It wasn't as severe here as in central and northern parts of Afghanistan; but most of the land was still uncultivated. The harvest from last year's seeds had been poor; just enough to feed a few families. The news had come of white men – most probably volunteers from the World Food Programme – distributing seeds in a nearby town. The news was good, but there remained the complicated negotiation about how to divide the subsequent harvest; then there was the long journey to the town, on foot and in trucks, past many checkpoints where the bribes – since corruption, despite draconian Islamic punishments, flourished as usual – could be very steep.

Outside in the courtyard, where tufts of grass grew wild in the cracks of the mud walls, an emaciated cow slumped on the ground; and somewhere inside the rooms around us I could sense the presence of women, could hear occasionally the rustle of thick cloth and the clink of pots and pans. I could imagine them: brisk, silent figures in the dusk, whose shapeless heavy chadors, with the narrow mesh across the eyes, resembled the habit of a viciously persecuted medieval sisterhood.

But this was the outsider's vision: the chador, I learned later, has usually been worn by village women as a status symbol – a sign of their husband's education or employment – and was more common in the towns and cities. Under the Taliban you could still glimpse women without it in the villages, where everyday life was traditionally autonomous of what went on in the cities. Women in rural Afghanistan, where 90 per cent of the country's approximately twenty million people still live, were less vulnerable to the Taliban's arbitrary brutality. Dupree mentions instances of women being beaten and killed outside Kabul, but on the whole they weren't as affected by the restrictions and controversies arising out of the Taliban's harsh gender policies as women in the cities. Of the minuscule 3 per cent of school-age Afghan females who went to school during communist rule, the majority came from the urban areas. It is the women in the cities, encouraged into education and employment by Zahir Shah, the communists, and, most recently, the UN agencies, who suffered most.

The rural–urban divide has always complicated the process of change in Afghanistan, as it has in many underdeveloped countries. So too have the heavy-handed ways in which change has often been imposed upon the countryside from above, by Afghanistan's tiny, Westernized, and mostly non-Pashtun, Persian-speaking urban elite in Kabul. The rural elite of religious and tribal leaders has tended to respond to their efforts at modernization by retreating even further in time. In 1929, conservative mullahs bullied women back into thicker chadors and sacked museums and libraries after overthrowing the liberal-minded King Amanullah, who had abolished the veil, opened co-ed schools, and ordered Afghans in Kabul to wear Western clothes. Not until 1959 did women appear without the chador on the streets of Kabul, and this continued for over thirty-five years, until they faced the cruellest restrictions yet on their freedom of movement and dress.

The Afghan communists had encouraged women in Kabul to wear skirts and employed them in the government. This was part of their plan to modernize Afghanistan. New textbooks sent out to the villages carried an image of three men in Western suits leading a traditionally dressed crowd to a glorious future. Volunteer teachers in the literacy campaign forced old men and girls to attend classes while at the same time, and often in the same villages, the communists were arresting and massacring tens of thousands of young Muslim men.

Much of the chaos and violence suffered in Afghan villages during the communist era was engineered by a Westernized elite at the head of an active government in Kabul – a city which, with its Persian-speaking population and apparently liberated women, was already alien to most Pashtuns. This may partly explain why the sons of Pashtun peasants and nomads who made up the Taliban imposed their harshest laws upon the women of Kabul soon after driving out the moderate Islamist Tajik commander Ahmed Shah Massoud from this most Westernized of Afghan cities in 1996 and forcing him to the north.

Suddenly, in yet another Afghan regression, women found themselves sentenced to the chador and confined to their homes. They could neither educate themselves nor work – Dupree estimates that the prohibitions directly affected anywhere between 40,000 and 150,000 working women and about 100,000 girls at school. Women had to be accompanied by male relatives outside their homes, where the possibility of public humiliation by the religious police was – usually beatings with sticks but also harsher punishments – ever-present.

The Taliban claimed they were shielding women from the sexual predation they had suffered in the days of the mujahedin warlords. A Taliban official, who had studied at a madrasa in Pakistan, told me that he couldn't trust his men with unveiled women; and in any case Mullah Omar, whose original mission had allegedly been to protect women from rapists and bandits, had to preserve at all costs the Taliban's reputation as uncorrupted men who had brought peace and security and 'true Islam' to Kabul.

The Taliban official wouldn't be drawn into a discussion of what 'true Islam' was or could be. But then what he really seemed to be articulating was the deep and long-standing fear and resentment of Western lifestyles, particularly the independence of women, among Pashtun men in the countryside – the modern ways that the communists had brutally imposed upon Afghanistan, and that Kabul, with the presence of foreign nationals there, represented. Mullah Omar expressed his contempt by staying away from what remained the official capital of Afghanistan and living in Kandahar. For the rural men who dominated the Taliban, the women in Kabul and other Afghan cities, the relatively modern Shi'ite and Persian-speaking minorities, the communists of the past, and the foreign aid workers of today were all part of the same large, undifferentiated threat to the Pashtun dictatorship that they, with some help from the sharia, or Islamic law, wished to maintain.

These complex social and economic resentments help to explain why the Taliban, while ruthless with the Shi'ites and NGO workers, did not curtail the religious practices of the 5,000 or so mostly poor Hindus and Sikhs in Afghanistan, even though the latter were briefly required – to avoid harassment from the religious police, the Taliban claim – to carry yellow identification badges at all times. They also help to explain the many incidents such as the one in which the religious police, who were answerable only to Mullah Omar in Kandahar, closed down an Italian-funded hospital in mid-May after they caught women workers dining with the male staff.

There were fewer such problems in the rural areas, where women, confined to looking after their families, already appeared part of the pre-modern moral order Mullah Omar apparently wished to recreate. You sensed that there was paradoxically a slightly greater freedom available to the women you saw travelling in the same buses as men, albeit in segregated rows, than was possible for women in Kabul, where the lines were clearly drawn.

UNESCO had supported the communist literacy campaign that was opposed by many Muslims; and during the anti-communist jihad in the 1980s many UN agencies and other NGOs carried on, among other development projects, the tasks of women's education and empowerment in communist-controlled Kabul. When the UN agencies argued that the Taliban had to allow Afghan women to work – particularly as nurses and doctors, since under the Taliban women could not be treated by men – the hardline leaders of the Taliban interpreted such insistence as further proof of the UN's complicity with the various forms of Western imperialism – cultural, social, and military – that they imagined were arrayed against them.

This is where some earlier exposure to the outside world might have helped – one can't overestimate the value, in these circumstances, of the small educated Afghan middle class that twenty years of war dispersed across the world. But the Pashtun village mullahs who formed the central leadership of the Taliban knew little else besides the Koran. This is why the Taliban, unlike such radical Islamist groups as the Muslim Brotherhood of Egypt and Pakistan's Jamiat-i-Islami, offered no coherent ideology or doctrine – as distinct from the fatwas that emanated randomly from Kandahar against women, idolatry, kite-flying, football, music, dancing, squeaky shoes, and American hairstyles.

The outlay for the Taliban's powerful Ministry of Promotion of Virtue and Prevention of Vice – which punished those whose beards were not the prescribed four inches long, and those who did not observe prayers and fasts, and worked hard to ensure that male minds remained free of the sinful thoughts incited by the presence of unveiled women – was three times as much as that for development. For Mullah Omar and his advisers from the rural clergy, it was enough to be pious and virtuous, and a healthy Islamic society would be created by itself. And the punishment for those who strayed from virtue was draconian: adulterers were stoned to death, while women were known to have the tips of their thumbs cut off for wearing nail polish. Not surprisingly, such cloud-cuckoo-land ideas – partly the result of their limited madrasa educations – and their brutal consequences made the Taliban increasingly unpopular among even the Pashtuns in the countryside who, oppressed by the mujahedin, had initially welcomed them as liberators.

Their aggressive puritanism – which includes a distrust of Shi'ite Muslims, hundreds of whom were massacred by Taliban soldiers – is far from the twentieth-century modernist ideologies of Islam that influenced an earlier generation of Afghan Islamists: Professor Burhanuddin Rabbani, the president of Afghanistan for two years in the early 1990s, was a graduate of the al-Azhar University in Cairo, while Mullah Omar doesn't have the basic educational qualifications required to be called a mullah.

The harsh arbitrariness of the mullahs in Kandahar and the religious police was justified under the name of 'true Islam', but sought for the most part to reconfigure the Pashtun dominance over Afghanistan's ethnic minorities – a new alignment of power that imposed Pashtun tribal ways over most of the country and made unassailable the Pashtun religious elites in the villages that had been, over the last century, continually threatened and undermined by the modernizing rulers of Afghanistan in Kabul.

The obstinacy and destructiveness of the Taliban now appear to be part of the history of Afghanistan's calamitous encounter with the modern world. Afghanistan missed the nineteenth century, which was a period of new beginnings for many old societies in the region. No country was less equipped to deal with the twentieth-century ideologies of communism, anti-communism, and radical Islam. No country was less prepared for the assortment of strategists and adventurers, people alien to and uncomprehending of Afghanistan, who managed to enlist the country's already great inner turmoil – the tragic violence and disorder of a near-primitive society modernizing too fast – into the wider conflict of the cold war; who managed to introduce more effective means of destruction and left behind a ruin more extensive than any the Afghans had known in their war-weary history.

The past two decades had probably weighed most heavily on the women in the country's small middle class, who had briefly flourished in the decade before 1979. In Kabul at Christmas 2004, I met Hawa Nooristani, a popular state TV anchor in Afghanistan. We sat in a damply carpeted room at the Ministry of Women's Affairs in Kabul. Pale light came through the windows, illuminating the dust on an old fax machine. A valentine in the form of a screen saver pirouetted on the screen of one of the two desktop computers in the room; the other screen displayed a message advising that its Norton AntiVirus subscription had expired. Two young women in headscarves appeared after five minutes or so with a large samovar and replenished our cups of green tea.

Born in Nangrahar province, Nooristani had gone to a local school and then in the late 1970s passed the entrance test for the medical faculty at Kabul University. But the anti-modern backlash had already begun in the country. Islamist mujahedin attacked schools in the provinces; they often kidnapped female students from the university in Kabul. Nooristani's father, a tribal leader, was 'open-minded' enough to educate his daughters, but he was worried. 'What will I do if they kidnap you?' he asked her. 'I will have to kill you.'

Nooristani joined the faculty of journalism at Nangrahar University. After three years, she married a government official and moved to Kabul, where she began to work for a women's magazine run by the communist government. She rose to be the magazine's deputy editor, reporting on such social issues as the marriage of minors, and profiling famous women singers and writers. She also wrote fiction and poetry in Pashto and raised a family of five children. This apparently placid life continued for twelve years, even as the war went on in Afghanistan. Then, in 1996, the Taliban came to Kabul, and closed down the magazine. They also detained her husband in Kandahar on false charges. Since the Taliban allowed women to work only in the health sector, Nooristani had to go underground while working for UN-Habitat, which was running a big project for widows. When the Taliban found out and began to look for her, then began a fearful phase for Nooristani. She and her five children had to seek shelter with friends and relatives, and move from house to house in order to avoid arrest. By now, her father and other relatives had already left for Pakistan. But she couldn't leave the country as long as her husband was in prison.

Nooristani smiled often, a sweet guileless smile, while describing her life, but tears suddenly brimmed in her eyes as she said, 'While I am talking to you, I remember those days and feel insecure once again. I realize again how weak were the foundations of our lives.'

The overthrow of the Taliban had given her fresh hope. She had restarted the women's magazine. She anchored news programmes on both TV and radio. She was also doing a computer course. Her teacher had told her, 'You are an intelligent student,' and as she reported this to me, she burst into girlish laughter. She was also working on a new collection of poems on computer. She had written her two previous collections in longhand; and lost both manuscripts. A friend had misplaced the first, and the other was destroyed when the Uzbek warlord Dostum bombed her home during the civil war in Kabul in 1992–4.

The United States lost interest in Afghanistan soon after the Soviet withdrawal from the country in 1989, although Afghans continued to pay a high price for having hosted one of the bloodiest battles of the cold war. In late 2001, the United States was faced with fresh responsibilities in Afghanistan after overthrowing the Taliban regime. It was obliged not only to engage in nation-building – a task President George W. Bush rejected during a presidential debate with Al Gore in 2000 as unsuitable for the United States – but also to provide basic security to more than twenty-five million people in a country as big as Texas. As it turns out, the way the Bush administration conducted the war, and dealt with its aftermath, has complicated both tasks.

Apart from Americans serving at bases in countries near Afghanistan and aerial bombing, the US committed only about 110 CIA officers and 316 Special Forces personnel to the overthrow of the Taliban. The Bush administration may have feared a stalemate in Afghanistan, where the armies of the British Empire and the Soviet Union have fared poorly in the past. Or, it may have planned to save ground troops for future military operations in Iraq. In any case, Defense Secretary Donald Rumsfeld preferred to use small, highly mobile forces supported by precision bombing in Afghanistan.

This forced the United States to recruit proxies on the ground. The most easily available of these turned out to be the anti-Taliban warlords in the so-called Northern Alliance, which consisted mainly of Tajiks, Hazaras, Uzbeks, and Turkmens, and which the Pashtun-dominated Taliban had repeatedly defeated. The CIA had helped arm many of these warlords during the anti-Soviet jihad. As the jihad had ended, the CIA and the State Department deferred to the Pakistani ISI and Saudi princes who had encouraged Muslims all over the world to join the jihad against the godless communist regime in Kabul, and who now tried to install the most extreme radical Islamists in power. Thus, billions of dollars of American taxpayer funding went into supporting a ruthless anti-American cabal of Islamists and Pakistani intelligence officers.

After the Soviet withdrawal in 1989, these uprooted mujahedin used brutal violence to assert their authority over the territories they controlled – hence the name *jang salar*, 'warlord', that Afghans came to use for many of the anti-Soviet mujahedin. Local mujahedin 'commanders' – the word in Afghanistan refers to men with guns and bands of loyal supporters – also set up toll tax checkpoints on roads. Extortion, arbitrary arrests, killings, kidnapping, and rape had become commonplace in many parts of Afghanistan in the early 1990s. Not surprisingly, many Afghans, including Hamid Karzai, initially welcomed the puritan Taliban as they arose in 1994 from the Pashtun-dominated southern and eastern provinces of Afghanistan to subdue by 1996 most of the warlords.

In the autumn of 2001, 'Operation Enduring Freedom' brought many of these mujahedin out of exile and retirement. In what President Bush has called one of the biggest 'bargains' of all time, CIA and Special Forces officers handed out 100-dollar bills totalling $70m. to such regional commanders of private militias as Ismael Khan in the west, Abdul Rashid Dostum, General Fahim Mohammed and Ustad Atta Mohammed in the north, and Hazrat Ali in the east.

Seeing that they were indispensable to the US war on terror, the warlords moved quickly and boldly as the Taliban regime collapsed. In November 2001, soldiers of the Tajik-dominated Northern Alliance raced into Kabul as soon as the Taliban abandoned it and occupied important government buildings, despite being told by their American supporters to await an orderly transition. Elsewhere in Afghanistan, the former mujahedin swiftly regained the power and influence that they had previously lost to the Taliban. Ismael Khan declared himself governor of the western province of Herat, and began to siphon off custom tolls on imports from Iran that then amounted to $9m. every month; he also reinstituted many Taliban-era restrictions on women.

Warlords in such border provinces as Nangrahar,

Kandahar, Khost, and Balkh resumed their battles to control the lucrative businesses of poppy cultivation and smuggling – fighting between the militias of Dostum and Atta Mohammed caused scores of civilian deaths in Balkh in 2002–3. They were soon associated with the kind of human rights abuses – extrajudicial killings, kidnapping, torture, rape, and human trafficking – that had caused the Taliban to be established in the first place. Warlords working with US Special Forces also committed atrocities, such as the death in the northern province of Shebarghan of up to 3,000 Taliban prisoners crammed by Dostum into sealed cargo containers.

In December 2001, the so-called Bonn agreement, an accord signed by militia leaders who fought with the United States against the Taliban, called for the UN to deploy an international security force in Kabul, and stipulated that all militias leave the city before the arrival of the UN-mandated forces. But this was never enforced. When Hamid Karzai arrived in Kabul in late 2001 as the US-backed interim president, he had to contend not only with General Fahim of the Northern Alliance and his tens of thousands of militia fighters ensconced in Kabul but also with the newly empowered warlords in the rest of the country.

Hazrat Ali is one of the more flamboyant and, with 18,000 armed supporters, most powerful of these warlords. He became briefly famous in late 2001 when US Special Forces hired him to hunt down Osama bin Laden in the caves of Tora Bora in the eastern province of Nangrahar. It is no longer clear whether bin Laden was in Tora Bora as American B-52s pulverized the area and commanders dazzled journalists with stories of high-tech terrorist caves inside the mountains. But Hazrat Ali continued to flourish. Backed by General Fahim in the Northern Alliance, and apparently favoured by US Special Forces, he threatened his rivals with American aerial strikes, and, after forcing out Karzai's candidate, appointed himself 'security chief' of the province of Nangrahar.

Such job titles in Afghanistan are rarely without grim irony. An investigator for the Afghan Independent Human Rights Commission in Nangrahar sighed before he went on to recite the cases of kidnapping, torture, and rape of women and young boys in which Ali's men were implicated. Since Tora Bora, Ali had also become one of the powerful men in Afghanistan involved in the drugs trade.

The farmers I met in Nangrahar province, among the 2.3 million Afghans employed in the drugs industry, described how Ali had encouraged and closely supervised the production and trafficking of opium. His men came to villages in pickup trucks and bought the poppy harvest, which, previously taken to Pakistan for processing, was now turned into heroin in laboratories within Nangrahar itself before being smuggled through Dubai and Pakistan onto the streets of London or Paris.

The new freedoms enjoyed by US-backed warlords like Hazrat Ali partly explain why Afghan opium poppy cultivation, abruptly curtailed when the Taliban enforced a ban in 2000–2001, jumped 64 per cent between 2003 and 2004, and why Afghanistan last year supplied 87 per cent of the world's heroin. Just as the CIA-sponsored radical Islam once connected Afghanistan to the modern world, so US-backed warlords have initiated Afghanistan into the globalized economy.

When I met Hazrat Ali in Jalalabad, the capital of

Nangrahar, near the Khyber Pass, in December 2004 at a compound teeming with Land Cruisers and heavily armed bodyguards, he had just returned from a tour of some poppy-growing districts. His assistant, a swarthy young man with wild eyes, was disappointed to see me. He had expected a white journalist, and he grew suspicious when I spoke to him in Urdu.

Hazrat Ali himself pleaded humility in the way a small-town hoodlum-turned-politician in India might. He was a 'very simple man', he said. Sitting cross-legged on a divan at one end of a long room, bare except for chandeliers, Ali repeatedly slapped the soles of his feet as he detailed his success in eradicating 95 per cent of the poppy grown in Nangrahar. He had not received clear enough instructions from Karzai, he said, otherwise he would have stopped poppy cultivation long ago. Now, within three days, there would be no poppy plant left in his province.

These claims were not entirely 'bullshit', as a Western diplomat in Kabul later described them. The efforts at eradication were largely successful in Nangrahar. But opium poppy can be stored for a long time, and many farmers in Nangrahar told me that Hazrat Ali was most likely waiting to sell his reserves after shortages caused by crop eradication in Afghanistan had inflated the international prices.

I asked him how the farmers whom he had forced to stop growing poppy would find another way of feeding their families. He said he didn't worry about that. Opium was immoral, banned by the sharia; it had to be eliminated. As for farmers in his province who complained about American soldiers breaking into their homes, searching for

terrorists and poppy, they needed, Ali said, to reform themselves; to stop growing poppy and supporting terrorists.

In his elegant mansion in the northern city of Mazar-I-
Sharif, some fifty miles from the Uzbekistan border,
the former warlord-turned-governor Atta Mohammed
described to me, as a television crew hovered around us,
how hard he had worked to eradicate poppy in Balkh
province, and how as a man of peace he had asked
hundreds of his fighters to voluntarily disarm. Feared
locally as an extreme Islamic fundamentalist, and previously seen in dirty camouflage khakis, Mohammed had
recently trimmed his long beard, and taken to wearing
pin-stripe suits while meeting foreign visitors in his wood-
panelled office.

Balkh TV news that evening showed Mohammed discussing the progress of Afghanistan with a visiting writer
from America. On television, Mohammed looked suave,
even persuasive. But Miriam, a long-standing American aid
worker I had met the previous evening, had already told
me that Mohammed's militia had stashed away large quantities of arms. Afghans in Mazar spoke casually of his role
in smuggling drugs across the nearby, largely unguarded,
border with Uzbekistan. In July 2004, Mohammed had
locked the Karzai-appointed local police chief in his own
home after the latter seized a consignment of opium.
British troops stationed in Mazar as part of the ISAF-run
Provincial Reconstruction Team had to supply the besieged
police chief with food and water until the stand-off ended.

When I met the military commander of the PRT in
December, he had just returned from what he described,
with British euphemism, as 'a frank talk' with Mohammed.

Apparently, there was little else that he and his few dozen troops in an area as large as Scotland could do.

Certainly, Afghanistan's weak central government is even less equipped to tackle the fact that twenty-eight out of the country's thirty-two provinces now grow poppy, often with the support and involvement of local officials, such as the chief of police in the remote northern province of Badakshan, who until recently was running the largest heroin factory in Afghanistan in his garden.

Karzai had initially offered cash incentives to poppy farmers in an attempt to make them destroy their crops. But many farmers never saw the money, which was swallowed up by corrupt government officials. Others accepted it and continued to cultivate poppy. Karzai later admitted his payments were a mistake.

The availability of high-yield seeds, cold-storage facilities, and microcredit may wean Afghan farmers away from what has become their most reliable source of income – poppy, which grows easily, even in areas without adequate water, and which can earn twenty-five times more than the traditional crops of wheat, rice, and cotton. But this will take years, if not decades. And long-term schemes for making Afghan agriculture and horticulture more profitable do not seem as important to the US counter-narcotics programme in Afghanistan as aggressive, quick-fix schemes for poppy eradication, which seem certain to invite resistance. In 2004, an American security company trained a 400-strong Afghan eradication team in just two weeks, and sent it out to the central province of Wardak, where it destroyed 1,000 hectares of poppy, but only after fighting off farmers who fired rockets and sowed their fields with land mines.

In November 2004, farmers in Nangrahar reported seeing a plane spraying poppy fields with chemicals. The governor of the province, Din Mohammed, who had to pacify the angry farmers, told me that only the Americans could have sent the plane, but US officials denied all knowledge of it. A European diplomat told me that 'very senior' members of the Bush administration had resolved to eradicate poppy aerially in Afghanistan, much to the consternation of Karzai, who feared that farmers would be incited to armed revolt by planes or helicopters destroying their fields.

It seems unfair to target, manually or aerially, hundreds of thousands of small poppy farmers without ensuring that they have alternative means of survival, especially while warlords and corrupt government officials continued to build great fortunes out of the narcotics business.

Many Afghans have asked why the 18,000 US troops in the country were unable to arrest the more notorious drugs traffickers. When I put this to a Western diplomat, he said that Al Capone was known as a mafia don for years before there was enough evidence to convict him. He then promised arrests of some big traffickers in early 2005. But no such arrests have happened, and until they do, it will be hard to dismiss Afghans as conspiracy-theorists when they claim the US ignored the extraordinary growth in poppy production over the last three years because it expected the money from drugs – Afghanistan's only major export – to spare it some of the costs of rebuilding the country's economy. Such short cuts, after all, have been taken before in Afghanistan, during the anti-Soviet jihad, when the CIA was complicit in the drugs trade.

*

Growing evidence that the Taliban and al-Qaeda were funding themselves through the narcotics trade may have finally alerted the Bush administration to the possibility that, as Antonio Maria Costa, executive director of the UN anti-narcotics programme wrote in a report in October 2003, 'Afghanistan will again turn into a failed state, this time in the hands of drug cartels and narco-terrorists.' In a more alarming survey published in November 2004, Costa warned that if the drug problem in Afghanistan persists, 'the political and military successes of the last three years will be lost'.

But Afghanistan will be unable to avoid this fate as long as the Bush administration considers warlords indispensable to its war on terror, and thus undercuts President Karzai's authority. Much of the country appears to be run largely by these warlords and their private militias, whom Karzai himself described, in a recent interview with the *New York Times*, as the greatest threat to Afghanistan's security – even more dangerous than Taliban insurgents, who killed more than 900 people in 2004, including reconstruction and aid workers, but are still largely confined to the southern and eastern provinces.

Defense Secretary Rumsfeld and his deputy, Paul Wolfowitz, have consistently refused to involve US troops in peacekeeping efforts in Afghanistan. More surprisingly, until September 2003, they opposed expanding the UN-mandated International Security Assistance Force (ISAF) beyond Kabul, especially in areas where, as the Human Rights Watch report for 2004 puts it, 'There are no real governmental structures or activity, only abuse and criminal enterprises by factions.' The 8,000-strong ISAF, which is under NATO command, will expand across Afghanistan over the next three years. But its presence will still compare poorly with 40,000 NATO soldiers in Bosnia, which is one-tenth the size of Afghanistan. Moreover, the ISAF has no mandate to take on drugs traffickers or even to intervene militarily in factional fighting.

In July 2004, Médecins Sans Frontières (MSF), which had remained in Afghanistan through the hard years of the civil war and the Taliban regime, finally withdrew from the country after five of its workers were killed by unknown gunmen. MSF claimed that Afghan officials gave them evidence that warlords in north-west Afghanistan were involved in the killings, but did nothing to arrest the suspects. MSF had previously 'condemned the distribution of leaflets by the coalition forces in southern Afghanistan in which the population was informed that providing information about the Taliban and al-Qaeda was necessary if they wanted the delivery of aid to continue'. It accused the United States of consistently using 'humanitarian aid to build support for its military and political ambitions', and thus compromising the neutrality of Western aid agencies in war zones.

In a response published in the *Wall Street Journal*, the novelist Cheryl Benard, who is married to the US ambassador Zalmay Khalilzad, advised MSF that 'it is a different world out there', and that 'humanitarians will have to operate under the cover of arms – or not at all'. But it is not clear whether the large-scale and expensive military offensives (costing $1bn. per month) against the Taliban and al-Qaeda are working, especially when compared to intelligence and police operations in Pakistan, where many senior al-Qaeda members have been captured.

Both bin Laden and Mullah Omar are still at large after

the highest bounties and most rigorous manhunts in history. This may attest not only to the difficulties of fighting a shadowy enemy in a vast and mountainous territory but also to the strength of tribal and religious loyalties and growing anti-American sentiment in the Pashtun-dominated provinces of Afghanistan and Pakistan. In October 2002, popular resentment of America helped a coalition of radical Islamist parties win elections in the Pakistani provinces bordering Afghanistan, where the Taliban appear to find ready support. More people in southern and eastern Afghanistan are likely to be drawn to radical Islamists as aerial bombings and raids on villages continue, and the US military places itself further beyond international law. No one among the thousands of Afghans detained by the US military at mostly unknown locations across Afghanistan since 2001 has been given prisoner-of-war status. Often released as arbitrarily as they are arrested, they have no access to legal counsel. Mistreatment during interrogation – beatings, sexual humiliation, and sleep deprivation – appears common. According to the Human Rights Watch report, eight Afghans have died in American custody. In 2004, two of these deaths were ruled homicides by US military doctors at Bagram air base near Kabul.

In Jalalabad, I met a diplomat from one of Afghanistan's powerful neighbours. He described in some detail his encounters with American diplomats and military officers, who he termed intellectually limited but very arrogant. He said, 'The Afghans in the south and east hate the Americans as much as they hated the Russians. They are too tired after twenty-five years of war. But give them two more years of Operation Enduring Freedom and they will start another jihad.'

Later that same evening, I was at the governor's mansion in Jalalabad, formerly a summer palace of the King of Afghanistan, when a delegation of tribal elders arrived. They had walked for much of the day from a remote district; mud covered their slippers and scaly feet. The governor attended to them immediately, after postponing his meeting with me. They sat on a terrace in two long rows, and the scene – long-bearded, turbanned men before their solicitous potentate, against a backdrop of gardens and pavilions – could have been that of a Mogul miniature painting.

The men had come to complain to the governor about heavy-handed American soldiers in their villages. After their leader spoke briefly and sombrely, the governor attempted a joke – possibly in order to hide his own inability to influence his American patrons. Afghanistan, he said, had become a Petri dish into which foreigners could throw in whatever they liked. Some of the men laughed, revealing toothless gums.

When their laughter subsided one of the elders began to speak. From where I sat, I couldn't see his face. I only heard his deep, urgent voice. He spoke about the dishonour caused to Afghan families by American soldiers barging into women's quarters, about the frustration and rage felt by him and others, and he spoke for a long time, his voice growing in passion until it broke. I began to believe that the diplomat, who I'd thought too embittered by his own encounters with powerful and abrasive Americans, might not have exaggerated much.

*

Many Afghans I spoke to felt that people in the West, absorbed with Iraq, had already grown indifferent to their fate, or saw in Afghanistan only what they wished to see: the dawn of democracy and freedom. But as Dr Sima Samar, the leading human rights activist in Afghanistan, suggested recently, 'Democracy and freedom are meaningless without justice and the rule of law.' The parliamentary elections may appear to be another milestone in the grand march to democracy and freedom; but they are also likely to give greater legitimacy to warlords, who are presently better placed than anyone else in Afghanistan to form political parties and influence voters.

For many Afghans, however, the future still appears to be full of opportunities. When I returned to Kabul, Karzai had announced his new cabinet. He had managed to exclude the more powerful warlords – Fahim and Dostum – and to choose what Massouda Jalal called 'qualified people', including of course Dr Jalal herself, who was asked to be the minister for women's affairs shortly after I met with her. The job seemed to have little political or financial power, and it would last only until the parliamentary elections, but she had accepted it.

I went to see her on her first day at work. On the afternoon I'd first met her it had been intensely cold and damp in her apartment in a Soviet-style housing estate. There was no power, and when she spoke of the 'dark ages' of the Taliban, a time that she spent largely at home, it had been hard to imagine a bleakness more lowering than the one she lived with. Now, at the ministerial chambers, brilliantly lit and expensively carpeted, her husband queued with many women waiting to be received by Dr Jalal.

The minister was busy, her assistant said, but granted

me time for one question. As she stood smiling and chatting with bouquet-laden visitors, I asked Dr Jalal what she thought the international community, which she had previously criticized, ought to do. It was the wrong question. Dr Jalal had yet to adjust her political opinions to her new official role, and she struggled briefly while the Afghan women around her stared at me. Then, she blurted out, 'Don't forget us.' As I left, she appeared slightly embarrassed by the sentimental words. But they expressed well, I thought later, the weary but still hopeful mood of many Afghans as they compete for the attention and goodwill of an easily distracted world.

Part III

Nepal:
The 'People's War'

IN KATHMANDU IN MARCH 2005, I met a Nepalese businessman who said he knew what had provoked Crown Prince Dipendra, supposed incarnation of Vishnu and former pupil at Eton, to mass murder. On the night of 1 June 2001, Dipendra appeared in the drawing room of the royal palace in Kathmandu, dressed in combat fatigues, apparently out of it on Famous Grouse and hashish, and armed with assault rifles and pistols. In a few frenzied minutes, he killed his parents, King Birendra and Queen Aishwarya, a brother, a sister and five other relatives before putting a pistol to his own head. Anointed king as he lay unconscious in hospital, he died two days later, passing his title to his uncle Gyanendra.

Dipendra's obsession with guns at Eton, where he was admired by Lord Camoys as a 'damn good shot', his heavy drinking, which attracted the malice of the *Sun*, his addiction to hashish and his fondness for the films of Arnold Schwarzenegger – all this outlines a philistinism, and a potential for violence, commonplace among scions of Third World dynasties (Suharto, Nehru–Gandhi, Bhutto). And it is not so hard to believe the semi-official explanation for his

actions: that his parents disapproved of his fiancée. However, the businessman, who claimed to know the royal
family, had a more elaborate and intriguing theory.

We sat in a rooftop café in Thamel, Kathmandu's tourist
centre, a few hundred feet from the royal palace. March,
the businessman said, was a good season for tourists in
Nepal. 'But look,' he continued, pointing to the alleys
below us, where the bookshops, trekking agencies, cyber-
cafes, bakeries, malls, and restaurants were empty. In
recent years, the tourist industry has been damaged by
news in the international press about the Maoist guerrillas, who model themselves on the Shining Path in Peru, and
whose 'people's war' has claimed more than 11,000 lives
since 1996. Even fewer tourists have ventured to Nepal
since 1 February 2005, when King Gyanendra, citing the
threat presented by the Maoists, grounded all flights, cut
off phone and internet lines, arrested opposition politicians
and imposed censorship on the media.

A portly man wearing a cotton tunic, tight trousers and
a cloth cap, the businessman had the prejudices of his class,
the tiny minority of affluent Nepalese whose wealth comes
largely from tourism and foreign aid; and that morning –
the spring sun growing warm and burning off the smog
over the Kathmandu Valley; the vendors of carpets,
Gurkha knives, pirate DVDs and Tibetan prayer flags sul-
lenly eyeing a stray tourist in tie-dye clothes – he aired them
freely.

He said that Maoists had bombed the private school he
sent his children to; he worried that his servants might join
the guerrillas, who controlled 80 per cent of the countryside and were growing strong in the Kathmandu Valley. He
said that he was all for democracy – he had been among

the protesters demanding a new constitution in the spring of 1990 – but peace and stability were more important. What the country needed now, he declared, was a strong and principled ruler, someone who could crush the Maoists. He said that he missed Dipendra: he was the man Nepal needed at this hour of crisis.

According to him, Dipendra's three years as a schoolboy in Britain had radicalized him. Just as Pandit Nehru had discovered the poverty of India after his stints at Harrow and Cambridge, so Dipendra had developed a new political awareness in England. He had begun to look, with mounting horror and concern, at his homeland. Returning to Nepal, he had realized that it would take more than tourism to create a strong middle class, accelerate economic growth, build democratic institutions, and lift the ninth poorest country in the world to the ranks of modern democratic nations. As it turned out, he had been thwarted at every step by conservative elements in the royal palace. He had watched multi-party democracy, introduced in 1991, grow corrupt and feeble while enriching an elite of politicians and bureaucrats; equally helplessly, he had watched the new rulers of Nepal fail to tackle the Maoists. Frustration in politics rather than love, the businessman claimed, had driven Dipendra to alcohol, drugs, guns, and, finally, to regicide.

It's often hard to know what to believe in Nepal, the only Hindu kingdom in the world, where conspiracy and rumour have long fuelled a particularly secretive kind of court politics. Independent newspapers and magazines have been widely available only since 1990, and though intellectually lively, the press has little influence over a largely illiterate population easily swayed by rumour. In December 2000, news that a Bollywood actor had insulted Nepal incited riots and attacks on Indians and Indian-owned shops across the country. Little is known about Dipendra, apart from his time at Eton, where his fellow pupils nicknamed him 'Dippy'. There is even greater mystery surrounding Pushpa Kamal Dahal, or Prachanda, the middle-aged, articulate leader of the Maoists, who has been in hiding for the last two decades.

King Gyanendra appeared on national television to blame the palace massacre on a 'sudden discharge by an automatic weapon'. A popular conspiracy theory, in turn, blamed it on the new king himself, who was allegedly involved in smuggling artefacts out of Nepal, and on his son, Paras, much disliked in Nepal for his habit of brandishing guns in public and dangerous driving – he has run over at least three people in recent years, killing one. More confusingly, the Maoists claimed that they had an 'undeclared working unity' with King Birendra, and accused Gyanendra, and Indian and American imperialists, of his murder.

This atmosphere of secrecy and intrigue seems to have grown murkier since February, when Gyanendra adopted the Bush administration's rhetoric about 'terrorism' and assumed supreme power. Flights to Nepal were resumed after only a few days, and the king claimed to have lifted the emergency on 30 April, but most civil rights are still suspended today. When I arrived in Kathmandu, fear hung heavy over the street crossings, where soldiers peeped out from behind machine-gun emplacements. Men in ill-fitting Western suits, with the furtive manner of inept spies, lurked in the lobby of my hotel. Journalists spoke of threatening phone calls from senior army officers who tended to finger as Maoists anyone who didn't support the king. Many of the people I wanted to meet turned out to be in prison or in exile. Appointments with underground activists, arduously made, were cancelled at the last minute, or people simply didn't turn up.

Sitting in her gloomy office, a human rights activist described the routine torture and extrajudicial killing of suspected Maoists, which had risen to a startling average of eight per day. Nothing was known about the more than 1,200 people the army had taken from their homes since the beginning of the 'people's war' – the highest number of unexplained disappearances in the world. She spoke of the 'massive impunity' enjoyed by the army, which was accountable only to the king. She claimed that the governments of India, the US, and the UK had failed to understand the root causes of the Maoist phenomenon and had decided, out of fear and ignorance, to supply weapons to the Royal National Army: 20,000 M16 rifles from the US, 20,000 rifles from India, helicopters from the UK.

She said that the 'international community' had chosen the wrong side in a conflict that in any case was not likely to be resolved by violence. Though recently expanded, and mobilized against the Maoists in 2001, the army was no more than 85,000 strong, and could not hold the country-side, where, among the high mountains, ravines and rivers – almost perfect terrain for guerrillas – it faced a formidable enemy.

She spoke with something close to despair. Much of her work – particularly risky at present – depended on international support. But few people outside Nepal cared or knew enough about its human rights record, and the proof lay in her office, which was austerely furnished, with none of the emblems of Western philanthropy – new computers, armed guards, shiny four-wheel drives in the parking lot – that I had seen in December in Afghanistan.

'People are passing their days here,' she said as I left her office, and the remark, puzzling at first, became clearer as I spent more time in Kathmandu. In the streets where all demonstrations were banned, and any protest was quickly quashed by the police, a bizarre feeling of normality prevailed, best symbolized by the vibrant billboards advertising mobile phones (banned since 1 February). Adverts in which companies affirmed faith in King Gyanendra appeared daily in the heavily censored newspapers, alongside news of Maoist bombings of police stations, unverified reports of rifts between Maoist leaders, promotional articles about Mercedes Benz cars and Tag Heuer watches, and reports of parties, and fashion shows and concerts in Kathmandu.

Thamel opened for business every day, but its alleys remained empty of tourists. Months of Maoist-enforced blockades and strikes were also beginning to scare away the few foreign investors who had been deceived by the affluence of Kathmandu into thinking that Nepal was a big market for luxury consumer goods. Interviewed in a local newspaper, a Dutch investor described the Nepalese as an 'extremely corrupt, greedy, triple-faced, myopic, slow, inexperienced and uneducated people', and declared that he was taking his hair-replacement business to Latvia. Western diplomats and United Nations officials – darting in their SUVs from one walled compound to another – speculated about a possible assault on the capital by guerrillas.

But it is the middle-class Nepalese, denounced by the

Maoists as 'comprador capitalists', who appear to live most precariously, their hopes and anxieties echoed in the newspapers by royalist journalists who affirm daily that Nepal needs a strong ruler and Gyanendra is best placed to defend the country, by means of a spell of autocratic rule, from both Maoist 'terrorists' and corrupt politicians.

Often while listening to them, I would remember the businessman I had met in Thamel and what he had told me about Dipendra; and I would wonder how the crown prince, if he had indeed been sensitized to social and economic distress during his three years in Thatcher's England, had seen his strange inheritance, a country where almost half of the twenty-six million people earned less than $100 a year and had no access to electricity, running water or sanitation; a country whose small economy, parasitic on foreign aid and tourism, had to be boosted by the remittances of Nepalese workers abroad, and where political forces seen as anachronisms elsewhere – monarchy and communism – fought for supremacy.

Histories of South Asia rarely describe Nepal, except as a recipient of religions and ideologies – Buddhism, Hinduism, communism – from India; even today, the country's sixty ethnic and caste communities are regarded as little more than a picturesque backdrop to some of the world's highest mountains. This is partly because Western imperialists overlooked Nepal when they radically remade Asia in the nineteenth and twentieth centuries.

While a British-educated middle class emerged in India and began to aspire to self-rule, Nepal remained a country of peasants, nomads, and traders, controlled by a few clans and families. Previously dependent on China, its high-caste

Hindu ruling class courted the British as they expanded across India in the nineteenth century. As in the so-called princely states of India, the British were keen to support despotic regimes in Nepal, and even reward them with territory; it was one way of staving off potentially destabilizing change in a strategically important buffer state to Tibet and China. The country was also a source of cheap mercenaries. Tens of thousands of soldiers recruited by the British from the western hills of Nepal fought during the Indian Mutiny, the Boxer Rebellion in China, and in the two world wars. The Gurkhas also helped the British suppress political dissenters in India, and then, more violently, communist anticolonialists in Malaya in the 1950s.

As the movement for political independence grew in India, Nepal came to be even more strongly controlled by Hindu kings and the elites they created by giving land grants to members of the high castes, Bahun and Chhetri, which make up less than 30 per cent of the population. The end of the British Empire in Asia didn't lead to rapid change in Nepal, or end its status as a client state. Indian-made goods flooded Nepalese markets, stifling local industry and deepening the country's dependence on India. In the 1950s and 1960s, as the cold war intensified, Nepal was the forward base of the CIA's operations against China.

American economists and advisers trying to make the world safe for capitalism came to Nepal with plans for 'modernization' and 'development' – then seen as strong defences against the growth of communism in poor countries. In the so-called Rapti zone, west of Kathmandu, where, ironically, the Maoists found their first loyal supporters in the 1990s, the US government spent about

$50m. 'improving household food production and consumption, improving income-generating opportunities for poor farmers, landless labourers, occupational castes and women'.

Modernization and development, as defined by Western experts during the cold war, were always compatible with, and often best expedited by, despotic rule. Few among the so-called international community protested when, after a brief experiment with parliamentary democracy in the 1950s, King Mahendra, Dipendra's grandfather, banned all political parties. A new constitution in 1962 instituted a partyless 'Panchayat' system of 'guided democracy' in which advisers chosen or controlled by the king rubber-stamped his decisions. The representatives of the Panchayat, largely from the upper castes, helped themselves to the foreign aid that made up most of the state budget, and did little to alleviate poverty in rural areas. The king also declared Nepal a Hindu state and sought to impose a new national identity on its ethnic and linguistic communities by promoting the Nepali language.

Such hectic nation-building could have lulled Nepal's many ethnic and linguistic communities into a patriotic daze had the project of modernization and development not failed, or benefited so exclusively and egregiously an already privileged elite. During the years of autocratic rule (1962-90), a few roads were built in the countryside, infant mortality was halved, and the literacy rate went up from 5 per cent in 1952 to 40 per cent in 1991. But Nepal's population also grew rapidly, further increasing pressure on the country's scarce arable land; and the gap between the city and the countryside widened fast.

What leads the sensitive prince to drugs and alcohol

often forces the pauper to migrate. Millions of Nepalese have swelled the armies of cheap mobile labour that drive the global economy, serving in Indian brothels, Thai and Malaysian sweatshops, the mansions of oil sheikhs in the Gulf, and, most recently, the war zones of Iraq. Many more have migrated internally, often from the hills to the sub-tropical Tarai region on the long border with India. The Tarai produces most of the country's food and cash crops, and accommodates half of its population. On its flat allu-vial land, where malaria was only recently eradicated, the Buddha was born 2,500 years ago; it is also where a generation of displaced Nepalese began to dream of revolution.

In Chitwan, one of the more densely populated districts in the Tarai, I met Mukti Raj Dahal, the father of the underground Maoist leader, Prachanda. Dahal was one of the millions of Nepalese to migrate to the Tarai in the 1950s. His son was then eight years old. He had travelled on to India, doing menial jobs in many cities, before return-ing to Chitwan, which American advisers and the Nepalese government were then developing as a 'model district' with education and health facilities. In Chitwan, Dalal bought some land and managed to give his eight children an edu-cation of sorts. Though he is tormented by stomach and spinal ailments, he exuded calm as he sat on the verandah of his two-roomed brick house, wearing a blue T-shirt and shorts under a black cap, a Brahmanical caste mark on his forehead.

He had the serenity of a man at the end of his life. And, given the circumstances, he had not done too badly. I had spent much of that day on the road from Kathmandu to the Tarai, shuffling past long queues of Tata trucks from

India, through a fog of dust and thick diesel smoke, ragged settlements occasionally appearing beside the road: shops made of wooden planks, selling food fried in peanut oil and tea in sticky clouded glasses, mud houses with thatched roofs – a pre-industrial bareness in which only the gleaming automatic guns of young soldiers and the tangle of barbed wire behind which they sat spoke of the world beyond Nepal.

The jittery soldiers who approached the car with fingers on their triggers were very young, hard to associate with stories I had heard in Kathmandu – stories no newspaper would touch – of the army marching men out of overcrowded prisons and executing them. My companion, a Nepalese journalist, was nervous. He knew that the soldiers in the countryside attacked anyone they suspected of being a Maoist, and journalists were no exception. Many of the soldiers barely knew what a journalist was.

There are few places in Nepal untouched by violence – murder, torture, arbitrary arrest – and most people live perpetually in fear of both the army and the Maoists, without expectation of justice or recompense. Dahal, however, appeared to have made a private peace with his surroundings. He told me that he spent much of his day at the local temple, listening to recitals of the *Ramayana*. He said that he still believed the king had good intentions. He appeared both bemused by, and admiring of, his own famous son, whom he had last seen at the funeral of his wife in 1996. The ideas of equality and justice, he thought, had always appealed to Prachanda, who was a sensitive man, someone who shared his food with poor people in the village. He couldn't tell me how his son had got interested in Mao or Marx in such a place as Chitwan, which had no bookshop or library. But he did know that Prachanda had got involved with communists when he couldn't find a good job with the government and had to teach at a primary school in his native hills of Pokhara.

In his speeches, which claim inspiration from Mao and seek to mobilize the peasants in the countryside against the urban elite, Prachanda comes across as an ideologue of another era: he's an embarrassment to the Chinese regime, which is engaged in the un-Maoist task of enriching Chinese coastal cities at the expense of the hinterland, and feels compelled to accuse Nepalese Maoists of besmirching the Chairman's good name.

In the few interviews he has given, Prachanda avoids answering questions about his background and motivation, which have to be divined from details given by Dahal: the haphazard schooling, the useless degree, the ill-paid teaching job in a village school, all of which seem to lead inexorably to a conflict with, and resentment of, unjust authority.

The 'modernization' and 'development' of Nepal during the 1950s and 1960s created millions of men like Prachanda, lured away from their subsistence economies and abandoned on the threshold of a world in which they found they had, and could have, no place. Nepal's agricultural economy offered few of them the jobs or the dignity they felt was their due, and they were too aware of the possibilities thwarted by an unequal, stratified society to reconcile themselves to a life of menial labour in unknown lands, and an old age spent in religious stupor. Educated, but with no prospects, many young men like Prachanda must have been more than ready to embrace radical ideas about the ways that an entrenched urban elite could be challenged and even overthrown if peasants in the countryside were organized.

Growing up in Nepal in the 1960s, Prachanda watched these ideas grow in the Naxalbari movement in India. Communist activists lived and worked secretly in parts of Nepal during the Panchayat era – in the 1950s, a famous communist leader called M.B. Singh travelled in the midwestern hills and acquired followers among the Magars, one of Nepal's more prominent ethnic groups now supporting the Maoists. But Prachanda says that the 'historic Naxalbari movement' of India was the 'greatest influence' on the communists of Nepal.

In the late 1960s, thousands of students, many of them middle class and upper caste, joined an armed peasant uprising led by an extremist faction of the Communist Party of India (Marxist) in West Bengal and Bihar. Known as Naxalites, after the Naxalbari district where the revolt first erupted in 1967, they attacked 'class enemies' – big landlords, policemen, bureaucrats – and 'liberated' territories which they hoped would form bases for an eventual assault on the cities, as had happened in China. The Indian government responded brutally, killing and torturing thousands. Driven underground, the Naxalite movement splintered, and remained dormant for many years.

In the 1990s, when India began to move towards a free market, the Naxalite movement revived in some of the poorest and most populous Indian states. Part of the reason for this is that successive Indian governments have steadily reduced subsidies for agriculture, public health, education, and poverty-eradication, exposing large sections of the population to disease, debt, hunger, and starvation. Almost 3,000 farmers committed suicide in the southern state of Andhra Pradesh after the government, advised by McKinsey, cut agricultural subsidies in an attempt to initiate farmers into the world of unregulated markets. In recent years, Naxalite movements, which have long organized landless, low-caste peasants in Bihar and Andhra Pradesh, have grown quickly in parts of Uttar Pradesh and Madhya Pradesh – where an enfeebled Indian state is increasingly absent – to the extent that police and intelligence officials in India now speak anxiously of an unbroken belt of communist-dominated territory from Nepal to South India.

The Naxalite uprising in the late 1960s invigorated the few communists in Nepal, who, like the members of the Nepali Congress, the main underground political organization, sought guidance and encouragement from India. In 1971, some Nepalese communists living across the border from Naxalbari declared a 'people's war' against the monarchy. They killed seven 'class enemies' before being suppressed by the king. As fractious as their Indian counterparts, the Nepalese communist parties split and split again over petty doctrinal or personality issues. In 1991, after the restoration of multi-party democracy, several of them contested elections, and even did well: a communist coalition became the biggest opposition party, and briefly held power in 1994. In the early 1990s, however, few people in Nepal could have predicted the swift rise of Prachanda and the obscure faction he led.

The Maoists under Prachanda resolved as early as 1986 to follow Mao's strategy of capturing state power through a 'people's war'. They did not start the war until the mid 1990s, however, when disillusionment with parliamentary democracy created for them a potentially wide popular base in the countryside. Still, hardly anyone noticed when on 4 February 1996 the Maoists presented the government with a list of forty demands, which included abrogating existing treaties with India, stripping the monarchy of all power and privileges, drafting a new constitution by means of a constituent assembly, nationalizing private property, declaring Nepal a secular nation, and ending all foreign aid. These demands were not likely to be met; and as though aware of this, the Maoists began their 'people's war' by attacking police stations in six districts four days before the deadline.

For the next five years, the Maoists forced their way into the national consciousness with their increasingly bold tactics. They financed themselves by collecting 'taxes' from farmers, and they exacted 'donations' from many businessmen in the Kathmandu Valley. They indoctrinated schoolchildren; they formed people's governments in the areas they controlled and dispensed rough justice to criminals and 'class enemies'. But much of the new power and charisma of the Maoists came from their ability to launch audacious attacks on the police and the army.

The military wing of the Maoists initially consisted of a few ill-trained men armed with antique rifles and home-made weapons. But they chose their first target cannily: the police, almost the only representatives of the central government in much of Nepal. Poorly armed, often with little more than sticks and .303 Lee Enfield rifles, the police retreated swiftly before the Maoists, who also attacked roads, bridges, dams, administrative offices, bridges, power plants – anything they felt might aid the counter-insurgency efforts of the government.

In recent years, the Maoists have grown militarily strong, mostly through conscription in the countryside, and regular training – allegedly provided by Indian Naxalites. They have acquired better weapons by looting police stations and buying from the arms bazaars of India; they have also learned how to make roadside explosives, pipe and 'pressure cooker' bombs. In November 2001, the Maoists launched forty-eight attacks on the army and the police in a single day, forcing the Nepalese government to impose a state of emergency. More than 5,000 people died in the next fifteen months, the bloodiest period in Nepal's modern history.

But violence is only a part of the Maoists' overall strategy. In an interview in 2000, Prachanda criticized Indian communist groups for their lack of vision and spoke of the importance of developing 'base areas'. Since 1996, the Maoists have spread out from their traditional home in the midwestern hills of Rolpa and Rukum districts. Their cadres – estimated to number as many as 100,000 – travel to deprived areas, addressing, and often recruiting from, the large and growing mass of people deeply unhappy with Nepal's new democratic dispensation.

Some measure of democracy was inevitable in Nepal by the 1980s. In previous decades, the state's half-hearted efforts at development had produced many low-level bureaucrats, small businessmen, teachers, students, and unemployed graduates. This new class resented the continuing dominance of upper-caste clans and families. The conflict between the old elite and its challengers was aggravated by a series of economic crises in the late 1980s. In 1985–6, Nepal had negotiated a loan with the IMF and World

Bank. The bank's euphemistically named (and free-market oriented) 'structural adjustment programme', which was then causing havoc in Latin American economies, forced the Nepalese government to cut farm subsidies and jobs in the public sector. GDP grew as a result but the gains were cancelled out by inflation of up to 10 per cent and a trade and transit embargo imposed by India in 1989, which caused severe fuel shortages and price rises.

The protesters who filled the streets of Kathmandu in the spring of 1990 were convinced that the decaying Panchayat system could not deal with the shocks of the new world and needed to be reformed. In acceding to demands for multi-party democracy, the king appeared to acknowledge the strength of the new educated class and to recognize that the old political system needed a degree of popular legitimacy if it was to survive. It's clear now that what happened in 1990 was less a revolution than a reconfiguration of power, sanctified by elections, among the old royalist oligarchy and an emerging urban middle class. Many courtiers and sycophants of the king managed to reinvent themselves as parliamentary politicians, often joining the Nepali Congress, the political party that ruled Nepal for all but one of the next thirteen years. There were few ideological differences between the Nepali Congress and the main opposition party, the radical-sounding Communist Party of Nepal (United Marxist-Leninist), both of which continued to be led by upper-caste men motivated largely by a desire for money and power. Elections were held frequently, and a procession of governments – thirteen in as many years – made Nepalese democracy appear vibrant. But the majority of the population, especially its ethnic communities, went largely unrepresented.

In 1992, when democracy still promised much, and Maoism was no more than another rumour on the streets of Kathmandu, Andrew Nickson, a British expert on Latin America, wrote prophetically:

> The future prospects of Maoism in Nepal will . . . depend largely on the extent to which the newly elected Nepali Congress government addresses the historic neglect and discrimination of the small rural communities which still make up the overwhelming bulk of the population of the country. As in the case of Peru, this would require a radical reallocation of government expenditures towards rural areas in the form of agricultural extension services and primary healthcare provision.

Needless to say, this didn't happen. In 2002, Dalits, low-caste Hindus, had an annual per capita income of only $40, compared to a national average of $210; fewer than 10 per cent of Dalits were literate. The upper-caste men who dominated the new democratic regime were competing among themselves to siphon off the money pouring into Nepal from foreign donors. A fresh convert to the ideology of the free market, the Nepalese government dedicated itself to creating wealth in urban areas. Trying to boost private investment in Kathmandu, it neglected agriculture, on which more than 80 per cent of the population depend for a living. Not surprisingly, absolute poverty continued to increase in the late 1990s, even as Kathmandu Valley benefited from the growth in the tourist, garment, and carpet industries, and filled up with new hotels, resorts, and villas.

In such circumstances, many people are likely to be attracted to violent, extra-parliamentary groups. The

Maoists in Nepal had their first ready constituency among rural youths, more than 100,000 of whom fail their high-school examination every year. Unemployed and adrift, many of these young men worked for other political parties in the countryside before becoming disillusioned and joining the Maoists.

Mohan was one of the young men who joined a newly legitimate political party after 1990 and then found himself remote from the spoils of power. He then worked with the Maoists for almost five years, living in jungles, once travelling to the easternmost corner of Nepal, before deciding to leave them. He couldn't return to his village, which lay in the Maoist-dominated region of Rolpa, and so had gone to India for a while. He was now trying to lie low in Kathmandu, and although he didn't say so, he seemed to be 'passing his days' and making a living through odd jobs, like so many other people in the city.

We had arranged to meet in Boudhanath, Kathmandu's major Buddhist site. Sitting in the square around the white stupa, among monks in swirling crimson robes and often with white faces, Mohan spoke of 'feudal forces' and the 'bourgeoisie': their corruption had paved the way for the Maoists, whom he described as 'anarchists'. He used the foreign words with a Nepalese inflection. He said that he had picked them up while accompanying a Maoist propagandist on tour; and it occurred to me, as he described his background, that he still used them despite having left the Maoists because he had no other vocabulary with which to describe his experience of deprivation and disappointment.

He was born and brought up in a family of Magar

shepherds in a corner of Rolpa district that had no proper roads, schools or hospitals. Educated at a school which was a walk of several miles from his village, he had joined the Nepali Congress in 1992, when still in his late teens, and had become a personal aide to a prominent local politician. There were many such young men. They received no money for their services, but slept in the politician's house, ate the food prepared for his family, and travelled with him to Kathmandu. Mohan said that it was a good time, the early years of democracy. He liked being in Kathmandu, especially with someone who had a bit of power. But he couldn't fail to notice that the politician returned less and less often to his constituency in the hills and often refused to meet people who came to his door asking for jobs, money, and medical help. He was surprised to hear that the politician was building a new house for himself in Kathmandu. Soon, he felt he was not needed, and one day the politician's wife told him to eat elsewhere.

Clashes between Nepali Congress activists and the Maoists were common in his area; he felt that he could be useful to the Maoists with his knowledge of politics. He was also attracted to the idea of ethnic autonomy that the Maoists espoused. He had seen in his time with the politician how the upper-caste-dominated government in Kathmandu possessed an unjust share of the country's wealth and resources. Many people he knew had already joined the Maoists, and in 1995, one of his friends introduced him to the Maoist 'squad commander' in the region.

As he spoke, I wondered if this was the whole truth, if he hadn't joined the Maoists for the same reason he had joined the Nepali Congress, the reason many young men like him in India joined political parties: for food and shelter. In any case, he joined the Maoists at a bad time: it was in 1995 that the Nepalese government launched Operation Romeo.

This scorched-earth campaign is described as an instance of 'state terror' in a report by INSEC (Informal Sector Service Centre), Nepal's most reliable human rights group. According to the report, the police attacked Rolpa and Rukum districts, killing and torturing young men and raping women. When I mentioned this to Mohan, he said that things weren't as bad as they were made out to be by the 'bourgeois' intelligentsia in Kathmandu, who, he thought, were soft on the Maoists. He said the Maoists were simply another opportunistic political group; this was why he had left them. They were interested in mobilizing ethnic communities only to the extent that this would help them capture 'state power'; they weren't really interested in giving them autonomy. He had also been repelled by their cruelty. He had heard about – if not actually seen – instances of Maoists punishing people who refused to pay taxes, defied their alcohol ban or were suspected of being police informers. Using rocks and hammers, they often broke all the bones in their victims' bodies before skinning them alive and cutting off their tongues, ears, lips, and noses.

Many of these stories appear in reports by Nepalese and international human rights groups. The Maoist leaders were, I often heard in Kathmandu, riding a tiger, unable to prevent their angry and frustrated cadres from committing torture and murder. Criminals had infiltrated their movement, and some Maoists now made a living from extortion and kidnapping. When confronted with these excesses, Maoist leaders deny or deplore them. They probably realize that they are losing many of their original supporters, who are as tired of the organization's growing extremism as of the years of indecisive fighting. Nevertheless, these leaders can often seem constrained in their political thinking by revolutionary methods and rhetoric created in another time and place. Prachanda, for instance, is convinced that 'a new wave of revolution, world revolution, is beginning, because imperialism is facing a great crisis'.

When the subject is not world revolution but the specific situation of Nepal, he can be shrewdly perceptive. A police officer in India told me that many of the Indian communists he interviewed confessed to learning much from the Maoists in Nepal, who were not as rigidly doctrinal as communists in India and Afghanistan. As Prachanda put it:

> The situation in Nepal is not classical, not traditional. In the Tarai region we find landlords with some lands, and we have to seize the lands and distribute them among the poor peasants. But in the whole mountainous regions, that is not the case. There are smallholdings, and no big landlords . . . How to develop production, how to raise production is the main problem here. The small pieces of land mean the peasants have low productivity. With collective farming it will be more scientific and things can be done to raise production.

It is not clear how much collective farming exists, or what non-military use the Maoists make of the taxes they collect. In fact, there is little reliable information about what goes on in the countryside. Few journalists venture out of their urban bases, and the Maoists aren't the only obstacle. Most of the very few roads outside Kathmandu are a series of large potholes, and then there are the nervous soldiers at checkpoints. And once you move away from the highway, no soldiers or policemen appear for miles on end. In Shakti Khor, a village in the Tarai region populated by one of the poorest communities in Nepal, a few men quietly informed us that Maoist guerrillas were hiding in the nearby forest, where no security forces ever ventured and from where the Maoists often escaped to India. At a small cooperative shop selling honey, mustard oil, turmeric, and herbal medicines, two men in their mid twenties appeared very keen to put in a good word for the Maoists – who the previous night had painted red anti-monarchy slogans on the clean walls.

In the other Maoist-dominated regions I visited, people seemed too afraid to talk. At Deurali Bazaar, a village at the end of a long and treacherous drive in the hills near Pokhara, a newly constructed bamboo gate was wrapped with a red cloth painted with a hammer and sickle and the names of Maoists either dead or in prison. The scene in the square appeared normal at first – women scrubbing children at a municipal tap, young men drinking tea, an old tailor hunched over an antique sewing machine, his walking stick leaning against his chair – but the presence of the Maoists, if unacknowledged, was unmistakable. When I tried to talk to the men at the tea-shop, they walked away fast, one of them knocking over the tailor's stick. The shopkeeper said that he knew nothing about Maoists. He didn't know who had built the bamboo gate; it had simply appeared one morning.

When I got back to Pokhara that evening, the news was of three teenage students killed as they tried to stop an army car on the highway. The previous day I had seen newspaper reports in which the army described the students as 'terrorists' and claimed to have found documents linking them to the Maoists. But it now seemed clear that they were just collecting donations for Holi, the Hindu festival of colours. There were eyewitnesses to the shooting. The parents of the victims had exhumed their corpses from the shallow graves in which the army had quickly buried them and discovered that two of them had been wearing their school uniforms. Like much else in Nepal, this would not appear in the newspapers.

The bloody stalemate in Nepal may last for a long time. The army is too small and poorly equipped at present decisively to defeat the Maoists. In some areas it has recently tried arming upper-caste villagers and inciting them to take action against the Maoists. In the southern district of Kapilavastu, vigilante groups organized by a local landlord and armed by the government claim to have killed more than fifty Maoists in February. Such tactics are likely not only to lead to a civil war but also to increase support for the Maoists in areas where the government is either absent or disliked.

Though unlikely at present, talks may offer a way forward. The Maoists have shown themselves willing to negotiate and even to compromise: in July 2001, they dropped their demand that Nepal cease to be a monarchy. More recently, Prachanda hinted at a flexible stance when he called for a united front of mainstream political parties against the monarch. He probably fears that the guerrilla force might self-destruct if its leaders fail to lead their more extreme cadres in the direction of moderate politics. But any Maoist concessions to bourgeois democracy are unlikely to please Gyanendra, who clearly wants to use the current chaos to help him hold on to his power.

If he periodically evokes the prospect of terrorists taking over Nepal, Gyanendra can count on the support of India, the US, and the UK. In late 2001, the US ambassador to Nepal, Michael Malinowski, a veteran of the CIA-sponsored anti-Soviet jihad in Afghanistan, said that 'These terrorists, under the guise of Maoism or the so-called "people's war", are fundamentally the same as terrorists elsewhere – be they members of the Shining Path, Abu Sayaf, the Khmer Rouge or al-Qaeda.' The then Hindu nationalist government in Delhi, just as eager to name new enemies, also described the Maoists as 'terrorists'.

The present Indian government has a more nuanced view of Nepal. But it is worried about India's own communist rebels and their links with the Nepalese Maoists, and it believes that, as Malinowski put it, 'all kinds of bad guys could use Nepal as a base, like in Afghanistan'. Responding to fears that the army in Nepal was running out of ammunition, India resumed its arms supply this year, partly hoping to contain the Maoists and wanting too to maintain its influence over Nepal in the face of growing competition from the US.

There is no evidence that bad guys, as defined by the Bush administration, have flocked to Nepal; the Maoists are far from achieving a military victory, and the communists in India are unlikely to extend their influence beyond the poverty-stricken districts they presently control. The rise of an armed communist movement in a strategically important country nevertheless disturbs many political elites, who believe that communism died in 1989 and that history has arrived at the terminus of liberal–capitalist democracy.

A European diplomat in Kathmandu told me that although Western countries hoped the political parties and the king would put up a joint front against the Maoists, they knew they might at some point have to support the king and his army if he alone was left to protect the country from the Maoists and keep alive the prospects for democracy. I did not feel that I could ask him about the nature of a democracy that is protected by an autocrat. Perhaps he meant nothing more by the word 'democracy' than regular elections: the kind of democracy whose failure to contain violence or to limit systemic poverty and inequality does not matter so long as elections are held, even if, as in Afghanistan and Iraq, under a form of martial law, and in which the turnout of voters does nothing but empower and legitimize a native elite willing to push the priorities of its Western patrons.

Such a form of democracy, which is slowly coming into being in Pakistan, could be revived again in Nepal, as the king repairs his relationship with the mainstream political parties. It is possible, too, that the excesses of the Maoists will cause them to self-destruct. Certainly the international revolution Prachanda speaks of will prove a fantasy. Yet it's hard to wish away the rage and despair of people who, arriving late in the modern world, have known its primary ideology, democracy, only as another delusion – the disenchanted millions who will increasingly seek, through other means than elections, the dignity and justice that they feel is owed to them.

Tibet:
A Backward Country

IN 1992 I LEFT Delhi and began to live in a small village in the Indian Himalayas. It was spring when I arrived. Every cloudless morning I got up and walked out onto the balcony of my cottage to see the white mountains towards the east straining high on their plinth of deep blue air. I could gaze upon these mountains for hours on end, especially in the long evenings, when the distant snow would refuse to disappear beneath the encroaching darkness, glowing an imperious red late into the night. My landlord often joined me on the balcony. One evening he asked me if I knew what lay beyond the mountains. I shook my head. 'Tibet,' he said.

When I finally travelled to Tibet in 2004, I remembered how surprised I had been by my landlord's reply back then. How had I managed to lose sight of this basic geography – Tibet, the broad high plateau between India and China, bigger than even western Europe, and the source of most of the great rivers of Asia (the Indus, the Yangtze, the Brahmaputra, and the Sutlej) – something so immediately obvious in all the atlases I had? How could I not have known that the Indian Himalayas bordering Tibet, a bus ride away from my own village, were predominantly Tibetan in culture and Buddhist in religion?

But then, Tibet was to me, as it had been to many others, a fantasy rather than a real place: a resonant cliché, 'the roof of the world', rather than a clearly defined area on a map.

Growing up in a Hindu Brahmin family in India, I had inherited a religious idea about Tibet: it was the sacred homeland of great seers and sages, people capable of levitation and astral travel. Later, while reading nineteenth- and early twentieth-century travellers and explorers from the West, I came across similarly romantic, if more apparently rational, notions of Tibet: it was the isolated, inaccessible country that had remained untouched by the drastic transformations imposed by railways, roads, steamships, and industries in the nineteenth century; a civilization where religion and tradition were a living force, and whose peoples radiated a serenity and gentleness long extinct in the frantically modern and aggressive societies of Europe and America.

Living in the Himalayas, remote at last from the squalor of Delhi and the small towns where I had spent most of my life, I had little trouble entering this Virtual Tibet. It became more compelling as I began to travel to the Indian border with China/Tibet. In the cold deserts and high valleys, where monks and hermits lived in tiny caves cut into steep hillsides, dressed in cotton vests in sub-zero temperatures, I could easily believe in the miraculous powers attributed to lamas and other spiritually exalted people – the benign, medieval religiosity that many Western travellers found in Tibet, recently commemorated in such

Hollywood films as *Seven Years in Tibet* and Martin Scorsese's *Kundun.*

There was little place in this vision for the hundred thousand or so Tibetan refugees in India – people who had escaped the country's Chinese communist rule. Expelled from their ostensible paradise of Tibet, they stood on the narrow, broken pavements of Indian hill-towns, selling woollen jackets, socks, gloves, calculators, Walkmans, and wrist-watches.

I had read of how the Chinese, who first invaded Tibet in 1950, had killed hundreds of thousands of Tibetans and destroyed many hundreds of monasteries and temples. I had read that the traditional society and culture of Tibet were gravely threatened. But I still didn't know what to make of the Tibetan refugees, and their oddly Westernized ways. In their jeans and American college sweatshirts, most young Tibetans didn't seem the heirs to a traditional culture, not with karaoke bars and video-game parlours standing next to Buddhist temples in Dharamsala, the home of the Dalai Lama, the spiritual leader of the Tibetan community in exile.

Our modern fantasies of a simple and whole past are fragile. Perhaps that's why we hold onto them so tenaciously. In Tibet, I sought to confirm everything I had imagined about it, and, for the first few days at least, I was not disappointed.

The magic began on the flight to Lhasa from Kathmandu when, defying predictions of bad weather and low visibility, Mount Everest unexpectedly emerged, all sheer rock and ice, looming well above the thick cloud cover at 25,000 feet; and then, after a long, snowbound mountain range, the Tibetan plateau revealed itself in all its purity and vastness.

Chinese military officials supervised our arrival at Gongkar airport. Their stern faces and green uniforms were the first reminder of the political status of Tibet. Outside, tour guides with Land Cruisers waited to attach themselves to tourists, and bilingual banners – on which Chinese ideograms dwarfed the elegant Tibetan script – proclaimed Tibet part of the rapidly progressing Chinese 'motherland'.

But less than a mile outside the airport, the empty countryside began: barley fields next to a very broad river, whose still surface reflected with spellbinding clarity the deep-blue sky, the surrounding bare hills, and, occasionally, the white massifs guarding the remote horizon.

This was the Yarlung Valley, the cradle of Tibetan civilization, where the first known ruler of Tibet emerged in the seventh century, and from where the Tibetan empire once spread as far as Afghanistan and Bengal. At Yambulagang, the site of the first known building in Tibet, yaks with smooth black horns and bushy white tails waited to carry us to the hilltop temple where monks pored over open manuscripts of rough paper, amid an overpowering aroma of rancid yak butter and sandalwood incense. After the blinding light of the valley, the chapels were dark and mysterious, crowded with gilded statues of the Buddha and Tibetan kings, the walls hectic with murals of the sharp-toothed multi-armed demons that the Tibetans revere as protector deities.

In these first few days it seemed to me that many centuries happily coexisted in Tibet. On the small ferry that took us next morning across the Tsangpo river to the eighth-century Samye monastery – the oldest in Tibet – there were two yaks and a young monk wearing blue jeans and sneakers under his habit.

The sun was warm, dazzling when reflected in the water and on the snow peaks and sandy banks. A handsome old man in a trilby hat twirled a prayer wheel. Two young women sat silently, holding stylish parasols in one hand and rosaries in the other; they turned out to be pilgrims, like most people on the ferry. A young couple in jeans and embroidered boots sat on the floor with their lively red-cheeked baby.

At the ferry beach, a ramshackle bus waited to take us across sand dunes to the monastery. I spent the long afternoon walking around the circular walled compound of the recently renovated monastery, which was designed originally to represent the Tibetan Buddhist cosmos, and was once fringed with 1,008 gold-encrusted *chortens* (reliquary mounds). Chinese, Indian, and Tibetan architectural styles rendered distinctive each of the three floors of the central building, whose wide assembly hall was full of the guttural chants of monks sitting amid riotously colourful silk drapes and shafts of sunlight.

In one of the darker chapels, a young monk whispered to me in Hindi. In our brief hurried conversation – Chinese spies were everywhere, he said – he explained that he had left Tibet illegally in order to spend a couple of years in Dharamsala, the home of the Dalai Lama, the spiritual leader of Tibetan Buddhists. Educated at Samye, he had not taken his vows until after his visit to the Dalai Lama. And now his younger brother was planning a risky journey to Dharamsala.

*

Part 3

To travel from Samye to Lhasa, past ruins of hillside
monasteries and fortresses, was to enter a more fraught
world. It was to confront the knowledge that had shad-
owed me at Yambulagang and Samye: that I was looking
at the ghosts of buildings almost entirely destroyed by Chinese and Tibetan fanatics before and during the Cultural
Revolution (1966-76).

'Religion is poison,' Mao Zedong had told the Dalai
Lama in 1955, early during the Chinese occupation of
Tibet. After 1959, when the Dalai Lama fled to India, the
Chinese had moved swiftly to undercut the power of the
monasteries which owned most of the arable land, and
loaned money to and educated poor villagers. At Samye,
where the first Tibetans were ordained as monks, and from
where Buddhism travelled to the rest of Tibet, Red Guards,
fired up by Mao's denunciation of religion and tradition,
had pounded *chortens* and statues into dust. Some of the
chortens have been restored and with their mix of concrete
and gold-leaf encrusting they embody well the tawdry
kitsch produced by Chinese-led restoration efforts in Tibet.
The destruction was most extensive in the region of Lhasa,
where all the major monasteries – Drepung, Sera, Ganden
– were reduced to ruins and only the seventeenth-century
Potala Palace, the traditional home of the Dalai Lama,
escaped the fury of the Red Guards.

The communist leadership in Beijing now admit, if
grudgingly, to 'excesses' and 'mistakes' during the Cultural
Revolution, when tens of thousands of Tibetans were
condemned as 'reactionaries', 'rightists' and 'capitalist
roaders', and imprisoned, tortured, and murdered. Ambi-
valence now clouds the official memory of Mao, the 'Great
Helmsman', who steered his country into famine and

{ 418 }

chaos. This is partly because in the early 1980s the Chinese regime embraced the free market after scorning 'capitalist roaders' for decades and decided that 'to get rich', as the late communist leader Deng Xiaoping described, 'is glorious'.

It wasn't easy, however, to get rich in Tibet. The hard ground and extreme cold precluded extensive agriculture – most Tibetans still depend on yak meat and barley flour – and little infrastructure for heavy industries existed outside Lhasa. The high altitude – an average elevation of 3,500 metres – and low oxygen deterred many outsiders. The only thing that Tibet seemed to possess in great quantity was its religion, and an exotic past that the Chinese discovered could be packaged and sold to tourists.

Since the early 1980s, the Chinese authorities have promoted tourism in Tibet, despite occasional setbacks, such as the anti-Chinese riots and demonstrations in Lhasa in 1987 and 1989. They remain suspicious of the growing popularity of Buddhism among young Tibetans and even Chinese – in Eastern Tibet in 2001 they partly demolished a monastic encampment that had attracted thousands of Tibetan and Chinese students of Buddhism. But they hope to attract visitors to the more famous old monasteries and temples, and have rebuilt and renovated a few of them. They have also improved telecommunications, built roads, and even a new railway that will link Lhasa with China.

New government hotels aiming, not always successfully, at an international style have appeared in Lhasa and the towns of Shigatse and Gyantse. There are fewer visa and travel restrictions for foreigners, and groups of tourists from the rich cities of coastal China throng the monasteries, posing with monks, and clambering up steep ladders to peer eagerly at the murals depicting tantric sex.

Encouraged by the government in Beijing, which wishes to open up Tibet, like the rest of China, to private enterprise and consumerism, hundreds of thousands of Han Chinese – the ethnic majority of China – have moved to Tibetan cities in order to take advantage of tax breaks and incentives to small businesses. Han Chinese are said to outnumber the Tibetans in Lhasa by two to one.

With its wide avenues, billboards with neon ideograms, shopping malls, discotheques, Sichuan restaurants, and brothels (usually disguised as massage parlours, as I discovered with some embarrassment), Lhasa now resembles a Chinese city on the make, as fanatically devoted to consumerist excess as it had previously been to communist austerity.

The Lhasa of my imagination – pilgrims with rosaries shuffling through a mist of incense, past old mud houses with painted wood window frames in narrow alleys – existed only for a few blocks around Jokhang temple, the most sacred spot in Tibet. Here at least the hustling that gives much of Lhasa the raw vulgarity of a frontier town was relatively absent. Tibetans dominated the crowd of pilgrims, tourists, policemen, and trinket-sellers flowing clockwise around the temple. Women from Eastern Tibet, magnificently adorned with turquoise headdress, necklaces, brooches, and bangles, mingled with young Tibetan city slickers in reversed baseball caps.

But at the monastery of Sera, tourists clicked their cameras frantically as young monks debated Buddhist philosophy in the traditional way, underscoring their point by leaning forward and bringing their hands together with a loud clap. But the event seemed staged; an American woman with a money-belt around her waist moved slowly through the crowd of tonsured men.

The Potala Palace still appears fabulous, as it abruptly rises, tier by tier, above the city on its own steep hill, and gazes equably at the mountains surrounding Lhasa. But looking directly down from the roof of the palace, I saw ugly squat blocks of concrete stretching to all four corners, and the palace with its vast magnificent hulk suddenly appeared marooned in the city. As I stood there one after-noon a shampoo salesman harangued passers-by on a megaphone in the huge Chinese-built square below the Potala – a desert of tarmac created by razing the old quar-ters; the echo penetrated the melancholy empty apartments of the present Dalai Lama, still touchingly preserved.

From this transplanted China that is modern-day Lhasa, I was relieved to return to Tibet. I rode in the ubiquitous Land Cruiser – an essential vehicle in a country where there are hardly any paved roads. And every step of the way – trailing clouds of dust across barren white valleys; past the black tents of nomads, from which children emerged, waving, holding their happy mucus-smudged faces up to us; on the high passes where prayer flags rippled in the strong wind; and then bowling alongside a turquoise lake cradled by yak-encrusted hills – I again felt the enchant-ment of Tibet's immense empty spaces.

It was evening when we drew into the town of Gyantse, the place where Tibet had first encountered the modern world: in 1903–4, in the shape of invading British troops. The British claimed that the Tibetans and the Russians were conspiring against the British Empire in India, and that there were Russian guns in the capital, Lhasa. This turned out to be yet another imperial self-deception, reinforced in equal measure by arrogance, paranoia, and flawed intelligence. The Tibetan government, mostly run by monks, had geopolitical ambitions only to the extent that they wished their country to be left alone by its powerful neighbours. Certainly, the small Tibetan army possessed no Russian guns, and was armed with nothing more dangerous than matchlock rifles, stones, sticks, and amulets blessed by the Dalai Lama.

Near Gyantse, the British trained two Maxim machine guns on the hapless Tibetan defenders. As one of the gunners later wrote, 'The slaughter was terrible . . . the Tibetans fell in heaps where the Maxims struck them.' Instead of ducking out of sight from the hail of bullets, the remaining Tibetans slowly walked away from the battlefield, their heads bowed as if in mourning. The sight confused the British. As a journalist embedded with the British troops tried to explain later, 'They were bewildered. The impossible had happened. Prayers, and charms, and mantras, and the holiest of their holy men, had failed them.'

More than 400 Tibetans were killed, and many more wounded, in what was only the first of several massacres in Tibet enabled by the Maxim gun, whose usefulness to imperial conquest was commemorated by Hilaire Belloc ('Whatever happens, we have got/ The Maxim gun, and they have not.') As Francis Younghusband, the Central Asian expert and leader of the punitive British expedition, acknowledged, it was a 'terrible and ghastly business'. He forgot to add, probably because he took it for granted, that

it was also a necessary business: the work of empire, intimidating weaker peoples, pre-empting present and potential
enemies.

Tibet's isolation had not been much disturbed during the
nineteenth century, when the imperial states of Europe –
Britain, Russia, Germany, France – exported their rivalries
to Asia and Africa and conquered native peoples in the
name of a superior civilization. As the Europeans saw it,
the country was too big and sparsely populated; and nothing much seemed to grow in its empty spaces apart from a
ritualistic, lama-ridden Buddhism. Its importance was –
and has remained – largely strategic.

The massacre near Gyantse initiated Tibet into the
modern world, its new rivalries, and its newfangled
weapons of mass destruction. After the British invaders
imposed humiliating terms upon the Tibetans and withdrew, Tibet suffered another invasion in 1910, this time by
the doddery Manchu rulers of China. It recovered its independence the next year, as the Manchu empire collapsed,
and then held on to it for almost four decades. In 1950,
however, it was invaded by Chinese communists attempting to 'unify' a China they claimed had been carved up by
foreign imperialists.

As part of the Chinese 'motherland', the area once controlled by the Dalai Lama and his government in Lhasa is
now called the Tibetan Autonomous Region (TAR); and its
past is partly rewritten by Chinese ideologues. At the fort
of Gyantse, a Chinese-built 'Memorial Hall of Anti-British'
describes the bloody events of 1903–4. It lauds, in broken
English, Tibetan soldiers for their efforts on behalf of the
'motherland' and denounces Tibet's British violators. A

tombstone marks the spot from where Tibetan soldiers, bewildered by the superior firepower of the British, allegedly plunged to their death.

The suicides, which have never been proved, seem a figment of the Chinese nationalist imagination, designed to reinforce the idea that the Tibetans were a weak, barbarian race and uniquely vulnerable to greedy foreigners. This is a common theme in Chinese writings about Tibet: that before its 'peaceful liberation' it was a benighted country where 'feudal' and 'reactionary' aristocrats together with monasteries and monks oppressed a majority population of serfs and slaves, mostly by addling their minds with ritual and religion. This unholy ruling elite was unable to modernize and develop Tibet, and didn't even learn the lessons of the rout near Gyantse: the importance of secular education, a modern army, transport, administration, and a productive population.

Before the Chinese invasion in 1950, Gyantse had been an important town on the trading route to India, then Tibet's closest trading partner. Now, cheap Chinese-made goods fill the shops and the stalls that spill onto the dusty pavements; and in the lobby of my resoundingly empty hotel, very young Chinese girls stood smiling vacantly in identical red silk dresses under a barber shop sign offering '24-hour massage service'.

China is developing and modernizing Tibet, taking the country into a glorious future: it was hard to get away from this message, which was garishly advertised on the welcome arches and billboards along the empty roads, to which my Tibetan guide always pointed with a wry smile. But the extreme youth of the prostitutes was proof that although the future might be glorious, the present was an ordeal for many people: the Tibetans as well as the large number of drifting Chinese who sought work in what to them was a remote, strange, and inhospitable land.

I had read in several books and articles on post-Mao China about its 'floating population', estimated to be over 100 million, looking for work away from home. Such large-scale uprooting was said to be one of the effects of the country's economic policies. However, Chinese-led modernization and development appeared to have affected only the few urban areas in Tibet, where most economic migrants from China lived. It seemed to have left untouched the labourers repairing the roads, the farmers in the small villages, and the idle Tibetans playing pool everywhere in roadside dwellings. And it had not diminished, and may even have reinforced, the role of religion in Tibetan society.

Almost all reports about contemporary Tibet attest that despite being under continuous assault for almost three decades, Buddhism remains central to most Tibetan lives. For the majority of Tibetans, the Chinese liberalization that began in the early 1980s primarily meant the freedom to worship their old gods rather than playing the new stock market in Lhasa. Some of the pilgrims I saw at Gyantse's famous octagonal stupa had travelled hundreds of miles. Half bent under the weight of their wooden-framed rucksacks, they walked around the monastic complex, feeding the mangy dogs, reflexively doling out money to the beggars, while spinning their prayer wheels. Inside the dark chapels, they squeezed yak butter out of yellow plastic bags into lamps burning at altars, and with greasy hands stuck one and five yuan notes in the shrines, their small-denomination notes with idealized pictures of Chinese peasants easily out-numbering the large-denomination notes left by tourists from Buddhist Taiwan, Japan, and Thailand.

The Chinese overlords of Tibet weren't without good intentions. It is mostly due to them that many Tibetans enjoy better education and health care. But the majority of Tibetans are still peasants and nomads; and even the educated Tibetans I spoke to seemed discontented with Chinese rule. Like all traditional people faced with mod-ernization, their choices are drastically limited. To embrace the glittering new world of China is to become as ruthlessly materialist and secular as the post-communist Chinese. It is to lose what is still precious to them: their religious and cultural identity.

The fear of 'Sinicization' seemed to weigh most heavily on the Tibetan refugees I met in Dharamsala after return-ing from Tibet. They were convinced that Han Chinese settlers would overwhelm the Tibetans with their alien ways and that soon, with the new rail connection to China, Tibetan society and culture would cease to exist.

Although these Tibetans are a politically diverse group, they generally agree that since the Chinese communists invaded Tibet in 1950, they have killed – mostly through execution, torture, and starvation – up to 1.2 million people and have destroyed tens of thousands of Buddhist monasteries and temples.

In May 1980, four years after Mao's death, the Chinese premier Hu Yaobang visited Tibet, where he apologized for these 'earlier errors', and promised Tibetans greater reli-gious freedom and economic development, along with a measure of political autonomy. But the Tibetans insist that the Chinese regime in Beijing continues to treat Tibet as a colony and has consistently sought to undermine its society and culture, and exploit its economic resources without much regard for its physical environment. There view was supported by the Human Rights Watch report in 2004 which claims that the communist regime in Beijing continues to behave brutally in Tibet, often detaining without trial, torturing, and executing those it suspects of being separatists or sympathizers of the Dalai Lama.

Many of these Tibetan exiles see their political leaders as being constrained by too many religious scruples. They may be right. As Samdhong Rinpoche, the prime minister of the Tibetan government in exile, explained to me in an interview in the spring of 2004, he has reservations about even such a commonplace tactic of resistance groups as economic boycott, since this hurts ordinary people more than the governments. He pointed out that the Dalai Lama supported a ban on Chinese toys only because they were produced by force in prison camps and boycotting them did not impair the livelihood of Chinese labourers.

When Mao Zedong informed the Dalai Lama in 1955 that 'Religion is poison', he probably meant that religion saps a nation's will to struggle and succeed in a competitive world. Rupert Murdoch, one of the over-eager investors in the liberalized Chinese economy, seemed to agree with Mao when he asserted that 'The main problem in Tibet is that half the population still thinks that the Dalai Lama is the "son of God"[*sic*].'

Such dismissals of Tibetan religion and culture are not confined to ultra-leftists or free-market libertarians. The Indian prime minister Nehru once confided to a British diplomat that the Tibetans 'were rather difficult people to help, for they were so ignorant of the modern world and its ways'. In a speech in 1997, Chen Kuiyuan, one of the hard-line Chinese technocrats to have ruled Tibet in recent years, pointed out that 'When the Dalai ruled Tibet, there was not a single regular school; children of the working people had no right or opportunity to receive an education, and more than 90 per cent of the Tibetan people were illiterate.'

When I quoted this speech to Samdhong Rinpoche, he did not fundamentally disagree with it: he readily admitted that Tibet under the *ancien regime* was no Shangri-La. In 1959, Samdhong Rinpoche was twenty years old and training for a degree in philosophy at the Tibetan monastery of Drepung, when he heard that the fourteenth and present Dalai Lama had fled Chinese-occupied Tibet to neighbouring India. Samdhong Rinpoche joined the thousands of Tibetans who followed the Dalai Lama and has not been back to Tibet since. In India, where he has spent most of his life, he is known for his learned advocacy of non-violent politics and his admiration for Gandhi and the Indian freedom struggle against the British.

In 2001, his election as prime minister, with an impressive 80 per cent of the votes cast, signalled the growing democratization of the Tibetan community in exile, of which the Dalai Lama has been the undisputed supreme leader. His vigorous self-criticism reveals the depth of introspection among the Tibetan community in exile.

As a young monk from the provinces in Lhasa, Samdhong Rinpoche saw that 'Members of religious orders failed to follow their moral codes and both in public and in private they were mostly occupied with sales, profits, usury, economic affairs, and other unspiritual matters.' Much of this occurred in his own monastery in Lhasa, Drepung. He also has little time for the Tibetan aristocracy that collaborated with the Chinese. 'Most of our leaders were involved in immoral practices aimed simply at fulfilling their own self-interests.' Predictably, when the Chinese came, 'Tibetans unhesitatingly sold off their country, for the sake of money and goods and their own narrow self-interests.' Samdhong Rinpoche attributes the sufferings of the Tibetan people to their 'collective negative karma'.

Dressed in a maroon robe, Samdhong Rinpoche spoke softly and precisely, in unaccented Hindi. He described to me how as a young, inexperienced refugee monk in India he first came across Gandhi's writings and began to clarify his political thinking. He said that he did not oppose the Chinese people or even Chinese sovereignty over Tibet. What he objected to was the quality of Chinese rule, its injustice and violence, which he called upon all Tibetans to actively reject through acts of non-cooperation and disobedience, without hating or harming the Chinese people.

Non-violence, he said, wasn't a tactic, or a means to a predetermined end. As a form of self-control and carefully measured action, it was an end in itself. A whole way of being in the world, it entailed respect and compassion for all living things.

He sees a free Tibet as a demilitarized zone of peace, devoid of nuclear, chemical, and biological weapons. He claims his government will do all it can to restore Tibet's ecological balance, which has been upset by Chinese-built dams and mining projects. He also said that one of his priorities was to educate more Tibetan refugees in the philosophical underpinning of satyagraha: the respect for human life, and the natural environment. He has already made a beginning by reorienting agriculture-based Tibetan settlements in India to organic farming.

This sounds appropriately small-scale and achievable. But it is still hard to avoid the question: Can Buddhistic non-violence have any role in a world ultimately shaped by brute force and economic interest?

In 1987, the Dalai Lama dropped his earlier demand for full independence for Tibet, describing it as 'unrealistic', and saying that he was willing to negotiate an autonomous status for Tibet within China. His desire to seek a 'middle way' of compromise did not result in any significant concessions from the Chinese; it also angered and alienated many Tibetan intellectuals and activists, who want to settle for nothing less than independence.

In Delhi in 1998, a former monk called Thupten Ngodup publicly immolated himself after Indian police forcibly ended a fast unto death undertaken by six Tibetan activists. The Tibetan Youth Congress, a radical group, had organized the hunger strike, despite the initial disapproval of the Dalai Lama and Samdhong Rinpoche.

Many Tibetan exiles increasingly question his effectiveness against a political opponent as apparently hard-nosed as the Chinese regime in Beijing, which becomes ever more respectable and attractive internationally as China's economy grows at the extraordinary rate of 10 per cent each year.

The award-winning novelist Jamyang Norbu, one of the founders of the Tibetan Youth Congress, is one of those Tibetans who believe that the Dalai Lama's religious commitments diminish his political role, and that his Buddhistic desire to compromise with the Chinese does not serve the Tibetan cause.

'Some people don't want to be enlightened, at least not immediately,' Norbu said in a PBS television documentary on Tibet. 'They are really happy in their landscape and in Tibet. They have a kind of affinity to their place they live in. And they don't want the Chinese there. And his Holiness cannot understand this . . .'

Norbu rejects the Western stereotype of Tibetans as innately non-violent – a romantic notion, which he thinks gratifies many Western people discontented with the aggressive selfishness of their societies, but obscures the political aspirations of the Tibetan peoples, and the variety of means available to them to achieve independence. In 1989, he published a book about one of the Khampa warriors of Eastern Tibet, who fought the invading Chinese army in 1950, and then initiated the bloody revolt against Chinese rule that eventually led to the Dalai Lama's departure for India.

'We are ordinary Tibetans,' Norbu told PBS. 'We drink; we eat; we feel passion; we love our wives and kids. If someone sort of messes around with them, even if they're an army, you pick up your rifle.'

In the early 1970s, Norbu dropped out of boarding school in Darjeeling and picked up a rifle and joined the Tibetan guerrillas operating out of Mustang, a piece of Nepalese territory that juts into Tibet. The CIA secretly funded these guerrillas and arranged for them to be trained in Colorado. American support was half-hearted at best, intended to undermine communist China, not to achieve Tibetan independence; it ended in the 1970s after Kissinger

and Nixon decided to befriend Mao, initiating the appeasement of China, which culminated in 1994 when Bill
Clinton decided to separate trade with China from the
problematic issue of human rights.

Abandoned by their sponsors, many Tibetan guerrillas
were attacked and killed by the Nepalese army. Finally, the
Dalai Lama told the Mustang guerrillas in a taped message
to give up arms and return to India.

Lhasang Tsering, who is now a bookseller in Dharamsala, was one of the Tibetan guerrillas in Mustang. He later
headed the Tibetan Youth Congress, and even worked for
the Tibetan government in exile before resigning in protest
against the Dalai Lama's decision to drop the demand for
full independence.

He told me what I have heard from many other
Tibetans: that in the last decade, the Chinese government
has encouraged Han Chinese to migrate in large numbers
to Tibet, with the result that the Tibetans are a minority in
their own country. Tibet faces a cultural genocide, Tsering
said, and will be wiped out unless some radical and quick
action is taken.

He didn't specify what form that action should take.
But he reminded me that Tibetans had fought fiercely for
their rights even during the exceptionally fearful days of
the Cultural Revolution. Armed with swords and spears,
Thrinley Chodron, a young nun, and her followers had
attacked their local Communist Party headquarters, killing
Chinese officials and their Tibetan collaborators. Tsering
was convinced that the freedom struggle for Tibet would
become militant after the Dalai Lama, who will be seventy
next year, passes away.

*

Many younger refugees I met in Dharamsala also stressed the need for immediate and extreme action; they complained that the Buddhist methods of dialogue and negotiation advocated by the Dalai Lama had proved futile. They pointed to the world attention given to the radical Islamists in Palestine and elsewhere after their spectacular acts of violence.

I knew that such views were popular among many Tibetan refugees; they were part of their Westernized general outlook. But I didn't argue with them; I didn't feel that I had earned the right to do so. My own views were as timid and mixed as those of any traveller to a beautiful country under a despotic regime.

When I think of Tibet now, I first remember that morning on the Tsangpo: the austere landscape, where small things – the water slapping against the boat, the bare hills brown against a blue sky, and a man in a trilby hat twirling his prayer wheel – possessed the power to bestow happiness.

I remember watching snow blow off the rocky summit of Mount Everest one chilly and windy evening on the half-collapsed mud roof of Rongbuk monastery. I remember the peasant Tibetan women in Lhasa, the garish symbol of Chinese capitalism, slowly circumambulating the Potala Palace, measuring the miles of concrete in a series of energetic prostrations, lying on their bellies on the ground one moment, and then rising up, their bangled arms outstretched before them, ready to plunge again onto the hard ground.

These images are commonplace in the books I read before visiting Tibet: the Tibetan landscape and people always

appear in them with a religious aura of humility and compassion. I liked to think that I was immune to these
stereotypes, which often managed to hide Tibet's harsh
political reality. I didn't believe that all Tibetans were
apogees of loving kindness and non-violence. But it was
hard not to feel that I had travelled to the heart of a unique
civilization: one whose achievement lay not in imposing
monuments and museums but in the refined personal culture – the humility and warmth – of its men and women.
I had little doubt that Buddhism had helped create a distinctive and sophisticated civilization in Tibet.

I had become aware, too, of the great dignity and inner
strength with which Tibetans have protected their tradition
and identity while living amid the physical rubble of this
civilization – the rubble of destroyed monasteries and
temples over which a profit-driven, and still repressive,
Chinese regime is building a Disneyland of Tibetan culture.

Many dejected Tibetan exiles probably agree with
Jamyang Norbu when he says that the Chinese are turning
the Tibetans into a 'sort of broken third-rate people, who
like ten, twenty, thirty, forty years from now will just be
someone who's begging from tourists'.

Samdhong Rinpoche, too, is convinced that time is running out for the Tibetans. But he firmly rejects using
violence as a tactic against the Chinese, saying that it
couldn't be an option even if he were certain that it would
win independence for Tibet overnight. 'You cannot achieve
a good end through the wrong kind of means.'

He added that it would be wrong to think of an armed
struggle as the difficult option and satyagraha as the
weapon of the weak. It is easy to respond to injustice with
hatred and violence, but harder to persuade one's adver-

sary of the wrongness of his actions. Non-violent protest isn't for the fainthearted, he said; it was an arduous practice, requiring much effort and discipline.

Perhaps this is why monks and nuns currently form the most visible resistance to Chinese rule in Tibet. According to Tsering Shakya, the leading historian of modern Tibet, monks and nuns 'command the loyalty and respect of the local population', which sees them as 'defenders of Tibetan culture and traditions'. In September 1987, monks from Samdhong Rinpoche's alma mater, Drepung, unfurled the Tibetan flag in central Lhasa – the first major political demonstration in Tibet in years. Monks and nuns from other monasteries followed. They were arrested and severely beaten, sparking clashes between Tibetans and the police, which in turn provoked Hu Jintao, the then Chinese administrator in Tibet, now China's president, to declare martial law in Tibet.

Correctly identifying monasteries as a source of trouble, in 1996 the Chinese government began to subject them to 'patriotism education', asking monks and nuns to denounce the Dalai Lama. But from Tibet, talking to ordinary Tibetans, and watching the great crowds of pilgrims in the rebuilt monasteries and temples, it seemed clear to me that despite official restrictions Buddhism was flourishing in Tibet.

Chinese heavy-handedness merely confirms the Dalai Lama's political and spiritual authority in Tibet. But it is not easy for Tibetan exiles to translate this reverence for the Dalai Lama into political advantage. It looks unlikely at present that the Chinese Communist Party will suffer the fate of its counterparts in the Soviet Union and Eastern

Europe. In any case, its successors may not look too kindly upon the prospect of an independent Tibet, the likely playground of 'foreign imperialists' on China's border. Given this, the Dalai Lama's scaled-down demand for Tibetan autonomy within China appears to be based on a realistic assessment of the strength of Chinese nationalist feeling. For even such Chinese dissidents as Wei Jingsheng, who have suffered greatly at the hands of the current regime in Beijing, assert that Tibet is and will remain part of China.

This is partly why Tibetan leaders in exile rule out a militant nationalist movement, despite the fact that Buddhism in Tibet is 'a powerful nationalist ideology', as Tsering Shakya acknowledges, and has the 'ability to mobilize the public and to contest the authority of the [Chinese Communist] Party'. As Samdhong Rinpoche explained to me, violence against China is likely to make it harder for the Dalai Lama to persuade Chinese dissident intellectuals to support autonomy for Tibet. And the Chinese government would be likely to severely punish the entire Tibetan population for the acts of a few armed dissenters. This seems a fair supposition: the Chinese regime has dealt brutally with its restive Muslim minorities in the north-western province of Xinjiang.

In any case, as Samdhong Rinpoche sees it, the Tibetans are fighting not so much to gain political freedom as to preserve their unique Buddhistic culture. 'What will we gain', he asked me, 'if we win political freedom but lose the culture that gives value to our lives? It is why we reject violence; why the Dalai Lama has said he will resign his leadership of the Tibetan community if it takes to violence. For non-violence is an inseparable aspect of the Tibetan culture we are fighting for.'

He explained that the Gandhian political method of satyagraha wasn't aimed so much at achieving large-scale results such as national independence and autonomy as at helping powerless individuals achieve dignity and confidence in their daily encounters with repressive authority. He said that satyagraha properly begins with small, achievable things, at the grass roots level; it seeks large-scale structural change through a profound change in basic human attitudes.

This, he said, had already happened in Tibet, where many monks and nuns saw non-violent politics as a spiritual duty: a form of self-control and carefully measured action. Samdhong Rinpoche said that it is partly because of the Dalai Lama's principled adherence to non-violence that Tibet remains a presence in the world's consciousness, and that Buddhism grows attractive to many people in the West.

This sounds right. But although many people see Tibet as a distinctive nation with an admirable religion and culture, no Western government dares lose lucrative business in China by recognizing the Tibetan right to self-determination. As China grows economically stronger, the great Tibetan dream – that the Dalai Lama will return to his homeland – appears unlikely to be fulfilled soon.

The Dalai Lama himself seems to know this. In a recent interview, he said that he would die happily in India if Tibet's political status did not change in his lifetime. Such statements are what make him seem insufficiently political. But the Dalai Lama's stance is in line with his Buddhistic distrust of immoral means and imaginary ends – the distrust, essentially, of violence and utopias, which another great exile, Alexander Herzen, expressed when he asserted that 'the end of each generation is itself' and that no generation should be asked to sacrifice itself for the sake of an unknown future.

In September 2004, the Dalai Lama's representatives visited China for the third time in two years and discussed Tibetan autonomy with mid-ranking communist leaders. The meetings between Tibetan and Chinese representatives were held again in June 2005. It is not clear whether these talks will lead to anything other than some diplomatic respectability for China as it prepares for the Beijing Olympics in 2008. However, given that they face a notoriously prickly opponent, the Tibetans have done well to keep alive the possibility of dialogue and negotiation.

And, perhaps, the Dalai Lama's insistence on non-violence will appear more fruitful over time, especially if China experiences democratic reform. It has been the strange fate of Tibet, once one of the most isolated places on earth, to function as a laboratory for the most ambitious and ruthless human experiments of the modern era: the Great Leap Forward, the Cultural Revolution, and now a state-imposed capitalism. After having suffered totalitarian communism, Tibetans now confront a dissolute capitalism: one that seeks arrogantly, and often violently, to turn all of the world's diverse humanity into middle-class consumers. But it seems wrong to think of Tibetans, as many outsiders do, as helpless victims of large, impersonal forces.

It is no accident that the Tibetans seem to have survived the large-scale communist attempt at social engineering rather better than most people in China itself. This is at least partly due to their Buddhistic belief in the primacy of empathy and compassion. And, faced with an aggressively secular materialism, they may still prove, almost alone in the world, how religion, usually dismissed (and not just by Mao) as 'poison', can be a source of cultural identity and moral values. They may prove how it can become a means of political protest without blinding the devout with hatred and prejudice; how it can help not only heal the shocks and pain of history – the pain that has led people elsewhere in the world into nihilistic rage – but also create a rational and ethical national culture – a culture that may make a freer Tibet, whenever it comes about, better prepared for its state of freedom than most societies.